THE HEINLE
Picture Dictionary

SECOND EDITION

NATIONAL GEOGRAPHIC LEARNING | HEINLE CENGAGE Learning·

Australia • Brazil • Japan • Korea • Mexico • Singapore • Spain • United Kingdom • United States

**The Heinle Picture Dictionary,
Second Edition**

Publisher: Sherrise Roehr

Senior Development Editor: Jill Korey
O'Sullivan

Development Editors: Brenden Layte,
Maureen Sotoohi

Director of Global Marketing: Ian Martin

Product Marketing Manager: Lindsey Miller

Director of Content and Media Production:
Michael Burggren

Content Project Manager: Mark Rzeszutek

Senior Print Buyer: Mary Beth Hennebury

Compositor: PreMediaGlobal

Cover Design: Michael Rosenquest

Cover Photo: Brian Skerry

Senior Technology Product Manager:
Scott Rule

Student Edition
ISBN-13: 978-1-133-56310-5

International Student Edition
ISBN-13: 978-1-133-56315-0

National Geographic Learning
20 Channel Center Street
Boston, MA 02210
USA

Cengage Learning is a leading provider of customized learning solutions
with office locations around the globe, including Singapore, the United
Kingdom, Australia, Mexico, Brazil, and Japan.

Cengage Learning products are represented in Canada
by Nelson Education, Ltd.

Visit National Geographic Learning online at: **ngl.cengage.com**
Visit our corporate website at **cengage.com**

Printed in the United States of America
2 3 4 5 6 7 18 17 16 15 14

Contents

1 Basic Words

Numbers	2
Time	4
Calendar	6
Money and Shopping	8
Colors	10
In, On, Under	12
Opposites	14
The Telephone	16

2 School

Classroom	18
Listen, Read, Write	20
School	22
Computers	24

3 Family

Family	26
Raising a Child	28
Life Events	30

4 People

Face and Hair	32
Daily Activities	34
Walk, Jump, Run	36
Feelings	38
Wave, Greet, Smile	40
Documents	42
Nationalities	44

5 Community

Places Around Town	46
Shops and Stores	48
Bank	50
Post Office	52
Library	54
Daycare Center	56
City Square	58
Crime and Justice	60

6 Housing

Types of Homes	62
Finding a Place to Live	64
Apartment Building	66
House and Garden	68
Kitchen and Dining Area	70
Living Room	72
Bedroom and Bathroom	74
Household Problems	76
Household Chores	78
Cleaning Supplies	80

7 Food

Fruits and Nuts	82
Vegetables	84
Meat, Poultry, and Seafood	86
Inside the Refrigerator	88
Food to Go	90
Cooking	92
Cooking Equipment	94
Measurements and Containers	96
Supermarket	98
Restaurant	100
Order, Eat, Pay	102

8 Clothing

Clothes	104
Sleepwear, Underwear, and Swimwear	106
Shoes and Accessories	108
Describing Clothes	110
Fabrics and Patterns	112
Buying, Wearing, and Caring for Clothes	114
Sewing and Laundry	116

9 Transportation

Vehicles and Traffic Signs	118
Parts of a Car	120
Road Trip	122
Airport	124
Taking a Flight	126
Public Transportation	128
Up, Over, Around	130

10 Health

The Human Body	132
Illnesses, Injuries, Symptoms, and Disabilities	134
Hurting and Healing	136
Hospital	138
Medical Center	140
Pharmacy	142
Soap, Comb, and Floss	144

11 Work

Jobs 1	146
Jobs 2	148
Working	150
Farm	152
Office	154
Factory	156
Hotel	158
Tools and Supplies 1	160
Tools and Supplies 2	162
Drill, Sand, Paint	164

12 Earth and Space

Weather	166
The Earth's Surface	168
Energy, Pollution, and Natural Disasters	170
The United States and Canada	172
The World	174
The Universe	176

13 Animals, Plants, and Habitats

Garden	178
Desert	180
Rain Forest	182
Grasslands	184
Polar Lands	186
Sea	188
Woodlands	190

14 School Subjects

Math	192
Science	194
Writing	196
Explore, Rule, Invent	198
U.S. Government and Citizenship	200

15 The Arts

Fine Arts   202
Performing Arts   204
Instruments   206
Film, TV, and Music   208

16 Recreation

Beach   210
Camping   212
City Park   214
Places to Visit   216
Indoor Sports and Fitness   218
Outdoor Sports and Fitness   220
Winter Sports   222
Games, Toys, and Hobbies   224
Camera, Stereo, and DVD   226
Holidays and Celebrations   228

Index   230
Credits   262

Acknowledgments

The publisher would like to thank the following reviewers, consultants, and participants in focus groups:

Susan Alexandre
Trimble Technical High School
Ft. Worth, TX

Lizbeth Ascencio
Dona Ana Branch
 Community College
Las Cruces, NM

Pam S. Autrey
Central Gwinnett High School
Lawrenceville, GA

JoEllen Barnett
K.E. Taylor Elementary School
Lawrenceville, GA

Linda Boice
Elk Grove Unified School District
Sacramento, CA

Chan Bostwick
Los Angeles Unified School District
Los Angeles, CA

Diana Brady-Herndon
Napa Valley Adult School
Napa, CA

Mona Brantley
Des Moines Area
 Community College
Ankeny, Iowa

Petra Callin
Child Services Center,
 Portland Public Schools
Portland, OR

David Chávez
Horizonte Instruction and
 Training Center
Salt Lake City, UT

Kathy Connelly
Ed Shands Adult School
Oakland, CA

María de Lourdes Colín Escalona
Toluca, Mexico

Sam Cucciniello
Belmont High School
Los Angeles, CA

Jennifer Daniels
Mesa County Valley School
 District 51
Grand Junction, CO

Jeff Diuglio
Boston University CELOP /
 Harvard IELP
Auburndale, MA

Dana Dusbiber
Luther Burbank High School
Sacramento, CA

Michal Eskayo
St. Augustine College
Chicago, IL

Sara Farley
Wichita High School East
Wichita, KS

Kathleen Flynn
Glendale Community College
Glendale, CA

Utzuinic Garcés
Mexico City, Mexico

Nancy Garcia
Riverbank High School
Riverbank, CA

Gerónima Garza
Cypress-Fairbanks
 Independent School District
Houston, TX

Sally Gearhart
Santa Rosa Junior College
Santa Rosa, CA

Julie Gomez-Baker
Mesa Unified School District
Mesa, AZ

Virginia Guleff
Miramar College
Escondido, CA

Katalin Gyurindak
Mt. San Antonio College
Walnut, CA

Orin Hargraves
Westminster, MD

Iordana Iordanova
Triton College
River Grove, IL

Ocean Jones
Merced High School
Merced, CA

Gemma Kang
Wonderland
Seoul, Korea

Vicki Kaplan
Adams 12 Schools
Thornton, CO

Dale R. Keith
Miami-Dade County
 Public Schools
Miami, FL

Alyson Kleiber
Stamford Public Schools
Stamford, CT

Jean Lewis
Clark County School District
Las Vegas, NV

Virginia Lezhnev
Center for Language
 Education and Development
Washington, DC

Mabel Magarinos
Orange County Public Schools
Orlando, FL

Elizabeth Minicz
William Rainey Harper College
Palatine, IL

Dianne Mortensen
John J Pershing Intermediate
 School
Brooklyn, NY

Kathryn Nelson
Wichita High School North
Wichita, KS

Andrea O'Brien
Lawrence Adult Learning Center
Lawrence, MA

Denis O'Leary
Rio del Valle Jr. High School
Oxnard, CA

Dianne Ogden
Snow College
Ephraim, UT

Bari N. Ramirez
L.V. Stockard Middle School
Dallas, TX

Nelda Rangel
Brownsville ISD Adult Ed
Brownsville, TX

David L. Red
Fairfax County Public Schools
Falls Church, VA

Eric Rosenbaum
BEGIN Managed Programs
New York, NY

Federico Salas
North Harris College—
 Community Education
Houston, TX

Claudia Sasía Pinzón
Instituto México de Puebla AC
Puebla, Mexico

Linda Sasser
Alhambra School District
San Gabriel, CA

Laurie Shapero
Miami Dade Community College
Miami, FL

Rayna Shaunfield
College of the Mainland
Texas City, TX

Carmen Siebert-Martinez
Laredo Community College
Laredo, TX

Luciana J. Soares de Souza
Britannia Juniors
Rio de Janeiro, Brazil

Susanne Stackhouse
Language Etc.
Washington, DC

Chris Lawrence Starr
Level Creek Elementary
Sewanee, GA

Betty Stone
SCALE—Somerville Center for
 Adult Learning Experience
Somerville, MA

Charlotte Sturdy
Boston, MA

Rebecca Suarez
University of Texas
El Paso, TX

Kathy Sucher
Santa Monica College
Santa Monica, CA

The Teachers of the Harvard
 Bridge Program
Harvard Bridge to Learning
 Program
Cambridge, MA

William Vang
Sacramento City Unified
 School District
Sacramento, CA

James R. Voelkel
Dibner Institute for the History of
 Science and Technology
Cambridge, MA

Wendell Webster
Houston READ Commission
Houston, TX

Colleen Weldele
Palomar College
San Marcos, CA

To the Teacher

About *The Heinle Picture Dictionary*

The Heinle Picture Dictionary, Second Edition is an invaluable vocabulary resource for students learning English. It presents the most essential vocabulary for beginning to intermediate students in a unique format. Unlike conventional picture dictionaries that illustrate target words in isolation, *The Heinle Picture Dictionary* conveys word meaning through the illustration of target words within meaningful, real-world contexts. It also offers students a multitude of opportunities to see, use, hear, and practice these words in context.

The dictionary is organized into 16 thematic units. Each two-page lesson within a unit focuses on a sub-theme of the broader unit theme. So, for example, in the *Housing* unit, there are lessons focusing on different styles of houses, specific rooms of a house, finding a house, household problems, household chores, and so on.

The focal point of each lesson is the word list and corresponding illustration(s) and/or photograph(s). The word lists are arranged for ease of navigation, with the words appearing in the order in which they are illustrated in the art. Singular words in the word list are preceded by an indefinite article (or the definite article, in special cases where the definite article would be more common or appropriate). Articles are included to help students understand when and how the articles should be used.

Each lesson includes *Words in Context, Words in Action,* and *Word Partnerships. Words in Context* is a short reading that features words from the word list. *Words in Action* is a pair of activities that help students put the words into meaningful use. *Word Partnerships* is a selection of collocations that exposes students to high-frequency English word pairings.

New to this Edition

Art: Much of the artwork in *The Heinle Picture Dictionary, Second Edition* has been updated to provide students with clear and consistent representations of the target words.

Word Lists: Word lists have been carefully reviewed and updated to provide students with the language they need.

High-Frequency Words: New to this edition is the indication of the ten most frequently used words of each word list. These high-frequency words were selected using the *Collins Bank of English*™. The *Bank of English* is a database of current English language usage that provides an accurate reflection of contemporary English. If you have limited time, you may choose to focus your teaching on these selected words. In each lesson, these ten high-frequency words are boldfaced for easy recognition.

Additional Ancillaries: The ExamView ® Assessment Suite, and the HPD IWB Classroom Presentation Tool are new to this edition. See below for more information about each of these.

Scientific Research Based

The Heinle Picture Dictionary was developed with research in mind. Research supports the idea that vocabulary is most effectively learned through repeated and varied exposure (Anderson, 1999) and through a strategic approach (Taylor, Graves, van den Broek, 2000). *The Heinle Picture Dictionary* provides students with not only clear illustrations to illuminate word meaning, but also numerous opportunities to encounter and use new vocabulary. The result is an approach to vocabulary learning that reinforces understanding of word meaning and helps students take ownership of new words.

The Heinle Picture Dictionary is adaptable to a variety of situations and purposes. Appropriate for both classroom and self study, *The Heinle Picture Dictionary* can be used as a stand-alone vocabulary and language learning resource or, using the array of available ancillaries, as the core of *The Heinle Picture Dictionary* program.

Word Lists

The target vocabulary can be practiced in a variety of ways.

- **Brainstorm to gather ideas.** With their books closed, ask students to brainstorm words they think might be in the lesson you are about to begin. Then have students check to see how many items they predicted correctly.

- **Check prior knowledge.** Ask students to cover the word lists and identify pictures by numbers.

- **Introduce vocabulary.** Present each word to the students. Ask them to listen to you or the audio and repeat. Help them with pronunciation and check for comprehension.

- **Quiz students.** Ask students to point to pictures that correspond to words you call out. *Or,* ask students to point to pictures that correspond to words embedded within a sentence or a paragraph that you read aloud.

- **Have students quiz each other.** Student A covers the word list and student B asks student A to point to the correct picture. *Or,* ask students to work in pairs to define the meaning of words in the list using their own words.

- **Classify.** Ask students to classify vocabulary on a chart or in a cluster diagram. Templates for many charts and diagrams are available on the *Activity Bank CD-ROM* or can be produced by the students.

- **Do a dictation.** Give students spelling tests, dictate the *Words in Context,* or dictate sentences containing vocabulary. This can also be done as a pairwork activity in which one student gives the words or sentences to another.

- **Have students create sentences/paragraphs.** Ask students to produce sentences or paragraphs using the vocabulary from the list.

- **Encourage discussion.** Discuss the theme of the lesson using the new vocabulary.

- **Provide real-life tasks.** Have students use the vocabulary in a real-life task, such as making floor plans, giving directions, giving instructions, completing forms, etc.

Words in Context

Words in Context introduces students to words from the word list in the context of a reading about the lesson topic. In addition to introducing vocabulary from the lesson in context, these readings can be used to stimulate classroom discussion. They can also be used for classroom dictations or as models for writing.

Words in Action

Words in Action provides students with multi-skill activities to practice and reinforce the vocabulary. These activities are especially useful as an application after the students become comfortable with the new vocabulary.

Word Partnerships

Word Partnerships provides students with common high-frequency collocations using words from the word list. Many of the "Word List" activities suggested above would work equally well with *Word Partnerships*.

Teaching Grammar with *The Heinle Picture Dictionary*

The scenes in *The Heinle Picture Dictionary* can be used as an effective tool for practicing grammar tenses. The following is an approach to using the dictionary to teach grammar.

Tell students to look at a scene in one of the lessons. Identify a time frame. For example, if you're teaching present continuous, tell the students to imagine that everything in the scene is happening now.

1. Identify the context—usually a story, a class discussion, or a task can work well here. Avoid correcting students at this point.
2. Reveal the objective. Let the students know the particular grammar point you will focus upon.
3. Present the structure using a simple chart. Remember to keep the context in mind.
4. Ask students to describe the picture, using the target tense. As an additional challenge, you may have students ask each other questions about the illustration.
5. Provide either written or oral practice.
6. Evaluate students' use and comprehension of the structure.
7. Provide an application that allows students to use the structure in a more independent and less guided way.

The same scene can be used over and over again to teach different tenses. The next time the scene is used to teach or review a tense, students will already be familiar with the vocabulary, so it will be easier for them to focus on the grammar.

Supplemental Materials

The Lesson Planner. The full-color *Lesson Planner* provides complete lesson plans at three different levels for each lesson in the dictionary. The levels are coded as follows:

★ = Beginning Low

★★ = Beginning

★★★ = Beginning High/Intermediate Low

The lesson plans take the instructor through each stage of a lesson, from warm-up, introduction, and presentation through to practice and application. The *Lesson Planner* includes the *Activity Bank CD-ROM*, which has additional activities for each unit, and the IWB Classroom Presentation Tool.

Each of the three lesson plans provided for every lesson in *The Heinle Picture Dictionary* is designed to be used in a full class period. The objective-driven lesson plans propose a variety of tasks and activities that culminate in an application and often an optional project. As you incorporate lesson plans into your instruction, you will discover how this approach ensures effective teaching and successful language learning. The lesson plan format consists of the following:

- **Warm-up and Review**—Students are given tasks or activities that will activate their prior knowledge, preparing them for the lesson.
- **Introduction**—Students are given the objective for the lesson. This is an essential step as students must know what it is they will be learning and why they will be learning it.
- **Presentation**—Teachers present new material, check student understanding, and prepare students for the practice.
- **Practice**—Students practice an activity provided by the teacher.
- **Evaluation**—The teacher checks the students' ability to do the previous practice as an indication of their readiness to perform the application.
- **Application**—Students demonstrate their ability to perform the objective of a lesson more independently, with less teacher guidance.

The HPD Workbooks. There are two HPD Workbooks: beginning level and intermediate level. Each level has its own supplemental audio program. The full-color workbooks are correlated page by page to the dictionary. They have a variety of activities, including listening activities to support student learning. New to this edition of the workbooks is the *Grammar Connection* where the content of each lesson is used to teach or review an appropriate grammar point.

The HPD Interactive CD-ROM. This interactive CD-ROM provides an abundance of interactive activities to reinforce the vocabulary learned in *The Heinle Picture Dictionary*. New to this edition, the CD-ROM will feature multiple language options for students.

The HPD Audio CDs include the readings and word lists.

ExamView® Use the HPD ExamView® test generation software to create personalized assessments of your students' learning. ExamView® makes it easy for you to create and administer student assessments and track student progress.

IWB Classroom Presentation Tool. Delivered on CD-ROM, the IWB Classroom Presentation Tool includes materials from *The Heinle Picture Dictionary* for use in the classroom with an interactive whiteboard or data projector with computer. These resources will help you create a dynamic classroom and increase student motivation, learner persistence, and language development.

Welcome to
THE HEINLE PICTURE DICTIONARY

Four thousand words are presented in 16 contextualized, thematic units. Each lesson in the unit presents vocabulary through color photographs and illustrations, contextualized readings, high-frequency word patterns study, and active learning opportunities.

"Words in Context" shows how the language is actually used through accessible, contextualized readings at a high-beginning level.

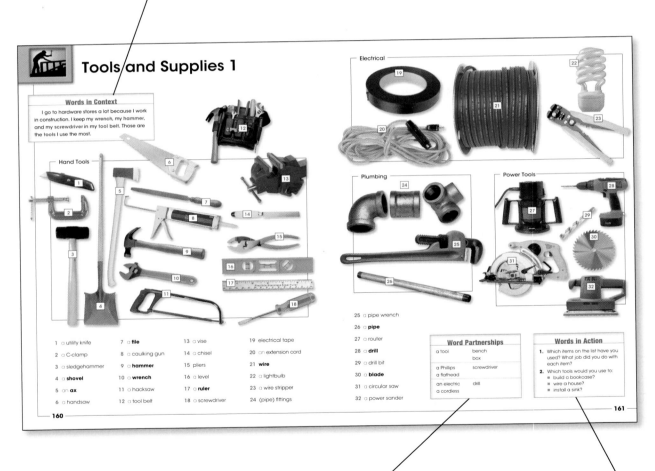

Tools and Supplies 1

Words in Context

I go to hardware stores a lot because I work in construction. I keep my wrench, my hammer, and my screwdriver in my tool belt. Those are the tools I use the most.

Hand Tools

Electrical

Plumbing

Power Tools

1 a utility knife	7 a **file**	13 a vise	19 electrical tape
2 a C-clamp	8 a caulking gun	14 a chisel	20 an extension cord
3 a sledgehammer	9 a **hammer**	15 pliers	21 **wire**
4 a **shovel**	10 a **wrench**	16 a level	22 a lightbulb
5 an **ax**	11 a hacksaw	17 a **ruler**	23 a wire stripper
6 a handsaw	12 a tool belt	18 a screwdriver	24 (pipe) fittings

25 a pipe wrench
26 **pipe**
27 a router
28 a **drill**
29 a drill bit
30 a **blade**
31 a circular saw
32 a power sander

Word Partnerships

a tool	bench
	box
a Phillips	screwdriver
a flathead	
an electric	drill
a cordless	

Words in Action

1. Which items on the list have you used? What job did you do with each item?
2. Which tools would you use to:
   - build a bookcase?
   - wire a house?
   - install a sink?

160

161

"Word Partnerships" expands students' use and understanding of high-frequency word patterns and collocations.

"Words in Action" gives critical thinking activities designed to help students put the vocabulary into meaningful use.

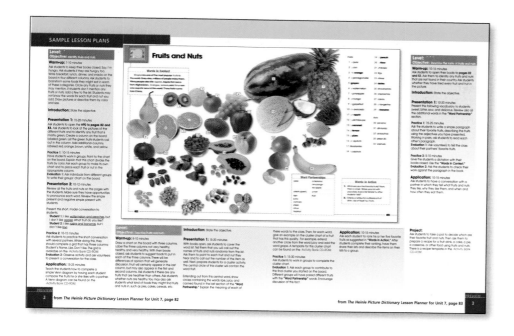

from *The Heinle Picture Dictionary Lesson Planner* for Unit 7, page 82

from *The Heinle Picture Dictionary Lesson Planner* for Unit 7, page 83

- The full-color **Lesson Planner** includes over 300 fully developed lesson plans that provide extensive support for the busy teacher.

  The **Lesson Planner** provides lesson plans at three levels for each lesson in the dictionary. The lessons are coded as follows:

  ★ = Beginning Low

  ★★ = Beginning

  ★★★ = Beginning High/ Intermediate Low

- **The Activity Bank CD-ROM** (included with the **Lesson Planner**) contains reproducible activity masters that can be customized for individual and classroom use.

- **The IWB Classroom Presentation** (included with the **Lesson Planner**) includes Student Book pages as well as audio and activities for classroom presentation.

- **The Heinle Picture Dictionary Workbooks,** beginning and intermediate, emphasize vocabulary and listening skills. Each workbook has its own audio program.

- **The Heinle Picture Dictionary Interactive CD-ROM** offers additional vocabulary practice through activities, games, and word webs. The CD-ROM also provides translations of the target vocabulary in multiple languages.

- **ExamView**® provides an easy way for teachers to create assessments and chart students' progress.

Numbers

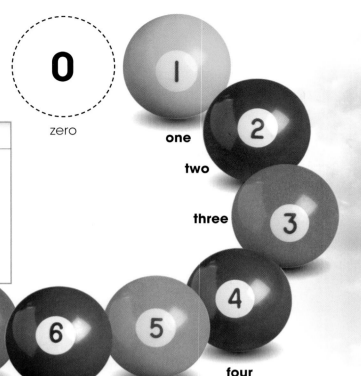

0
zero

one

two

three

four

Words in Context

Some cultures have special birthdays. In Mexico, a girl's **fifteenth** birthday is special. She has a party called the *quinceañera*. In Japan, **twenty** is the beginning of adulthood. In Japan, people celebrate their **twentieth** birthday on January 15, the Day of Adults. In Thailand and Korea, the **sixtieth** birthday is the most important one.

nine eight seven six five

ten

eleven

twelve

thirteen

30 thirty	**70** seventy	**1,000** one thousand
40 forty	**80** eighty	**10,000** ten thousand
50 fifty	**90** ninety	**100,000** one hundred thousand
60 sixty	**100** one hundred	**1,000,000** one million

fourteen fifteen sixteen seventeen eighteen nineteen twenty

Word Partnerships

an odd	number
an even	
a lucky	number

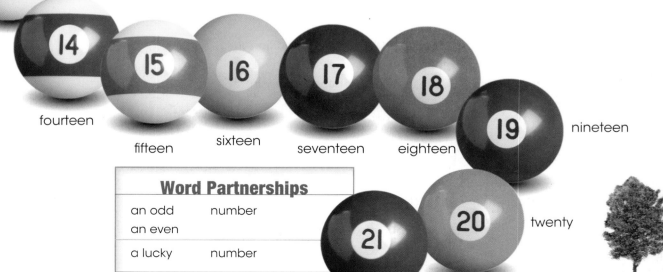

twenty-one

2

21st	twenty-first
20th	twentieth
19th	nineteenth
18th	eighteenth
17th	seventeenth
16th	sixteenth
15th	fifteenth
14th	fourteenth
13th	thirteenth
12th	twelfth
11th	eleventh
10th	tenth
9th	ninth
8th	eighth
7th	seventh
6th	sixth
5th	fifth
4th	fourth
3rd	third
2nd	second
1st	first

Fractions

$1/4$ = one-quarter / a quarter

$1/2$ = one-half / a half

$2/3$ = two-thirds

$3/4$ = three-fourths / three quarters

Words in Action

1. Work in a group. Practice reading the following:
   - 25 minutes / 62 students / 98 pages
   - 12th birthday / 16th floor / 21st of May
2. Work with a partner. Ask and answer these questions:
   - What's your street address?
   - What's your phone number?

Time

I usually get up at about eight o'clock. But sometimes I like to get up before **dawn**. I love the quiet of the **sunrise**. About once a **month** I sleep until **noon**. On those **days**, there aren't enough **hours** in the day. **Night** comes much too soon.

Periods of time

a second

a minute

an **hour**

a day

a week

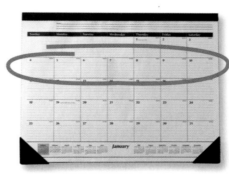

a month

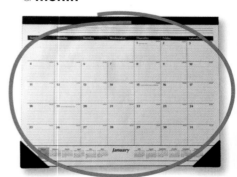

a **year**
2013–2014

a **century**
2001–2100

a decade
2011–2020

a millennium
2001–3000

Times of day

sunrise / dawn

morning

noon / midday

afternoon

evening

sunset / dusk

night

midnight

Clock times

 six o'clock

 six twenty-five /
twenty-five past six /
twenty-five after six

 six forty-five /
(a) quarter to seven /
(a) quarter of seven

 six-oh-five /
five past six /
five after six

 six-thirty /
half past six

 six fifty-five /
five to seven /
five of seven

 six fifteen /
(a) quarter past six /
(a) quarter after six

 six thirty-five /
twenty-five to seven /
twenty-five of seven

Word Partnerships	
at	ten o'clock
	night
in	the morning
	the evening
every	day
once a	week
	month
this	week
last	month
next	year
two hours	ago
five months	

Words in Action

1. What time do you usually get up? Have breakfast? Leave home in the morning? Have lunch? Go to bed?

2. What is your favorite time of day? Why? Discuss with a partner.

Calendar

Days of the week

5 **Monday**

6 **Tuesday**

7 **Wednesday**

8 **Thursday**

9 **Friday**

10 **Saturday**

11 **Sunday**

Words in Context

The Month Poem

Thirty days has **September**,
April, **June**, and **November**.
All the rest have thirty-one
Except **February**.
February has twenty-eight most of the time,
But one year in four it has twenty-nine.

TUESDAY

February
1 **4**
2014

February 2014

	January 2014	February 2014	March 2014
S M T W T F S	S M T W T F S	S M T W T F S
1 2 3 4	1	1
5 6 7 8 9 10 11	2 3 4 5 6 7 8	2 3 4 5 6 7 8
12 13 14 15 16 17 18	9 10 11 12 13 14 15	9 10 11 12 13 14 15
19 20 21 22 23 24 25	16 17 18 19 20 21 22	16 17 18 19 20 21 22
26 27 28 29 30 31	23 24 25 26 27 28	23 24 25 26 27 28 29
		30 31

5	Monday	February 3
2		

6	Tuesday	February 4
3		

7	Wednesday	February 5
4		

8	Thursday	February 6

9	Friday	February 7

10	Saturday	February 8

11	Sunday	February 9

Weekdays	Weekend

Seasons

12 spring

13 summer

14 fall / autumn

15 winter

Months of the year

16 January

17 February

18 March

19 April

20 May

21 **June**

22 July

23 August

24 September

25 October

26 November

27 December

2014

16 January

S	M	T	W	T	F	S
			1	2	3	4
5	6	7	8	9	10	11
12	13	14	15	16	17	18
19	20	21	22	23	24	25
26	27	28	29	30	31	

17 February

S	M	T	W	T	F	S
						1
2	3	4	5	6	7	8
9	10	11	12	13	14	15
16	17	18	19	20	21	22
23	24	25	26	27	28	

18 March

S	M	T	W	T	F	S
						1
2	3	4	5	6	7	8
9	10	11	12	13	14	15
16	17	18	19	20	21	22
23	24	25	26	27	28	29
30	31					

19 April

S	M	T	W	T	F	S
		1	2	3	4	5
6	7	8	9	10	11	12
13	14	15	16	17	18	19
20	21	22	23	24	25	26
27	28	29	30			

20 May

S	M	T	W	T	F	S
				1	2	3
4	5	6	7	8	9	10
11	12	13	14	15	16	17
18	19	20	21	22	23	24
25	26	27	28	29	30	31

21 June

S	M	T	W	T	F	S
1	2	3	4	5	6	7
8	9	10	11	12	13	14
15	16	17	18	19	20	21
22	23	24	25	26	27	28
29	30					

22 July

S	M	T	W	T	F	S
		1	2	3	4	5
6	7	8	9	10	11	12
13	14	15	16	17	18	19
20	21	22	23	24	25	26
27	28	29	30	31		

23 August

S	M	T	W	T	F	S
					1	2
3	4	5	6	7	8	9
10	11	12	13	14	15	16
17	18	19	20	21	22	23
24	25	26	27	28	29	30
31						

24 September

S	M	T	W	T	F	S
	1	2	3	4	5	6
7	8	9	10	11	12	13
14	15	16	17	18	19	20
21	22	23	24	25	26	27
28	29	30				

25 October

S	M	T	W	T	F	S
			1	2	3	4
5	6	7	8	9	10	11
12	13	14	15	16	17	18
19	20	21	22	23	24	25
26	27	28	29	30	31	

26 November

S	M	T	W	T	F	S
						1
2	3	4	5	6	7	8
9	10	11	12	13	14	15
16	17	18	19	20	21	22
23	24	25	26	27	28	29
30						

27 December

S	M	T	W	T	F	S
	1	2	3	4	5	6
7	8	9	10	11	12	13
14	15	16	17	18	19	20
21	22	23	24	25	26	27
28	29	30	31			

Words in Action

1. What's your favorite season? Month? Day? Why? Discuss with a partner.

2. What are three dates that are important to you? These can be birthdays, anniversaries, or holidays. Discuss with a partner.

Money and Shopping

Coins

1 a **penny** / one cent / 1¢

2 a nickel / five cents / 5¢

3 a **dime** / ten cents / 10¢

4 a **quarter** / twenty-five cents / 25¢

5 a half dollar / fifty cents / 50¢

Bills

6 one dollar / a one-dollar bill / $1

7 five dollars / a five-dollar bill / $5

8 ten dollars / a ten-dollar bill / $10

9 twenty dollars / a twenty-dollar bill / $20

10 fifty dollars / a fifty-dollar bill / $50

11 one hundred dollars / a one hundred-dollar bill / $100

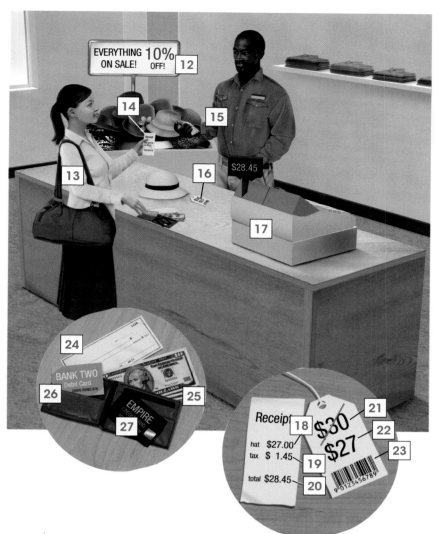

EVERYTHING ON SALE! 10% OFF! **12**

14

15

13

16

$28.45

17

24

BANK TWO Debit Card **26**

25

EMPIRE **27**

Receipt **18** **$30** **21**

hat $27.00 **22**

tax $ 1.45 **19** **$27**

23

total $28.45 **20**

9 012345 6789

Verbs

28 windowshop

29 shop

30 buy

31 exchange

32 return

33 shop online

Shopping

12 a **sale**

13 a **shopper**

14 a **receipt**

15 a cashier

16 a price tag

17 a cash register

18 the **price**

19 the sales tax

20 the **total**

21 the regular price / the full price

22 the sale price

23 a bar code

Methods of payment

24 a (personal) check

25 **cash**

26 a debit card

27 a **credit card**

Word Partnerships

buy things	on sale
pay by	check
	credit card
pay with	a check
	a credit card
pay (with)	cash
save	money
spend	
Saying prices	
$1.25 =	a dollar twenty-five
	one twenty-five
$10.50 =	ten dollars and fifty cents
	ten fifty

Words in Action

1. What do you pay for with a credit card? What do you pay for with a check? What do you pay for with cash? Discuss with a partner.

2. Do you have any bills in your pocket? Which ones? Do you have any coins? Which ones?

Colors

Words in Context

Colors can make us feel different ways. **Yellow** can make us happy. **Orange** can make us feel full of energy. **Black** can make us feel sad. **Blue** can make us feel calm.

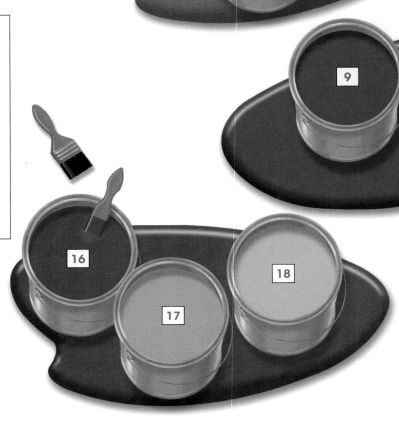

Primary colors

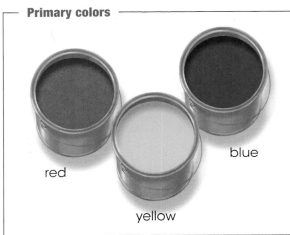

red

yellow

blue

1 **red**	7 lime green	13 **gold**	19 **orange**
2 maroon	8 teal	14 purple	20 **white**
3 coral	9 **blue**	15 violet	21 cream / ivory
4 pink	10 turquoise	16 **brown**	22 **black**
5 **green**	11 navy (blue)	17 beige / tan	23 **gray**
6 olive green	12 **yellow**	18 taupe	24 silver

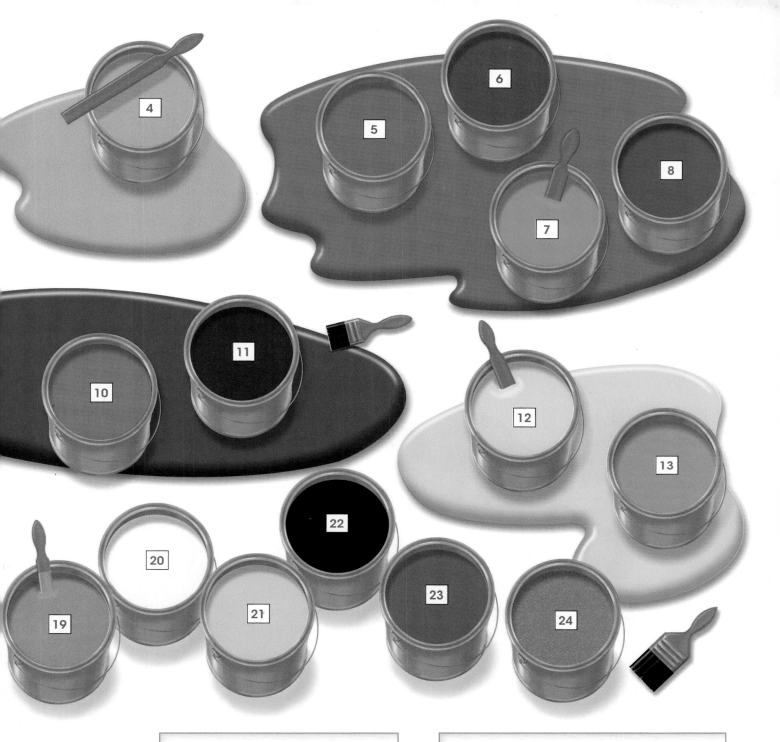

Word Partnerships		
light	pink	
dark	purple	
pale	gray	
	blue	
	green	
a	bright	color
	cheerful	
	rich	
	dull	

Words in Action

1. Look around the room. How many colors can you find? Make a list.

2. Work with a partner. Describe the color of one of your classmates' clothes. Your partner will guess the classmate.
   - Student A: *Someone is wearing green and blue.*
   - Student B: *It's Marcia!*

In, On, Under

Word Partnerships

right	under
	next to
just	behind
	in front of
	to the left of
	above

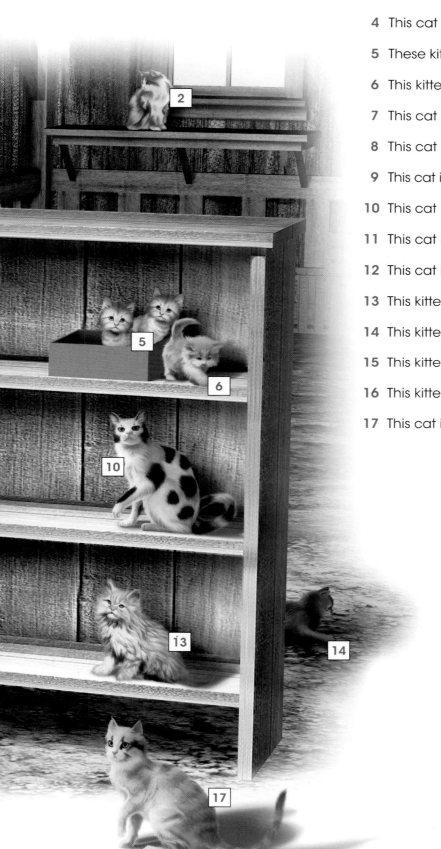

1 This cat is **on top of** the shelves.

2 This cat is **far from** the other cats.

3 This cat is **on** a box.

4 This cat is **between** two boxes.

5 These kittens are **in / inside** a box.

6 This kitten is **outside (of)** the box.

7 This cat is jumping **off** the shelves.

8 This cat is **on the left of / to the left of** cat number 9.

9 This cat is **on the right of / to the right of** cat number 8.

10 This cat is **above / over** cat number 13.

11 This cat is **next to / beside** the shelves.

12 This cat has a ribbon **around** its neck.

13 This kitten is **below / under** cat number 10.

14 This kitten is **behind** the shelves.

15 This kitten is **near / close to** the shelves.

16 This kitten is **underneath** the shelves.

17 This cat is **in front of** the shelves.

Words in Action

1. Cover the list of words. Ask a partner questions like this:
   - *Where is cat number 10?*

2. Describe where things are in your classroom. Write ten sentences using ten different prepositions.

Opposites

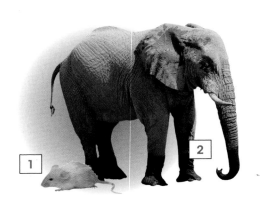

1
2

Words in Context

Opposites sometimes attract. **Women** with **light** hair sometimes like **men** with **dark** hair. Very **tall** men sometimes marry very **short** women. **Thin** people sometimes fall in love with **heavy** people.

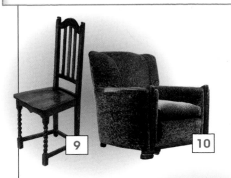

9
10

11
12

13

14

19
20

21
22

23

24

31
32

33

34

Word Partnerships

a cold	day
a hot	drink
	room
an open	window
a closed	door
	book
a clean	car
a dirty	dish
	room
a full	cup
an empty	stomach

1 **small / little**	9 hard	17 tall
2 **big / large**	10 soft	18 short
3 strong	11 alive	19 full
4 weak	12 dead	20 empty
5 dirty	13 ugly	21 **old**
6 clean	14 beautiful	22 **young**
7 easy	15 expensive	23 heavy
8 difficult	16 cheap	24 light

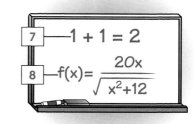

$$1 + 1 = 2$$

$$f(x) = \frac{20x}{\sqrt{x^2 + 12}}$$

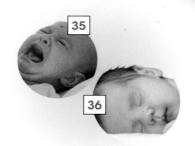

25 fat / heavy	**33** slow
26 thin	**34** fast
27 rich	**35** loud / noisy
28 poor	**36** quiet
29 hot	**37** **open**
30 cold	**38** closed / shut
31 **new**	**39** **man**
32 old	**40** **woman**

Words in Action

1. Work in pairs. Say one of the words on the list. Your partner will say the opposite.

2. Describe things that are the same or different about two people you know. Use words from the list.
   - *Leo and Ali are strong.*
   - *I'm tall. My brother is short.*

The Telephone

Words in Context

Do you want to make a **long-distance phone call** in the U.S.? **Pick up** the **receiver** and **dial** 1 + the **area code** + the **phone number**. Do you need **directory assistance**? You can dial **411**. Remember, there are four **time zones** in the U.S. When it is 9:00 P.M. in Los Angeles, it's midnight in New York!

1 a smartphone

2 an application / an app

3 911 / emergency assistance

4 411 / information / directory assistance

5 a touch screen

6 a calling card / a phone card

7 a charger

8 a text message

9 a local call

10 a long-distance call

11 an international call

12 time zones

13 a **caller**

14 a phone jack

15 a **cord**

16 a headset

17 an **operator**

18 a cordless phone

19 a **cell phone** / a mobile phone

20 an area code

21 a **telephone number** / a **phone number**

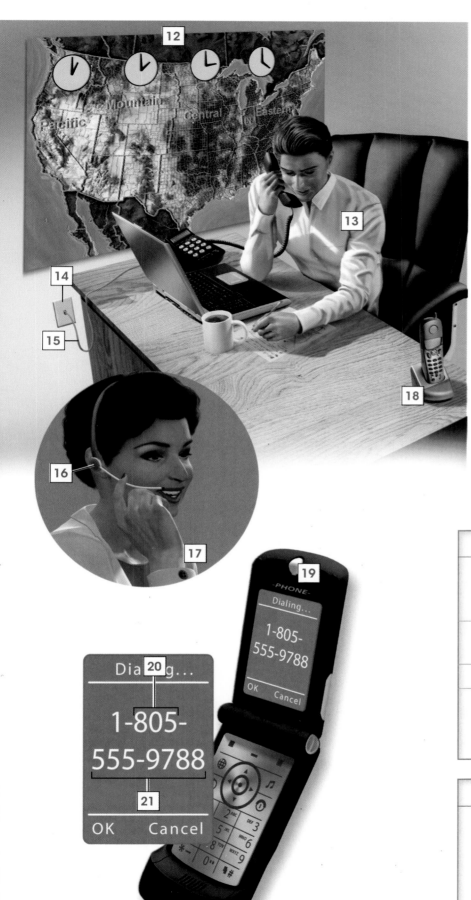

22 pick up the phone

23 dial a number

24 hear the phone ring

25 answer the phone

26 have a conversation

27 hang up the phone

28 send a text (message)

29 get a text (message)

Word Partnerships

make	an international call
	a long-distance call
	a local call
call	directory assistance
	911
look up	a phone number
telephone	company
	service
	bill

Words in Action

1. What is your area code and phone number?

2. How often do you make local, long-distance, and international calls? Who do you call? Why? Discuss with a partner.

Classroom

30 cheat on a test

31 fail a test

Words in Context

What does the ideal **classroom** look like? Some experts think that a classroom should look friendly. It should have comfortable **seats** and **desks**. It should have a large **bookshelf** with many **books**. It should also have bright **posters** and **bulletin boards** to show **students'** work.

1

Aa Bb Cc Dd Ee Ff Gg Hh Ii Jj Kk Ll Mm Nn Oo Pp Qq Rr Ss Tt Uu Vv Ww Xx Yy Zz

8

7

Homework for Friday:
Read page 78. **5**
Answer the questions.

6

2

3

4

9

1

1

12

22

20

21

Word Partnerships

go to	the board
write on	
erase	
a high school	student
a college	
an international	
a graduate	
a hard / difficult	test / exam
an easy	
a midterm	
a final	

26

25

24

23

32 study for a test

33 take a test

34 pass a test

1 the alphabet	**10** a globe	**20** a notebook
2 a **teacher**	**11** a bookshelf	**21** a pen
3 a marker	**12** a **book**	**22** a **desk**
4 a (whiteboard) eraser	**13** a **map**	**23** an eraser
5 a homework assignment	**14** a (black)board	**24** a pencil
6 a (white)board	**15** chalk	**25** a textbook
7 a bulletin board	**16** a poster	**26** a **student**
8 a clock	**17** an overhead projector	**27** a **chair** / a **seat**
9 a flag	**18** a **table**	**28** a **grade**
	19 a workbook	**29** a **test** / an **exam**

Words in Action

1. Work with a group. Make a list of everything in your classroom. Which group has the longest list?

2. Cover the word list. Find one word in the picture that starts with each of the following letters: a, b, c, d, e, f, g, h.

Listen, Read, Write

I think that...

K-I-M

I study English

1 **raise** your hand	7 **read**	12 **listen**
2 **hand in** your paper	8 **look up** a word (in the dictionary)	13 **spell** your name
3 **collect** the papers		14 **take a break**
4 **copy** the sentence	9 **close** your book	15 **sit down**
5 **exchange** papers	10 **open** your book	16 **go** to the board
6 **write** your name	11 **discuss** your ideas	17 **erase** the board

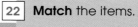

I Study English

22 **Match** the items.

　1. 3 ⤬ four
　　 4 　　 three

23 **Cross out** the wrong answers.

　1. 2 + 2 = ✗ 4 ✗

24 **Check** the correct answer.

　1. 2 + 2 = ___ 3 　✓4

25 **Correct** the mistake.

　1. 2 + 2 = ✗ 4

26 **Fill in** the blank.

　1. 2 + 2 = 4

27 **Underline** the correct answer.

　1. 2 + 2 = 　3 　<u>4</u> 　5

28 **Circle** the correct answer.

　1. 2 + 2 = 　3 　④ 　5

29 **Darken** the correct oval.

　1. 2 + 2 = ◯3 　⬤4

18	hand out papers	24	**check**
19	stand up	25	correct
20	**talk** with a group	26	fill in
21	**share** a book	27	underline
22	match	28	circle
23	cross out	29	darken

Word Partnerships

read	silently
	aloud / out loud
	to your partner
discuss	with a partner
	with a group
listen	to me
	carefully
	to your partner
	and repeat

Words in Action

1. Take turns giving and following classroom instructions. For example, one person says: *Stand up*. The other person stands up.

2. Which activities do you often do in class? Make a list.

School

LIBRARY

Class of "20__"

Extracurricular Activities

SPORTS

Principal

Extracurricular Activities

SPORTS

Soccer

Baseball

DRAMA CLUB

Join the Spanish Club

SCHOOL BUS

Word Partnerships

elementary	school
middle	
high	
join	a team
	a club

George Washington High School
1st Semester Grade Report

To the Parents of: **James**

HR	SUBJECT	TEACHER	1	EXAM	2	EXAM
1	Biology	Stephens	B-	B	C+	C
2	English 2	Geofferies	A	A	A	A
3	Intro Journal	Bennett	A	A	A	A-
4	Seminar	Hurst	CR		CR	
5	Algebra 2	Jakobs	F	D	D+	C

1st Semester	Monday	Tu
8:00–9:25	ogy	B
9:25–10:20	Orchestra	H
10:20–10:40	Study Hall	E
10:40–11:00	Break	Stu
11:00–11:55	Spanish I	Sp
11:55–12:30	Lunch	L
12:30–1:25	English II	Er
1:25–2:20	Algebra	A

CA COLL

22

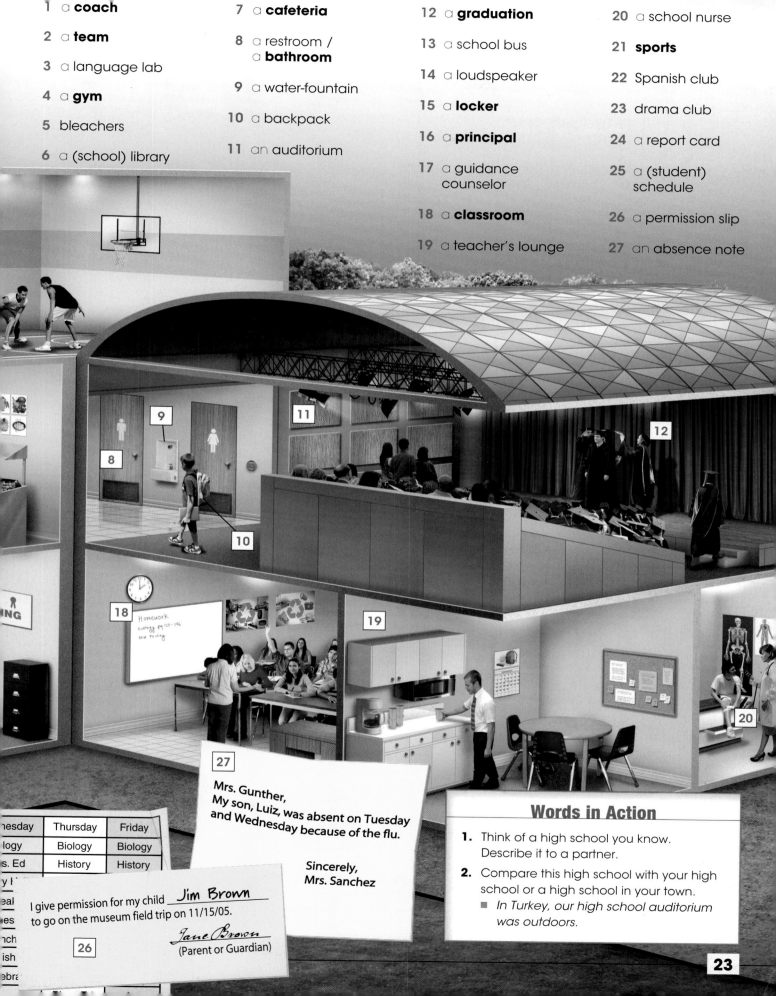

1 a **coach**
2 a **team**
3 a language lab
4 a **gym**
5 bleachers
6 a (school) library

7 a **cafeteria**
8 a restroom / a **bathroom**
9 a water-fountain
10 a backpack
11 an auditorium

12 a **graduation**
13 a school bus
14 a loudspeaker
15 a **locker**
16 a **principal**
17 a guidance counselor
18 a **classroom**
19 a teacher's lounge

20 a school nurse
21 **sports**
22 Spanish club
23 drama club
24 a report card
25 a (student) schedule
26 a permission slip
27 an absence note

Homework
ecology pg 99-146
test Friday

27

Mrs. Gunther,
My son, Luiz, was absent on Tuesday and Wednesday because of the flu.

Sincerely,
Mrs. Sanchez

	Thursday	Friday
...logy	Biology	Biology
s. Ed	History	History

I give permission for my child _Jim Brown_ to go on the museum field trip on 11/15/05.

26

Jane Brown
(Parent or Guardian)

Words in Action

1. Think of a high school you know. Describe it to a partner.
2. Compare this high school with your high school or a high school in your town.
   ■ *In Turkey, our high school auditorium was outdoors.*

23

Computers

1

2

Verbs

30 be online

31 enter your password

3

4

32 select text

33 click

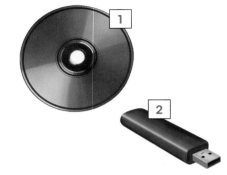

34 scan

35 print (out)

16

26

5

7

8

11

2013 Monthly Reports

Home

Work **5**

6

Expense Report

9

10

12

17

19

20

18

Enter

Shift

21

1   a CD-ROM
2   a flash drive
3   a **window**
4   a toolbar
5   a folder
6   a cursor
7   a **file**
8   a (drop down) menu
9   icons
10 a scroll bar
11 a **cable**
12 a power strip
13 a projector
14 a scanner
15 a printer
16 a tablet

17 a desktop (computer)
18 a **key**
19 a monitor
20 a **screen**
21 a keyboard
22 an **e-mail** (message)
23 a **laptop** (computer) /
    a notebook (computer)
24 a trackpad / a touchpad
25 **software** /
    a (computer) program
26 a USB port
27 a **mouse**
28 a CD-ROM drive
29 the **(Inter)net** /
    the (World Wide) Web

TO: Ivan@myletter.com
CC:
FROM: fjones@messages.com
SUBJECT: HI!!

Hi Ivan,
Thanks for your e-mail.
I'll give you a call tonight.
Fred

Words in Action

1. Draw a computer. Without looking at the word list, label each part of the computer.
2. Practice reading aloud these addresses:
    ■ president@whitehouse.gov
    ■ http://www.natgeo.com

25

Family

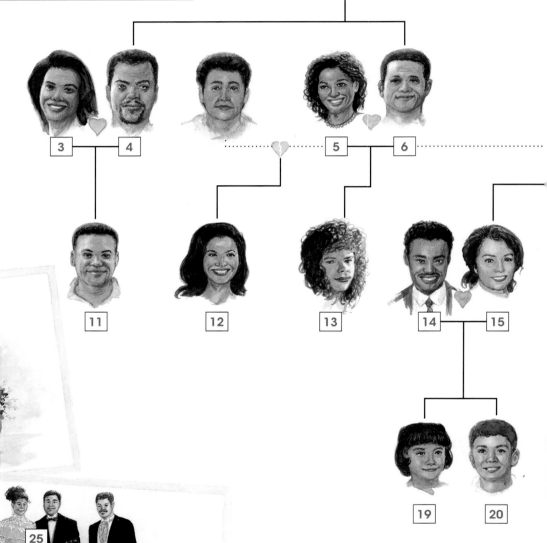

Words in Context

Children often look more like one **parent** than the other. Maybe you have your **mother**'s eyes, your **father**'s hair, your **grandmother**'s skin color, or your **grandfather**'s lips. Who do you look like?

27 be married   **28** be divorced

1 grandfather
2 grandmother
3 aunt
4 uncle
5 stepmother

6 father
7 mother
8 stepfather
9 mother-in-law
10 father-in-law
11 cousin

12 stepsister
13 half sister
14 brother-in-law
15 sister
16 sister-in-law
17 brother
18 husband
19 niece
20 nephew
21 son
22 daughter
23 grandchildren
24 grandparents
25 parents
26 wife

29 be a single mother   30 be remarried

Word Partnerships		
a first	wife
a second	husband
an ex-	
an older	brother
a younger	sister

Words in Action

1. Which members of your family look alike?
   - *I look like my sister.*
   - *My brother looks like my father.*
2. Draw a family tree or bring pictures to class. Tell a partner about your family.

Raising a Child

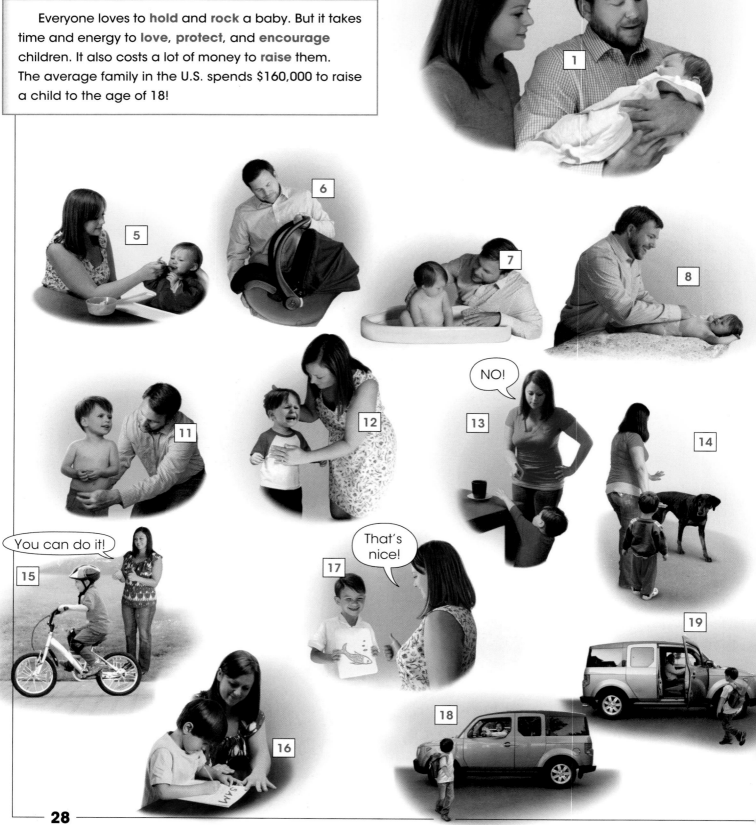

28

1 **love** him

2 nurse him

3 rock him

4 **hold** him

5 **feed** him

6 **carry** him

7 bathe him

8 **change** his diapers

9 **play** with him

10 pick him up

11 dress him

12 comfort him

13 discipline him

14 **protect** him

15 **encourage** him

16 **help** him

17 praise him

18 drop him off

19 pick him up

20 **read** to him

21 put him to bed

Word Partnerships		
grow (up)	fast	
	quickly	
read	a book	
	a story	

Verbs

22 crawl   23 cry

24 behave   25 misbehave

26 **grow**   27 grow up

Words in Action

1. Write a list of "Rules for Parents." Share your rules with the class.
   - *Parents must always protect their children.*

2. Talk with a group. What are the ten most important things to do for a child? Make a list. Put the most important things first.

Life Events

Words in Context

The Life of Steve Jobs

1973
Steve **graduates** from high school.

1976
Steve starts making computers in his garage.

2004
Steve **gets sick.**

2011
Steve Jobs **dies.**

1955
Steve Jobs **is born.**

1974
Steve **gets a job** at a video game maker.

1991
Steve **gets married.**

1998
Steve introduces a new computer.

2007
Steve introduces a new phone.

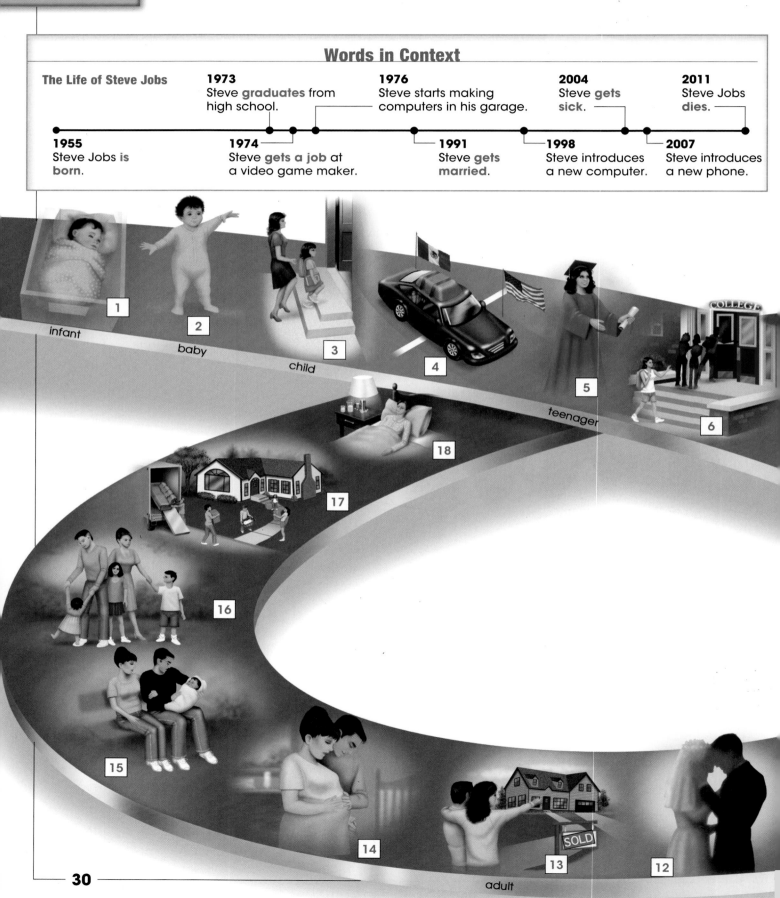

infant 1

baby 2

child 3

4

teenager 5

6

18

17

16

15

14

13

12

adult

1 be born	9 date	17 **move**
2 **learn** to walk	10 fall in love	18 get sick
3 **start** school	11 get engaged	19 take a vacation
4 immigrate	12 get married	20 celebrate a birthday
5 graduate from high school	13 **buy** a house	21 **become** a grandparent
6 **go** to college	14 be pregnant	22 retire
7 rent an apartment	15 have a baby	23 **travel**
8 **get** a job	16 **raise** a family	24 **die** / pass away

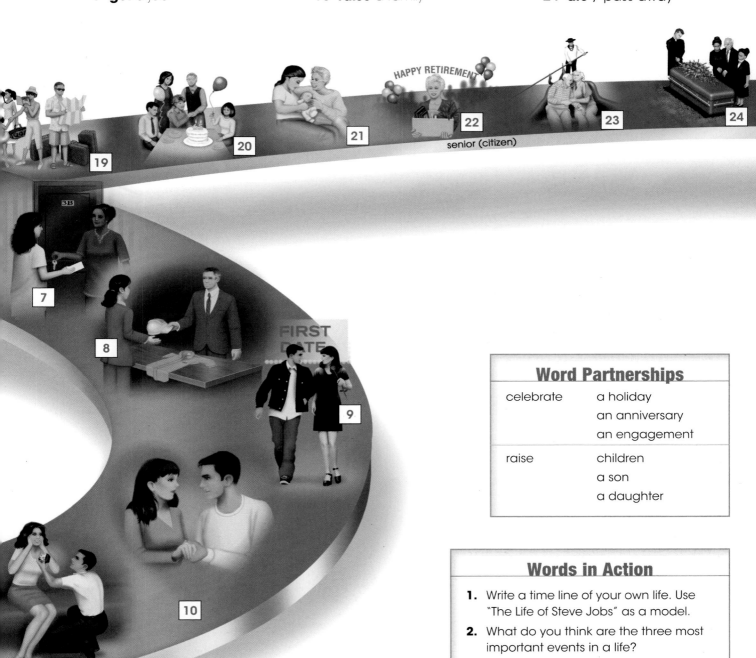

senior (citizen)

HAPPY RETIREMENT

FIRST DATE

Word Partnerships

celebrate	a holiday
	an anniversary
	an engagement
raise	children
	a son
	a daughter

Words in Action

1. Write a time line of your own life. Use "The Life of Steve Jobs" as a model.

2. What do you think are the three most important events in a life?

Face and Hair

Words in Context

The way people wear their hair changes often. One year, **long hair** is the fashion for women. The next year, it is **short hair**. Sometimes **curly hair** is popular. But then soon everyone wants **straight hair**. Men's fashions change too. Sometimes **sideburns** are long and sometimes they are short. **Beards** and **mustaches** come and go.

1

2

3

4

5

6

7

8

9

10

11

12

13

14

15

16

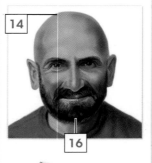

Word Partnerships

a friendly	face
a happy	
a pretty	
thin	hair
thick	
reading	glasses
prescription	

32

1 **red hair**

2 **brown hair**

3 **black hair**

4 blond hair

5 gray hair

6 freckles

7 a **scar**

8 a **mustache**

9 a dimple

10 a **wrinkle**

11 short hair

12 shoulder-length hair

13 **long hair**

14 **bald**

15 sideburns

16 a **beard**

17 straight hair

18 curly hair

19 wavy hair

20 pierced ears

21 braids

22 a bun

23 bangs

24 a ponytail

25 cornrows

26 pigtails

27 a mole

28 **glasses**

Words in Action

1. Compare yourself with a partner.
   - *We both have short hair.*
   - *I have freckles. Alex doesn't.*
2. Work with a partner. Take turns describing the face of someone you know. The other person will draw the face.

Daily Activities

1 wake up

2 **get up**

3 **brush** your teeth

4 **take** a shower

5 **comb** your hair

6 shave

7 **put on** makeup

8 get dressed

9 **eat** breakfast / **have** breakfast

10 **take** your child to school

11 **go** to work

12 **take** a coffee break

13 **eat** lunch / **have** lunch

14 **go** home

15 **take** a nap

16 **exercise** / work out

17 **do** homework

18 **make** dinner

19 **eat** dinner / **have** dinner

20 **take** a walk

21 do housework

22 take a bath

23 **go** to bed

24 sleep

25 **watch** television

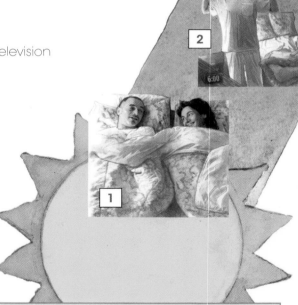

Words in Action

1. Take turns asking and answering questions about the picture.
   - Student A: *What does the family do in the morning?*
   - Student B: *They wake up, get dressed, and eat breakfast.*

2. Tell your partner about your typical morning.
   - *I wake up at 9:00. First I brush my teeth and then I take a shower.*

34

Walk, Jump, Run

1	fly	10	**fall**	19	sit (down)
2	**leave**	11	**run**	20	jump
3	**enter** / go in	12	**cross**	21	go up
4	march	13	get on	22	go down
5	**walk**	14	get off	23	crawl
6	get out (of)	15	squat	24	kneel
7	**get in**	16	**follow**	25	**push**
8	jog	17	**lead**	26	ride
9	slip	18	stand up	27	**pull**

Word Partnerships

fall	off
jump	down
	over
get in	a car
get out of	a taxi
get on	a train
get off	a bus
ride	a bicycle / a bike
	a motorcycle
	a horse
cross	the street

Antonio's

45|P

Words in Action

1. What five things do you do every day? Use words from the list.

2. Take turns acting out some of the verbs on the list. The other students will guess what you are doing.

Feelings

Words in Context

People cry when they feel **sad** or **homesick**. Sometimes they also cry when they are **happy**, **angry**, or **scared**. People laugh when they are happy. Sometimes they also laugh when they are **nervous** about something.

Words in Action

1. How do you feel right now? Use one or more words from the list.
2. Find a picture of a person in a magazine or newspaper. How do you think the person feels?
   - *She is not smiling. She looks bored or angry. Maybe she is in pain.*

1 proud
2 **happy**
3 **worried**
4 **sick** / ill
5 embarrassed
6 **full**

7 hungry
8 thirsty
9 in love
10 frustrated
11 homesick
12 lonely

13 tired
14 **surprised**
15 confused
16 **afraid** / scared
17 excited
18 sad

19 **comfortable**
20 uncomfortable
21 **angry**
22 **interested**

23 **calm**
24 nervous
25 bored

← ELM STREET   ELM ROAD →

?

ICE CREAM

Word Partnerships	
angry	about
embarrassed	
happy	
afraid	of
proud	
tired	
frustrated	by
confused	

Wave, Greet, Smile

1 **argue**

2 greet

3 **visit**

4 shake hands

5 **touch**

6 have a conversation

7 **give** a gift

8 **write** a letter

9 apologize

10 compliment

11 **agree**

12 disagree

13 comfort

14 bow

15 **introduce**

16 **call**

17 hug

18 **smile**

19 **help**

20 wave

21 kiss

22 dance

23 invite

24 congratulate

40

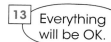

Word Partnerships

agree	with
dance	
argue	
apologize	to
bow	
wave	

Words in Action

1. How do men and women in your culture greet someone new? How do they greet good friends? Family members?

2. Write five sentences about your best friend. Use words from the list.

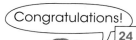

Documents

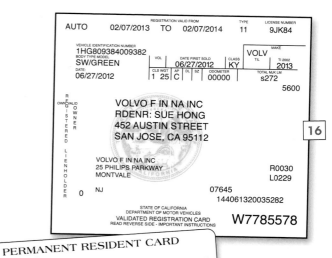

AUTO | 02/07/2013 | TO | 02/07/2014 | | TYPE 11 | | LICENSE NUMBER 9JK84 |

REGISTRATION VALID FROM

VEHICLE IDENTIFICATION NUMBER
1HG809384009382
BODY TYPE MODEL
SW/GREEN
DATE:
06/27/2012

VOL | DATE FIRST SOLD 06/27/2012 | CLASS KY | MAKE VOLV | TIL TI 2002 2013

CLS WGT 1 | AP 25 | DL C | SZ | ODOMETER 00000 | TOTAL MLK LM s272

5600

REGISTERED OWNER/VALID OWNER

VOLVO F IN NA INC
RDENR: SUE HONG
452 AUSTIN STREET
SAN JOSE, CA 95112

VOLVO F IN NA INC
25 PHILIPS PARKWAY
MONTVALE

0   NJ

R0030
L0229

07645
144061320035282

STATE OF CALIFORNIA
DEPARTMENT OF MOTOR VEHICLES
VALIDATED REGISTRATION CARD
READ REVERSE SIDE - IMPORTANT INSTRUCTIONS

W7785578

16

Words in Context

There are **documents** for almost every important event in life. When you are born, you get a **birth certificate**. When you graduate from school, you get a **diploma**. You get a **driver's license** when you are ready to drive. You apply for a **passport** before you travel to another country. And you get a **marriage certificate** when you get married.

PERMANENT RESIDENT CARD
NAME SUSAN HONG

INS A# 355–XX–9701
Birthdate: 01/05/74   Category IR1   Sex F
Country of Birth: Korea
CARD EXPIRES: 11/10/2020
Resident Since: 08/01/2008

C1USA0462474389EAC0026252433<<
7206214F1009055IRL<<<<<<<<<<<9
HONG<<SUSAN<<<<<<<<<<<<<<<<<<

17

Personal Information (please print)

| 1 | **Name** | Hong | 2 | John | 3 | E | 4 |
| | | LAST | | FIRST | | MIDDLE INITIAL | |

5 **Sex** 👨 Male ☒   👩 Female ☐

6 **Date of birth** 6 / 21 / 1970
MONTH   DAY   YEAR

7 **Place of birth** Los Angeles, CA

8 **Soc. Sec. No.** 135–XX–2887

9 **Telephone No.** 415 / 555 – 8765
AREA CODE

10 **E-mail** jhong@bower.com

Address

11 452 Austin St.
STREET

San Jose   CA   95112
12 CITY   **13** STATE   **14** ZIP

15 *John E Hong*
SIGNATURE

DMV **CALIFORNIA** DMV
DRIVER LICENSE
N89473
EXPIRES: 01-05-2018
CLASS: C
Susan Hong
452 Austin Street
San Jose, CA 95112
SEX: F   HAIR: BLK   EYES: BRN
HT: 5-01   WT: 98   DOB: 01-05-1974
Susan Hong
xxxxx   xxx xx   xxxx

18

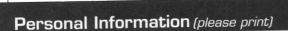

ℋAWTHORNE ℭOLLEGE

Student: Karen Hong
ID no: 349087

19

BT **Bower Technology**

John E. Hong
Engineer

38 Rawlson Circle
San Jose, CA 95112
www.bowertech.com

Phone: (408) 555-3982
Fax:(408) 555-3980

20

SOCIAL SECURITY

135–XX–2887
THIS NUMBER HAS BEEN ESTABLISHED FOR
JOHN E HONG

John E. Hong
SIGNATURE

21

A (registration) form

1 **name**

2 **last name** / surname / family name

3 first name

4 middle initial

5 **sex / gender**

6 date of birth

7 place of birth

8 Social Security number

9 **telephone number**

10 **e-mail address**

11 street address

12 **city**

13 **state**

14 zip code

15 **signature**

Documents

16 a vehicle registration card

17 a Resident Alien card / a green card

18 a driver's license

19 a student ID

20 a business card

21 a Social Security card

22 a **passport**

23 a visa

24 a birth certificate

25 a marriage certificate

26 a Certificate of Naturalization

27 a college degree

28 a high school diploma

24

State of California
UNITED STATES OF AMERICA

CERTIFICATE OF BIRTH
FROM THE RECORDS OF BIRTHS IN THE CITY OF
LOS ANGELES, CA U.S.A.

Record # 479

1 Full Name of Child	Karen Hong
2. Date of Birth	March 2, 1996
3. Gender and Plurality	

25

Certificate of **Marriage**

This Certifies That

John E. Hong
Born 6/21/1970   Place of birth   Los Angeles, CA

and

Susan Hong
Born 1/5/1974   Place of birth   Korea

THE UNITED STATES OF AMERICA

ORIGINAL
TO BE GIVEN TO
THE PERSON NATURALIZED

CERTIFICATE OF NATURALIZATION

No. A98-45H-937

Petition No   575

Personal description of holder as of date of naturalization. Date of birth   01/05/74   sex   F
complexion   Fair   color of eyes   Brown   color of hair   Black   height   5   feet   1   in
weight   98   pounds visible distinctive marks   None
Marital status   Single   former nationality   Korean
I certify that the description above given is true, and that the photograph affixed hereto is a likeness of...

Susan Hong
(Complete and true signature of holder)

355-XX-9701   ss:

Be it known that at a term of the   District   Cou
Los Angeles County
held pursuant to law at   California
on   5/2/95   the Court having found...
Susan Hong
then residing at   4501 Broward Ln
intends to reside permanently in the United States (when so required b...
Naturalization Laws of the United States), had in all other respects complied...
the applicable provisions of such naturalization laws, and was entitled th...
...citizen shift thereupon ordered that such person be and is...

26

Paulson University

27 by authority of the Board of Regents and on recommendation of the Faculty
hereby confers upon
John...

28 **John Kennedy High School**

this

the

In Witness Whereof the ... Signatures of the Officers of the same are hereunto affixed this eleventh day of June, 2014.

Hershel McLeod
Principal of High School

Ray A...
Chairman of the Board
Walter Marshall

43

22

PASSPORT

United...
of A...

23

Visas

January/Valid   February/Valid

JAPAN IMMIGRATION
3 NOV. 2012
Status: Temporary Visitor
Duration: **90 days**

7

Word Partnerships

apply for	a passport
get	a marriage license
have	a green card
sign	your name
print	
say	
fill in / fill out	a form
an application	form
an order	

Words in Action

1. Which documents do you have? Make a list.

2. Role-play. Student A is registering for a class. Student B is asking for personal information.
   - Student A: *Hi, I'd like to register for a class.*
   - Student B: *Sure. What's your last name?*

Nationalities

Words in Context

Women from many different countries have been in space. In 1963 Valentina Tereshkova, a **Russian** woman, was the first woman in space. Sally Ride was the first **American** woman in space. Chiaki Mukai was the first **Japanese** woman in space. A **French** woman, a **Canadian** woman, and an **English** woman have also been in space.

1 Canadian
2 **American**
3 Mexican
4 Venezuelan
5 Colombian
6 Peruvian
7 Brazilian
8 Chilean
9 Argentine / Argentinean
10 **British**
11 **German**
12 **French**
13 Spanish
14 **Italian**
15 Greek

16 Turkish
17 Iranian
18 Egyptian
19 Saudi Arabian
20 Nigerian
21 **Russian**
22 **Indian**
23 **Chinese**
24 **Korean**
25 **Japanese**
26 Thai
27 Vietnamese
28 Filipino
29 Malaysian
30 Australian

N
W   E
S

10 UNITED KINGDOM

11 GERMANY

12 FRANCE

13 SPAIN

14 ITALY

15 GREECE

16 TURKEY

17 IRAN

18 EGYPT

19 SAUDI ARABIA

20 NIGERIA

21 RUSSIA

22 INDIA

23 CHINA

24 REPUBLIC OF KOREA

25 JAPAN

26 THAILAND

27 VIETNAM

28 PHILIPPINES

29 MALAYSIA

30 AUSTRALIA

Words in Action

1. With a partner, practice matching countries and nationalities. One person will say a country. The other will say the nationality. Take turns.
   - Student A: *Brazil*
   - Student B: *Brazilian*

2. Do you have classmates or friends from other countries? Make a list of their nationalities.

45

Places Around Town

Words in Context

I come from Concon, a small town in Chile. There's a **church**, a **gas station**, a **school**, and a soccer **stadium**. There is no **mall**, no **hospital**, no **library**, and no **movie theater**. Concon is beautiful. There are **parks** in the town and beaches nearby. Sometimes I get homesick for my little town.

1 a factory

2 **a stadium**

3 a mall

4 a motel

5 a mosque

6 **a school**

7 a synagogue

8 **a hospital**

9 **a college**

10 a police station

11 **a theater**

12 a movie theater

13 **a church**

14 a post office

15 an office building

16 a fire station

17 a city hall / a town hall

18 **a library**

19 a courthouse

20 a gas station

21 a parking garage

22 a high-rise (building)

23 a car dealership

24 a sidewalk

25 **a corner**

26 an intersection

27 **a street**

28 **a park**

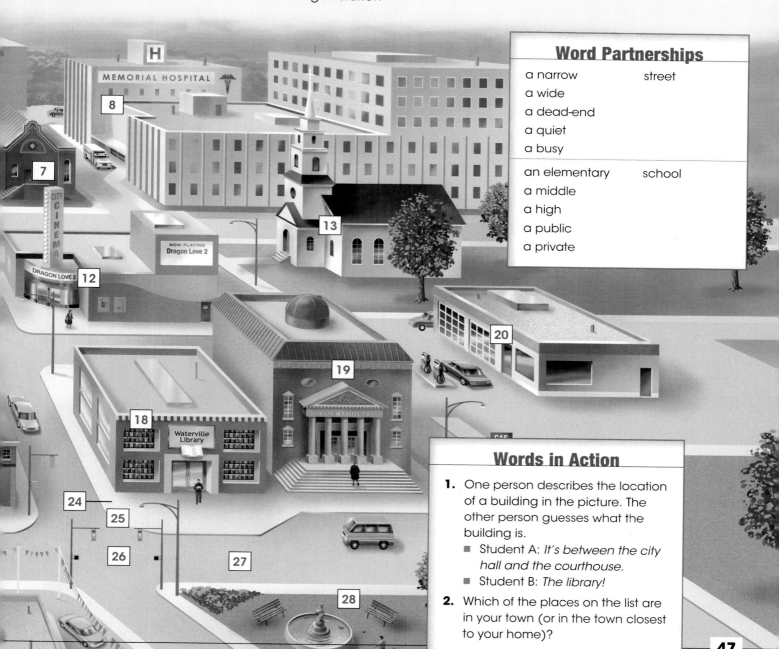

H
MEMORIAL HOSPITAL
8
7
CITY CINEMA
NOW PLAYING
Dragon Love 2
13
DRAGON LOVE 2
12
20
19
18
Waterville Library
24
25
26
27
28

Word Partnerships

a narrow	street
a wide	
a dead-end	
a quiet	
a busy	

an elementary	school
a middle	
a high	
a public	
a private	

Words in Action

1. One person describes the location of a building in the picture. The other person guesses what the building is.
   - Student A: *It's between the city hall and the courthouse.*
   - Student B: *The library!*

2. Which of the places on the list are in your town (or in the town closest to your home)?

47

Shops and Stores

Words in Context

Americans shop a lot before holidays. Before Thanksgiving, **supermarkets** sell a lot of food. Just before Christmas, **department stores** and **toy stores** are crowded. Around Valentine's Day, **florists** and **jewelry stores** are very busy.

1 an electronics store
2 a clothing store
3 a shoe store
4 **a gift shop**
5 a jewelry store
6 a sporting goods store
7 a toy store
8 a furniture store
9 **a bookstore**
10 **a music store**
11 a hair salon / a beauty salon
12 a barbershop
13 a health club / **a gym**
14 a thrift shop / a second-hand store
15 a copy shop
16 a nail salon
17 a (dry) cleaner
18 a flower stand
19 **a coffee shop**
20 a pet store
21 **a bakery**
22 a laundromat
23 a fast food restaurant
24 **a department store**
25 **a drugstore** / **a pharmacy**
26 **a supermarket**
27 an ice cream stand
28 a flea market

Word Partnerships

shop at	a bookstore
work at	a jewelry store
manage	a music store
own	a bakery

Words in Action

1. You need bread, dog food, aspirin, a swimsuit, and a CD. Which stores will you go to?

2. What three stores in the picture do you most like to go to? Why? Tell a partner.

Bank

2.5%

LOWEST RATES
3.0% 🎓
2.5% 🏠
2.0% 🚗

LOAN OFFICER

BANK MANAGER

Word Partnerships

a withdrawal	slip
a deposit	
write	a check
sign	
endorse	
cash	
deposit	
bounce	
earn	interest

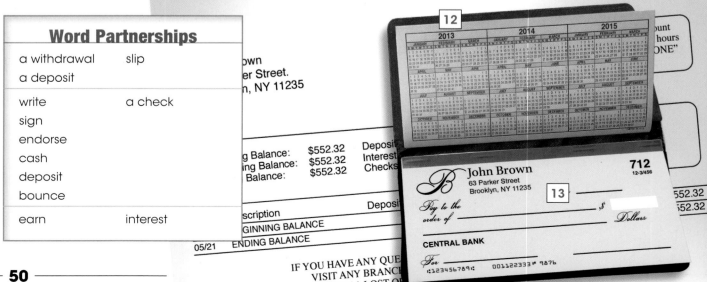

10 **C** Central Bank
5001 BAY ST. BROOKLYN, NY 11235

CHECKING
Monthly Statement   Account 00001546093
Statement Period: 04/22/14 through 05/21/14

Page 1 of 1
Enclosures: 0

...unt
...hours
...ONE"

...own
...er Street.
...n, NY 11235

...g Balance:	$552.32	Deposi...
...ing Balance:	$552.32	Interes...
...Balance:	$552.32	Checks...

...scription   Deposi...
...GINNING BALANCE
05/21   ENDING BALANCE

IF YOU HAVE ANY QUE...
VISIT ANY BRANC...
TO REPORT A LOST O...

B John Brown   **712**
63 Parker Street   12-3/456
Brooklyn, NY 11235

Pay to the
order of _____ $ _____
_____ Dollars

CENTRAL BANK

For _____
⑆123456789⑆ 001122333⑈ 9876

552.32
552.32

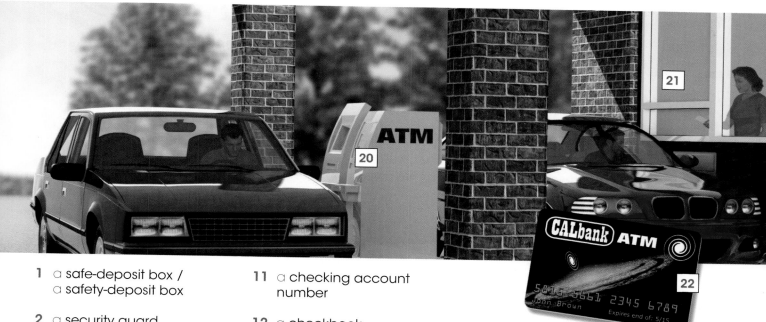

1 a safe-deposit box / a safety-deposit box

2 a security guard

3 a vault

4 a teller

5 a teller window

6 **cash** / **money**

7 a **customer**

8 a bank manager

9 a loan officer

10 a (monthly) statement

11 a checking account number

12 a checkbook

13 a check

14 a (savings account) passbook

15 **interest**

16 a deposit

17 a withdrawal

18 a balance

19 a money order

20 an ATM

21 a drive-up window

22 an ATM card / a bankcard

SAVINGS ACCOUNT				
NOTE	%INTEREST	+DEPOSITS	–WITHDRAWLS	BALANCE
24 Open account		$500.00		$500.00
24 Textbooks			$75.00	$425.00
11 Interest	$3.21			$428.21
25 Birthday gift from Mom		$25.00		$453.21
2 Interest	$3.68			$456.89

14 **15** **16** **17** **18**

UNITED STATES POSTAL SERVICE. POSTAL MONEY ORDER **19**

SERIAL NUMBER 03313978165
YEAR, MONTH, DAY 2014-03-27
POST OFFICE 017720
16-800 000
U.S. DOLLARS AND CENTS **$1,500.00¢**
PAY TO Chow Realty
ADDRESS 1125 W. 62 nd
Alameda 73 Blvd
AMOUNT **ONE THOUSAND FIVE HUNDRED & 00¢ *********
NEGOTIABLE ONLY IN THE U.S. AND POSSESSIONS
C.O.D. NO. OR USED FOR
FROM John Brown
ADDRESS 63 Parker St
Brooklyn NY
CLERK 004
⑆0000008003⑆ 03313978165⑈

Verbs

23 **wait** in line

24 **insert** your ATM card

25 **enter** your PIN

26 **withdraw** cash

27 **make** a deposit

28 **remove** your card

Words in Action

1. When was the last time you went to the bank? What did you do there? What part of the bank did you go to? Who did you speak to?

2. Work with a partner. One person says the steps to using an ATM. The other acts out the steps.

Post Office

Words in Context

Do you want the **mail** you **send** to arrive safely and on time? Be sure to use a **zip code** on every **letter** and **package**. Also be sure to use a **return address**. A **postal clerk** can **weigh** your mail so you will know how much **postage** to put on it.

1

Name:
Address:
Maria Garcia
456 Stone St.
Homeland, FL 33847

The Electric Company

Due date: 5-10-14

Balance Due: $70.00

3

2

Dear Elena,

Thanks for your letter. I was happy to hear from you. Everything is fine with me. I like my English class and I'm meeting many new friends. I'm living in a nice town. It has lots of good shops and stores. I am spending too much money!

How are you? How is your family? Write me again soon.

Love,
Maria

Maria Garcia
456 Stone St.
Homeland, FL
33847 — **4**

5

Happy Birthday!

Elena Ramírez
65 Oak Ave.
Pasadena, CA
91101 — **7**

6

8

16

15

2.00 oz

1 a **bill**	7 a **zip code**	12 a stamp machine	18 a postmark
2 a **letter**	8 an **envelope**	13 a post office box / a P.O. Box	19 overnight mail / next-day mail
3 a **greeting card**	9 a **mailbox**	14 a **catalog**	20 a (postal) clerk
4 a (return) address	10 a mail carrier / a letter carrier	15 a (postal) scale	
5 a **stamp**	11 a mail truck	16 a **postcard**	
6 a (mailing) address		17 a **package**	

52

Verbs

21 address

22 weigh

23 put a stamp on

24 mail / send

Tomorrow.

17 TARO SHIZAWA
56 POWELL ST.
QUEENS, N.Y.

Word Partnerships

a business	letter
a personal	
a love	
a first class	stamp
a book of	stamps
a sheet of	
a roll of	
a postage-paid	envelope
a self-addressed stamped	

Words in Action

1. What kinds of mail do you send? What kinds do you get? What is your favorite kind of mail to receive? What is your least favorite? Discuss with a group.

2. Describe your last visit to the post office. What did you do? Who did you talk to? What did you see? Tell your partner.

Library

25 look for a book

26 check out books

Words in Context

Libraries can change people's lives. In 1953, **author** Frank McCourt arrived in New York City from Ireland. One day a man told Frank to go to a library. So Frank did. He got a **library card**, **checked out** a **book**, and fell in love with reading. All of the reading he did at the library helped Frank McCourt become a successful **writer**. Now people can read his **autobiography** in 30 different languages!

Reading Room

Reference Desk

Title War and Peace
Author Tolstoy **5**

BigBook of Cheer by Mike Nichols

Observer
FIRE BURNS FOREST

WAR & PEACE
Leo Tolstoy

Chinese Cooking

27 read

Book Return

28 return books

1 the periodical section
2 a **magazine**
3 the reading room
4 the reference desk
5 an online catalog / a computerized catalog
6 the fiction section
7 the nonfiction section
8 a **dictionary**
9 an encyclopedia
10 a librarian
11 a library card
12 a hardcover (book)

13 a paperback (book)
14 an atlas
15 the circulation desk / the checkout desk
16 a **newspaper**
17 a **headline**
18 a **title**
19 a **novel**
20 an **author** / a **writer**
21 a cookbook
22 a **biography**
23 an autobiography
24 a **picture book**

Fiction **6**

Nonfiction **7**

Reference

8

9

Children's Section

24

Fishy, Fish, Fish

Gandhi's Life
22
By
Jane Smith

My Life
by
Abraham Lincoln
23

Word Partnerships

a library	book
a good	book
a boring	writer
a detective	novel
a romance	
a science-fiction	
a historical	

Words in Action

1. Imagine you will spend an afternoon in this library. What will you do?
2. Discuss the following questions with a group:
   - What is your favorite book?
   - What is your favorite magazine?
   - What is your favorite newspaper?

Daycare Center

Words in Context

Parents should check these things at a **daycare center**:

- Are the children busy and happy?
- Do the **childcare workers** take good care of the children?
- Is there a special room for **newborns**?
- Are the **potty chairs** and **changing tables** clean?

Word Partnerships

a cute	baby
a newborn	
baby	food
a clean	diaper
a dirty	
change	a diaper
play with	toys
put away	
share	

31 a newborn

32 an infant / a baby

33 a toddler

34 a preschooler

1 a **nipple**

2 a **bottle**

3 a **crib**

4 a playpen

5 a rest mat

6 a baby swing

7 a teething ring

8 a **parent**

9 a baby carrier

10 a rattle

11 a **stroller**

12 a cubby

13 a **girl**

14 a **boy**

15 **toys**

16 a **bib**

17 a childcare worker

18 a **high chair**

19 formula

20 a potty chair

21 a diaper pail

22 (baby) powder

23 (baby) lotion

24 (baby) wipes

25 a pacifier

26 a changing table

27 a (disposable) diaper

28 training pants

29 a (cloth) diaper

30 a diaper pin

Words in Action

1. Which are the 10 most important items for a newborn? Discuss and make a list with a group.

2. Imagine you have a one-year-old baby. You are taking a trip on an airplane. Which items will you take?

Formula

City Square

Words in Context

Prague and Marrakesh have interesting **city squares**. The squares have outdoor **cafés**, **street vendors**, **street musicians**, and **pedestrians**. There are many **hotels**, **museums**, and **restaurants**. At night, there are plenty of **tourists** in the squares.

1 a **hotel**

2 a **bank**

3 an art gallery

4 a streetlight

5 a traffic accident

6 a **(traffic) cop**

7 a **fountain**

8 a **café**

9 a **billboard**

10 a monument

11 a **(fire) hydrant**

12 a street vendor

13 a travel agency

14 a handicapped parking space

15 a **curb**

16 a **sidewalk**

17 a pedestrian

18 a crosswalk

19 a **sign**

20 a (parking) meter

Keep Our City Clean! 9

Cafe Rio

World Travel 13

Vincent **Van Gogh** EXHIBITION

24

23

21 a tourist
information booth

22 a street musician

23 a **statue**

24 a **museum**

25 a newsstand

Word Partnerships	
an art	museum
a science	
a natural history	
a street	sign
a neon	
a sidewalk	café
an outdoor	

Words in Action

1. Imagine you are a tourist in this city square. Where will you go? What will you do?

2. Think about the town or city you live in or near. Make a list of all the things you can find there.

Crime and Justice

Words in Context

Iceland has very little **crime**. There are only four **prisons**, and many of the **prisoners** are part-time! There are usually only one or two **murders** a year, and crimes like **armed robbery** are extremely rare. There are sometimes **muggings** in the capital city of Reykjavík, but Iceland is still one of the safest countries in the world.

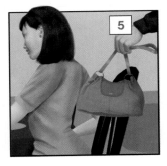

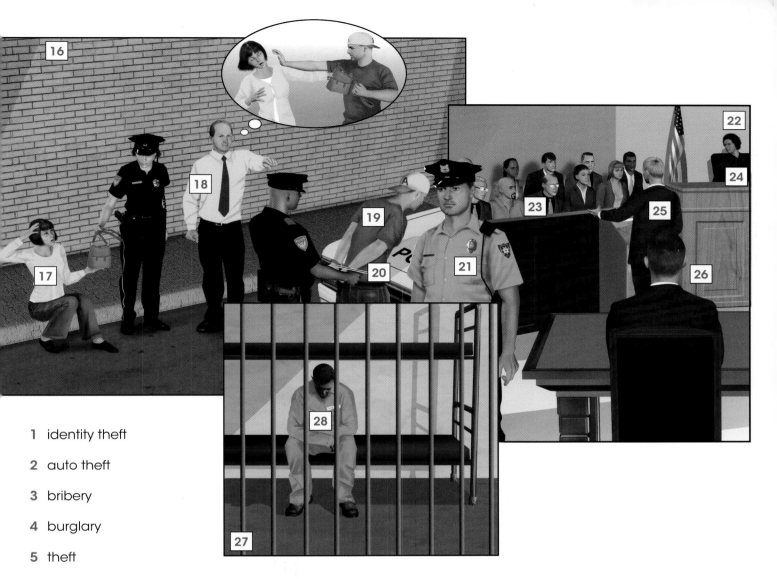

1 identity theft

2 auto theft

3 bribery

4 burglary

5 theft

6 drug dealing

7 drunk driving

8 arson

9 graffiti

10 mugging

11 **murder**

12 shoplifting

13 vandalism

14 gang violence

15 armed robbery

16 an **arrest**

17 a **victim**

18 a **witness**

19 a criminal

20 handcuffs

21 a police officer

22 a **trial**

23 a jury

24 a **judge**

25 a **lawyer /**
an **attorney**

26 a courtroom

27 a jail / a **prison**

28 a **prisoner**

Word Partnerships

a fair	trial
a speedy	
commit	a crime
witness	
report	
go to	prison
spend time in	
get out of	

Words in Action

1. Talk with a group. Which crimes are most common in your community?

2. Put the crimes in a list from the least serious crime to the most serious crime. Discuss your list with a partner.

Types of Homes

Words in Context

Do you live in a **house**, an **apartment**, or a **condo**? There are many other kinds of homes, too. For example, some people in the Sahara desert live in **tents**. Some people in the U.S. live in **mobile homes**. And some people near the North Pole live in **igloos**.

Word Partnerships

live in	a house
	an apartment
	a dorm
live on	a houseboat
	a ranch

1 a **house**

2 a **tent**

3 a **cottage**

4 a (log) cabin

5 a chalet

6 a duplex / a two-family house

7 a mobile home

8 a farmhouse

9 an **apartment**

10 a **condominium** / a **condo**

11 a villa

12 a townhouse

13 a houseboat

14 a **palace**

15 an igloo

16 a **ranch**

17 a retirement home

18 a dormitory / a **dorm**

19 a **castle**

20 the city / an urban area

21 the suburbs

22 a small town

23 the country / a rural area

Words in Action

1. What kinds of homes have you lived in or stayed in? Tell your class.

2. You can stay in three of these homes. Which three will you choose? Why?

Finding a Place to Live

Words in Context

Are you **looking for** an apartment? It isn't always easy. Read the classified ads in newspapers and talk to your friends. **Make** appointments to see a lot of apartments. Before you **sign** a lease, talk to the landlord. **Ask** questions like these:

- How much is the security deposit?
- When is the rent due?
- When can I **move in**?

Renting an Apartment

1 **look for** an apartment

2 **make** an appointment (with the landlord)

3 **meet** the landlord

4 **see** the apartment

5 **ask** questions

6 **sign** the lease

7 **pay** a security deposit

8 **get** the key

9 pack

10 load a van or truck

11 unpack

12 arrange the furniture

13 decorate the apartment

14 pay the rent

15 **meet** the neighbors

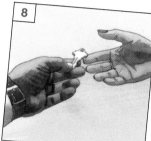

Buying a House

16 **call** a real estate agent

17 **look at** houses

18 **make** a decision

19 **make** an offer

20 **negotiate** the price

21 **inspect** the house

22 **apply for** a loan

23 **make** a down payment

24 **sign** the loan documents

25 **move in**

26 **make** the (house) payment

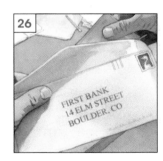

Word Partnerships		
look for	an apartment	in the classified ads
		online
		with a real estate agent
pay	the rent	early
		late
		on time

Words in Action

1. Work in pairs. Cover the words. Say what's happening in one of the pictures. Your partner will find and point to this picture. Take turns.

2. Have you rented an apartment or bought a house? Tell your group what steps you took.

Apartment Building

Words in Context

I'm the **superintendent** of an **apartment building** in Los Angeles. We have **30 unfurnished apartments**. Most of these are **studios**. We have a **laundry room** in the **basement**. There's no **doorman**, but I watch everyone who comes in the **lobby**. I take good care of my building.

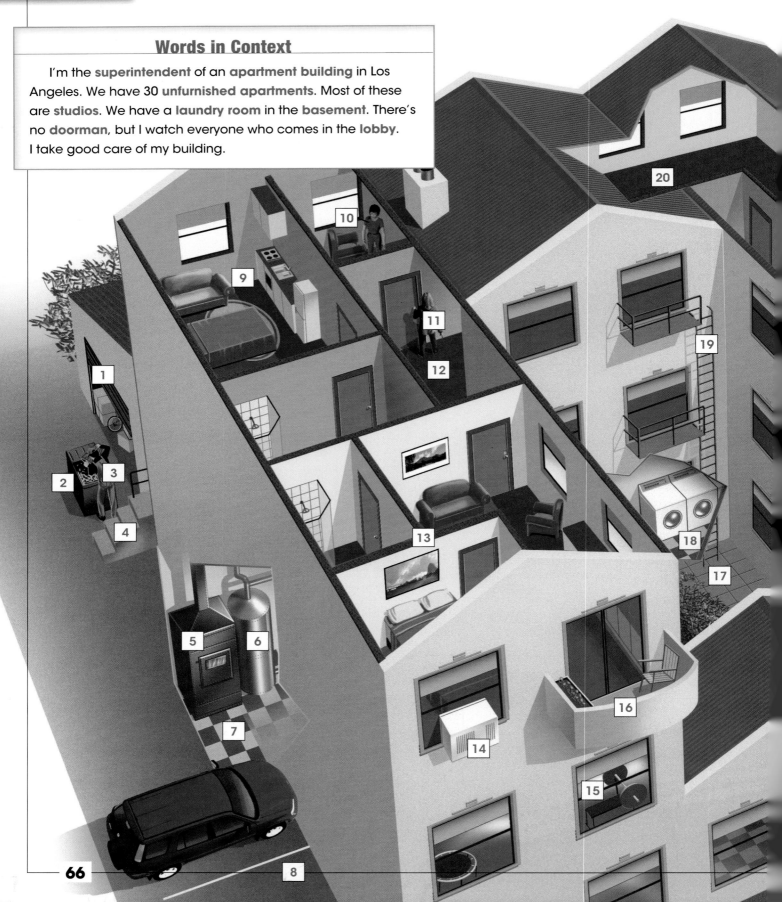

1 a storage space	7 a **basement**	20 an unfurnished apartment
2 a dumpster	8 a parking space	21 a furnished apartment
3 a **superintendent** / a super	9 a studio (apartment)	22 a **lobby**
4 **stairs**	10 a **tenant**	23 an **elevator**
5 a furnace	11 a roommate	24 a revolving door
6 a water heater	12 a **hallway**	25 a doorman
	13 a one-bedroom apartment	26 a peephole
	14 an air conditioner	27 a door chain
	15 a workout room / a **gym**	28 a dead-bolt (lock)
	16 a balcony	29 a doorknob
	17 a **courtyard**	30 an intercom
	18 a laundry room	31 a **key**
	19 a fire escape	

Word Partnerships

the ground	floor
the first	
the second	
the third	
the fourth	

Words in Action

1. Role-play with a partner. One of you is the super of this building. The other is looking for an apartment.
   - Student A: *Is there a laundry room?*
   - Student B: *Yes. It's in the basement.*

2. Describe an apartment building you know.

House and Garden

Words in Context

Different cultures have different kinds of **houses**. North American houses often have **yards** with **lawns**. People cook on their **grills** and relax on a **patio**, **porch**, or **deck**. Some Arab and Mexican houses have courtyards. Even **windows** are different from place to place. In France, windows open like **doors**. In Greece and North Africa, windows are often painted blue.

1 a chimney

2 an attic

3 a skylight

4 a **roof**

5 a **deck**

6 a grill / a barbecue

7 a hammock

8 a lawn / **grass**

9 a lawn mower

10 a **window**

11 a shutter

12 a **door**

13 a doorbell

14 a porch

15 **steps**

16 a **garage**

17 a rake

18 a driveway

19 a garbage can / a trash can

20 a **yard**

21 a **garden**

22 a patio

23 a **gate**

24 a fence

25 hedge clippers

26 a wheelbarrow

27 a (garden) hose

28 a walk(way)

29 a sprinkler

Word Partnerships

a flower	garden
a vegetable	
a chain-link	fence
a picket	
a barbed wire	
a front	door
a screen	
a garage	

Words in Action

1. Cover the word list. Name as many parts of the house as you can. Start at the top of the house and work your way down.

2. Draw your dream house. Label all the parts. Show your dream house to a partner. How are they similar? How are they different?

69

Kitchen and Dining Area

1	a microwave (oven)	21	a stool
2	a **cabinet**	22	a **chair**
3	**dishes**	23	a **plate**
4	a **shelf**	24	a **bowl**
5	a counter(top)	25	a **glass**
6	a stove	26	a placemat
7	a (tea) kettle	27	silverware
8	an oven	28	a **candle**
9	a potholder	29	a teapot
10	a coffeemaker	30	a mug
11	a spice rack	31	a napkin
12	a blender	32	a **table**
13	a toaster		
14	a dishwasher		
15	a sink		
16	a drying rack / a dish rack		
17	a garbage disposal		
18	a dish towel		
19	a freezer		
20	a **refrigerator**		

Word Partnerships

a dining room	table
a kitchen	chair
an electric	stove
a gas	
load	the dishwasher
start / turn on	
empty	

Living Room

Words in Context

Some people like lots of furniture in their living rooms—a **sofa**, a **love seat**, a **coffee table**, chairs, a **wall unit**, and several **lamps**. Others like just a rug and a couple of **easy chairs**. In the Middle East, people often sit on **cushions** or low **benches** instead of chairs. And in some Asian countries, people sit on the **floor**.

1 a **bench**	9 a (throw) pillow	17 a **ceiling**	25 a thermostat
2 a cushion	10 a window seat	18 a smoke detector	26 a mantel
3 an armchair / an easy chair	11 a love seat	19 blinds	27 a fireplace
4 an end table	12 a coffee table	20 a **curtain**	28 a fire screen
5 a **lamp**	13 an ottoman	21 a **wall**	29 a house plant
6 a lampshade	14 the **floor**	22 a bookcase	30 a **fire**
7 a wall unit	15 a curtain rod	23 a vent	31 a rocking chair
8 a **sofa** / a **couch**	16 a (ceiling) fan	24 a (light) switch	32 an **outlet**

Word Partnerships

a floor	lamp
a table	
a desk	

sit	in an armchair
	in a rocking chair
	on a sofa
	on the floor
	on a cushion

Words in Action

1. How is your living room similar to this one? How is it different? Discuss with a partner.
   - *I have a fireplace like the one in the picture.*
   - *My sofa is bigger than the one in the picture.*

2. Draw your perfect living room. Label all the items in the drawing.

Bedroom and Bathroom

Words in Context

Feng shui is a Chinese art. It suggests ways to make homes healthy and happy. For a calm **bedroom**, your **bed** should not face a door. Your **bedspread** should not touch the floor. In the **bathroom**, the **toilet** should not face the door. You should have many **mirrors**. Mirrors bring happiness.

1 a **closet**

2 a **blanket**

3 a **carpet**

4 a rug

5 a drawer

6 a dresser

7 a **mirror**

8 a (window) shade

9 an alarm clock

10 a night table

11 a pillowcase

12 a **pillow**

13 a mattress

14 a **bed**

15 a **sheet**

16 a comforter

17 a bedspread

18 a **shower**

19 a shower curtain

20 a drain

21 a medicine cabinet

22 a (bath)tub

23 a plunger

24 toilet paper /
toilet tissue

25 a **toilet**

26 a **towel**

27 a faucet

28 a sink

29 a washcloth

30 a toilet brush

31 a wastebasket

Word Partnerships

a twin	bed
a double	
a queen-size	
a king-size	
a bunk	
a fitted	sheet
a flat	
flush	the toilet
go to	bed
get out of	
make the	

Words in Action

1. Draw your bedroom and label the things in it. Then describe it to a partner.
   - *There is a big bed with three red pillows. There's also a dresser with five drawers.*

2. What things are usually already in a bedroom and bathroom when you move into a house or apartment? What things do you usually need to bring? Make lists with a partner.

Household Problems

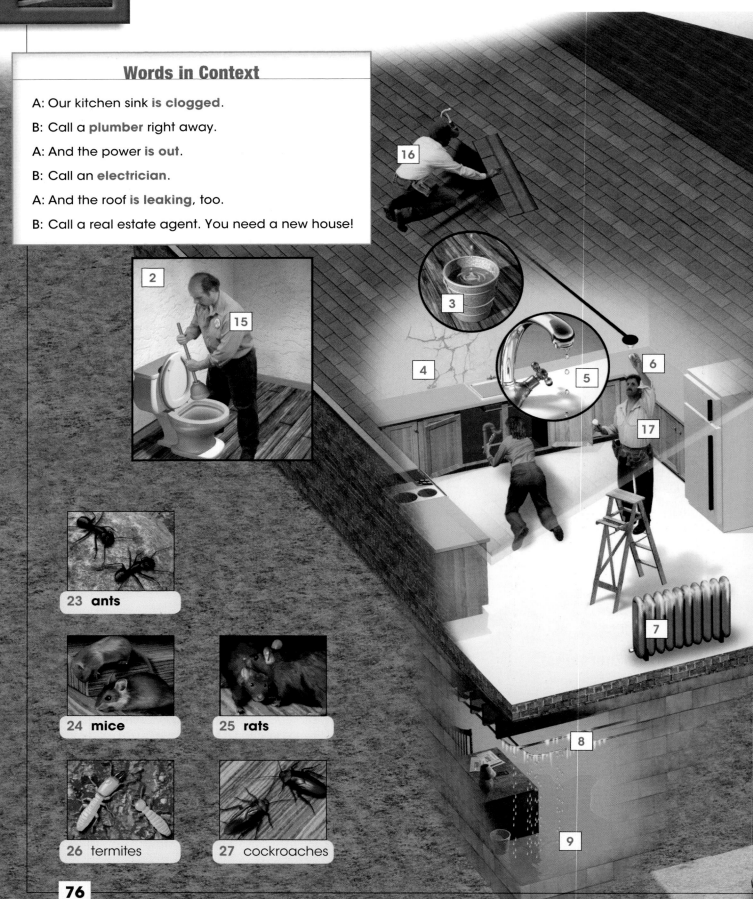

Words in Context

A: Our kitchen sink **is clogged**.

B: Call a **plumber** right away.

A: And the power **is out**.

B: Call an **electrician**.

A: And the roof **is leaking**, too.

B: Call a real estate agent. You need a new house!

23 **ants**

24 **mice**

25 **rats**

26 termites

27 cockroaches

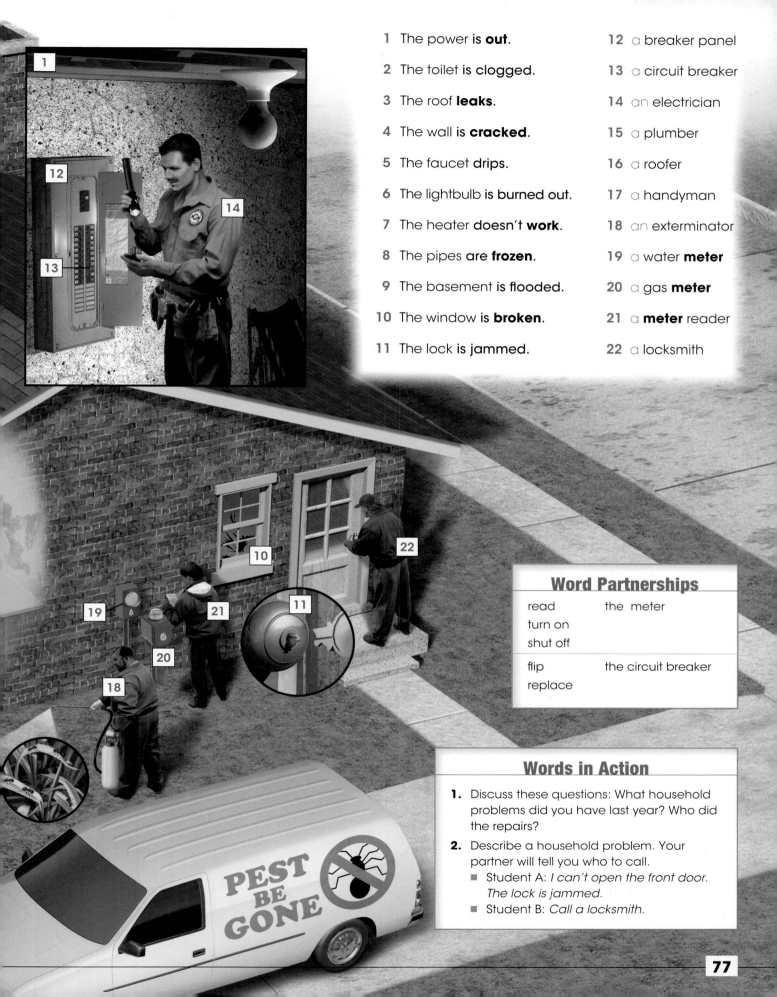

1 The power **is out**.
2 The toilet **is clogged**.
3 The roof **leaks**.
4 The wall **is cracked**.
5 The faucet **drips**.
6 The lightbulb **is burned out**.
7 The heater **doesn't work**.
8 The pipes **are frozen**.
9 The basement **is flooded**.
10 The window **is broken**.
11 The lock **is jammed**.

12 a breaker panel
13 a circuit breaker
14 an electrician
15 a plumber
16 a roofer
17 a handyman
18 an exterminator
19 a water **meter**
20 a gas **meter**
21 a **meter** reader
22 a locksmith

Word Partnerships

read	the meter
turn on	
shut off	
flip	the circuit breaker
replace	

Words in Action

1. Discuss these questions: What household problems did you have last year? Who did the repairs?
2. Describe a household problem. Your partner will tell you who to call.
   - Student A: *I can't open the front door. The lock is jammed.*
   - Student B: *Call a locksmith.*

Household Chores

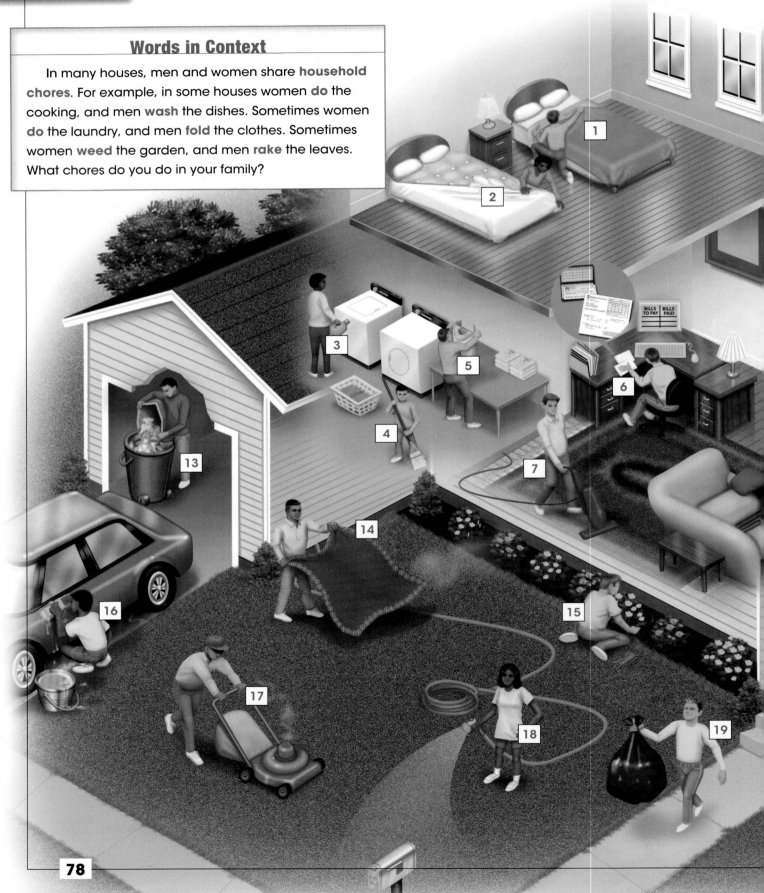

78

1 **make** the bed

2 **change** the sheets

3 **do** the laundry

4 **sweep** the floor

5 fold the clothes

6 **pay** the bills

7 vacuum the carpet

8 dust

9 polish the furniture

10 **clean** the sink

11 scrub the toilet

12 mop the floor

13 **empty** the wastebasket

14 shake out the rug

15 weed the garden

16 **wash** the car

17 mow the lawn /
mow the grass

18 **water** the lawn

19 take out the trash /
put out the trash

20 rake the leaves

21 **do** the dishes /
wash the dishes

22 cook / **do** the cooking

23 **dry** the dishes

24 put away the dishes

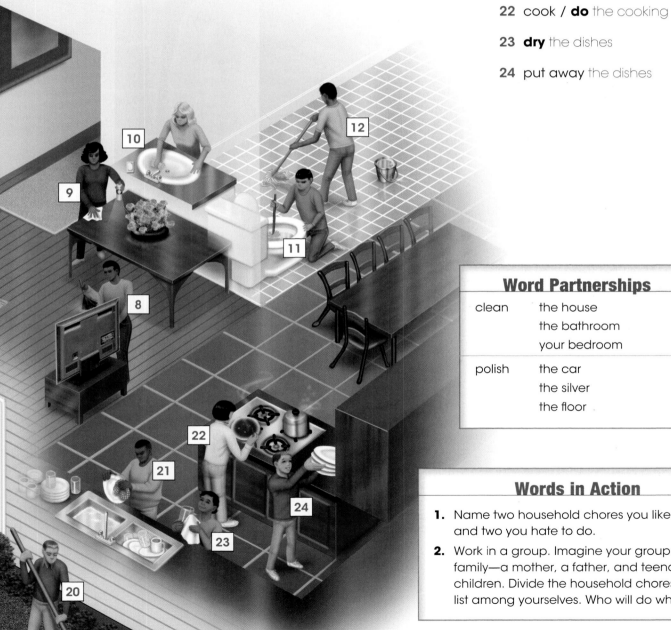

Word Partnerships

clean	the house
	the bathroom
	your bedroom
polish	the car
	the silver
	the floor

Words in Action

1. Name two household chores you like to do and two you hate to do.

2. Work in a group. Imagine your group is a family—a mother, a father, and teenage children. Divide the household chores on the list among yourselves. Who will do what?

Cleaning Supplies

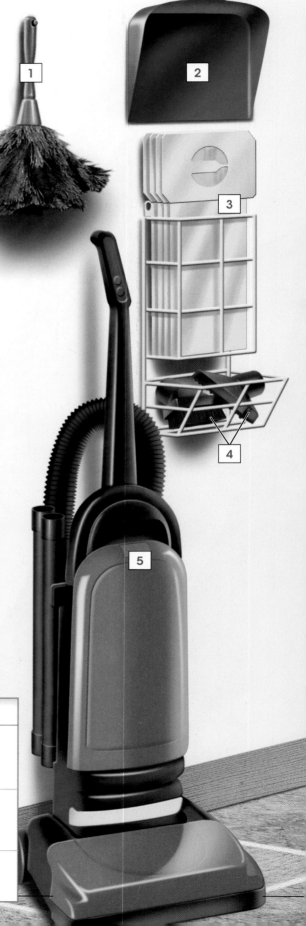

Words in Context

Do you want to wash a window? Follow these steps:

- Put on **rubber gloves**.
- Mix a gallon of warm water with a little ammonia.
- Put the liquid on the window with a clean **sponge**.
- Pull a **squeegee** across the window.
- Wipe the squeegee with a **rag** or a **paper towel** and repeat.

1 a feather duster

2 a dustpan

3 a vacuum cleaner bag

4 vacuum cleaner attachments

5 a **vacuum** (cleaner)

6 a squeegee

7 **paper towels**

8 trash bags

9 furniture polish

10 a dust cloth

11 glass cleaner

12 dishwasher detergent

13 dish soap / dishwashing liquid

14 a scouring pad

15 bug spray / insect spray

16 a **bucket** / a **pail**

17 a **rag**

18 **rubber gloves**

19 **cleanser**

20 a scrub brush

21 a **sponge**

22 a flyswatter

23 a stepladder

24 a mousetrap

25 a recycling bin

26 a **mop**

27 a dust mop

28 a **broom**

Word Partnerships

heavy-duty	trash bags
20-gallon	
plastic	
a sponge	mop
a string	
a floor	
a push	broom
a kitchen	

80

Words in Action

1. Name cleaning supplies you use often. What do you use each item for?

2. You need to clean your living room, your bathroom, and your kitchen. Which cleaning items will you use for each room?

Fruits and Nuts

82

Fruits

1 a pear
2 a kiwi
3 an **orange**
4 a pomegranate
5 **grapes**
6 a watermelon
7 a pineapple
8 a mango
9 a grapefruit
10 an avocado
11 an **apple**
12 a cantaloupe
13 a **coconut**
14 a **lemon**
15 a **plum**
16 an apricot
17 blueberries
18 a papaya
19 a **peach**
20 a **lime**
21 cherries
22 figs
23 olives
24 **dates**
25 strawberries
26 raspberries
27 raisins
28 a tangerine
29 a **banana**

Nuts

30 pecans
31 almonds
32 pistachios
33 peanuts
34 walnuts

Word Partnerships

peel	a banana
	an orange
	an apple
crack (open)	a nut
ripe	fruit
juicy	
canned	
dried	
citrus	
tropical	

Words in Action

1. What are your five favorite fruits? Rank them in order. Share your list with your class. Is your list similar to other students' lists?

2. Create a recipe for a delicious fruit drink. Use at least four fruits.

Vegetables

1 broccoli

2 beets

3 asparagus

4 spinach

5 **lettuce**

6 squash

7 a **tomato**

8 **cabbage**

9 pinto beans

10 chickpeas / garbanzo beans

11 a zucchini

12 an eggplant

13 an artichoke

14 celery

15 an **onion**

16 cauliflower

17 a turnip

18 kidney beans

19 a **carrot**

20 bean sprouts

21 lima beans

22 a sweet potato

23 a bell pepper

24 **corn**

25 a cucumber

26 a **potato**

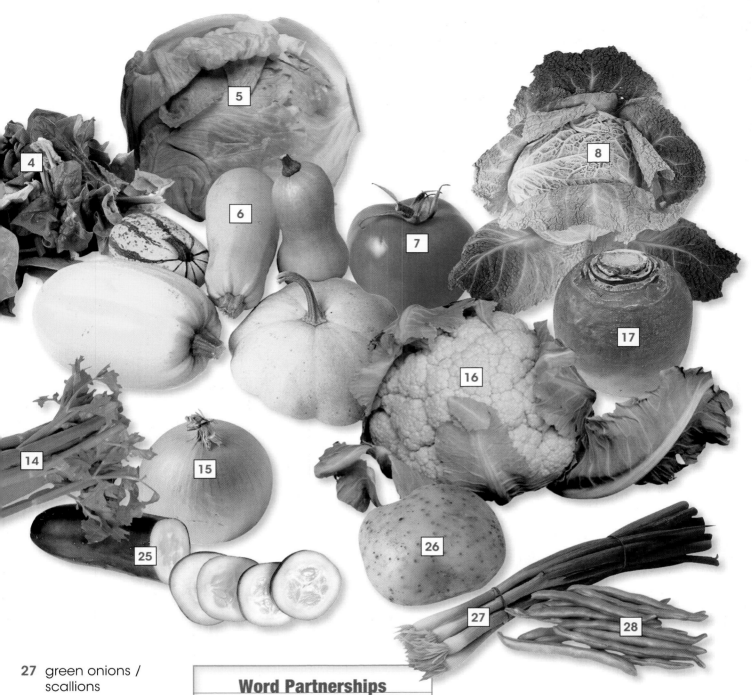

27 green onions /
scallions

28 green beans /
string beans

29 **garlic**

30 **peas**

31 a radish

32 a **mushroom**

Word Partnerships

a head of	cabbage
	cauliflower
	lettuce
an ear of	corn
a spinach	leaf
a lettuce	
fresh	vegetables
frozen	
raw	
organic	

Words in Action

1. Which vegetables do you have in your house right now? Which ones do you eat raw? Which ones have you never eaten?

2. Make two lists: *Vegetables I like* and *Vegetables I don't like*. Compare your lists with a partner.

Meat, Poultry, and Seafood

Words in Context

Fish and **shellfish** are healthy foods. They contain very little fat. The Koreans and the Japanese eat a lot of **seafood**. **Clams**, **oysters**, **shrimp**, and **tuna** are favorite foods in these countries. However, Americans love **meat**. The average American eats 27 pounds (12.3 kilograms) of **ground beef** a year—mostly in hamburgers.

MEAT

BEEF

PORK

LAMB

POULTRY

1 lamb chops
2 leg of lamb
3 pork chops
4 ham
5 salami
6 sausages
7 pork roast
8 ground beef
9 ribs
10 **steak**

11 roast beef
12 **liver**
13 veal cutlets
14 lobster
15 oysters
16 clams
17 mussels
18 crab
19 scallops
20 shrimp
21 filet of sole

22 cod
23 swordfish
24 **salmon**
25 trout
26 tuna
27 **thighs**
28 **wings**
29 **breasts**
30 **turkey**
31 **chicken**
32 **duck**
33 drumsticks / **legs**

Word Partnerships

raw fresh frozen grilled	fish
fatty lean	meat
a rare a medium a well-done	steak

Words in Action

1. Pick your favorite items from the meat, poultry, and seafood sections. Compare your favorites with a partner.

2. Imagine you are having a barbecue. What meat, poultry, and seafood will you buy?

87

Inside the Refrigerator

1   frozen vegetables
2   frozen waffles
3   **ice cream**
4   ice tray
5   **soda**
6   margarine
7   mayonnaise
8   sour cream
9   iced tea
10 pickles
11 tofu
12 yogurt
13 syrup
14 **cream**
15 bottled water
16 **cake**
17 **jam**

18 **salad**
19 (salad) dressing
20 **bacon**
21 cold cuts
22 (cheddar) cheese
23 **butter**
24 (Swiss) cheese
25 **eggs**
26 **milk**
27 orange juice
28 apple juice

Word Partnerships

fruit	salad
potato	
pasta	
scrambled	eggs
fried	
hard-boiled	
poached	
mozzarella	cheese
Parmesan	
cottage	

Frozen Vegetables 1

Frozen Waffles 2

Real Ice Cream 3

4

Soda 5

6 Margarine

MAYONNAISE 7

8 Sour Cream

9

10 Pickles

Tofu 11

22 Cheddar Cheese

23

24

Yogurt 12

13 Syrup

CREAM 14

15 SPRING WATER

16

17 Strawberry Jam

25

18

19 Salad Dressing

Farm Fresh BACON 20

21

26 Freshest LO FAT MILK

27 Orange Juice

28 Apple Juice

Words in Action

1. Think about the foods in the refrigerator. Make three lists: *Very healthy*, *Less healthy*, and *Not healthy*. Discuss your list with a partner.

2. Plan your dinner tonight using the food in this refrigerator.

Food to Go

Words in Context

Do you eat at the **food court**? Health experts have some advice for you. Don't order a **hot dog** and **french fries**. Order a salad instead. Don't have a **hamburger**. Have **beans** and **rice** instead. And finally, don't order **coffee** or soda. Have water or juice.

1	**pizza**	7	french fries	13	**tea**
2	lasagna	8	a **hot dog**	14	a doughnut
3	spaghetti	9	a baked potato	15	a muffin
4	a **hamburger**	10	a **sandwich**	16	**mustard**
5	a bagel	11	a **straw**	17	ketchup
6	fish and chips	12	**coffee**	18	chopsticks

Word Partnerships

sticky	rice
steamed	
fried	
black	beans
pinto	
refried	
a slice of	pizza
a piece of	
a small	
a medium	
a large	

Rice
Fried Brown
white

Stir Fried Vegetables
Chicken
Shrimp
Beef

Chicken Teriyaki
Chicken
Shrimp
Beef

Egg Rolls
Spring

HOT SALSA

BURRITOS
beef chicken egg
cheese special

TACOS
beef
chicken
fish

19 **rice**

20 stir-fried vegetables

21 chicken teriyaki

22 an egg roll

23 sushi

24 soy sauce

25 a burrito

26 a taco

27 salsa

28 **beans**

29 a tortilla

Words in Action

1. Which take-out foods do you like? Which ones don't you like?

2. Work with a partner. Role-play ordering food at one of the places in the picture.
    - Student A: *Can I help you?*
    - Student B: *Yes, I'd like two egg rolls.*
    - Student A: *Do you want something to drink?*
    - Student B: *Yes. Coffee, please.*

Cooking

Shish Kebab Recipe

1 **Measure** $^1/_4$ cup of olive oil.

2 **Dice** 1 tablespoon of garlic.

3 **Whisk** the oil and garlic with a little lemon juice.

4 **Add** 1 pound of lamb cubes.

5 **Marinate** overnight in the refrigerator.

6 **Grill** the kebabs for 5 minutes on each side.

Breakfast Burrito Recipe

7 **Scramble** 2 eggs in a bowl.

8 **Fry** the eggs.

9 **Broil** 2 slices of bacon.

10 **Steam** a cup of broccoli.

11 **Grate** $^1/_4$ cup of cheese.

12 **Fold** everything into a tortilla.

13 **Microwave** for 30 seconds.

Roast Chicken with Potatoes Recipe

14 **Season** the chicken with garlic and rosemary.

15 **Roast** at 350°F (175°C). (20 minutes per pound)

16 **Baste** frequently with pan juices.

17 **Boil** the potatoes.

° = degrees

Pea Soup Recipe

18 **Slice** 1 large onion.

19 **Sauté** the onion in oil.

20 **Stir** the onion and 1 pound of split peas into 2 quarts of water.

21 **Simmer** for 2 hours.

22 **Peel** 4 large carrots.

23 **Chop** the carrots and add to the soup.

24 **Cook** for 30 minutes more.

25 **Puree** the soup in a blender.

Candy Pecans Recipe

26 **Grease** a cookie sheet.

27 **Beat** 1 egg white.

28 **Sift** ¹/₂ cup of sugar with 2 teaspoons of cinnamon.

29 **Mix** 3 cups of pecans and the sugar and cinnamon into the egg white.

30 **Spread** the mix on a cookie sheet.

31 **Bake** at 250°F (120°C).

Word Partnerships

bake	bread
	a cake
steam	vegetables
chop	
cook	
peel	potatoes
boil	

Words in Action

1. Which recipe looks the best to you? Why?

2. Write down your favorite recipe. Put your recipe together with your classmates' recipes to make a class cookbook.

Cooking Equipment

Words in Context

Every country has its own **cooking equipment**. For example, Italian kitchens usually have a big **pot** for cooking pasta. Many Mexican kitchens have a special **pan** to make tortillas. Asian kitchens often have a **grill** for meat and a special **vegetable steamer**. Many kitchens around the world have a **set of knives**, a **cutting board**, **measuring cups**, and **measuring spoons**.

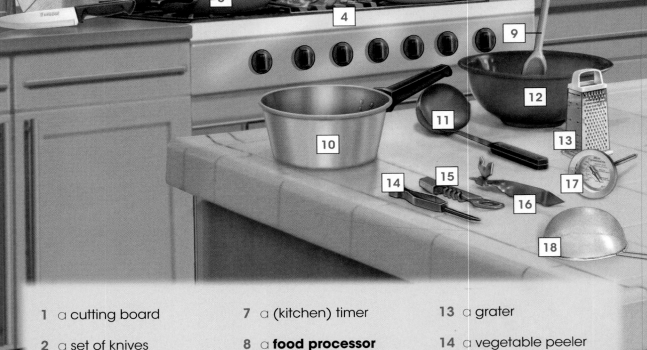

1 a cutting board

2 a set of knives

3 a (frying) **pan**

4 a **grill**

5 a **pot**

6 a **lid**

7 a (kitchen) timer

8 a **food processor**

9 a wooden spoon

10 a **saucepan**

11 a ladle

12 a **mixing bowl**

13 a grater

14 a vegetable peeler

15 a bottle opener

16 a can opener

17 a (meat) thermometer

18 a strainer

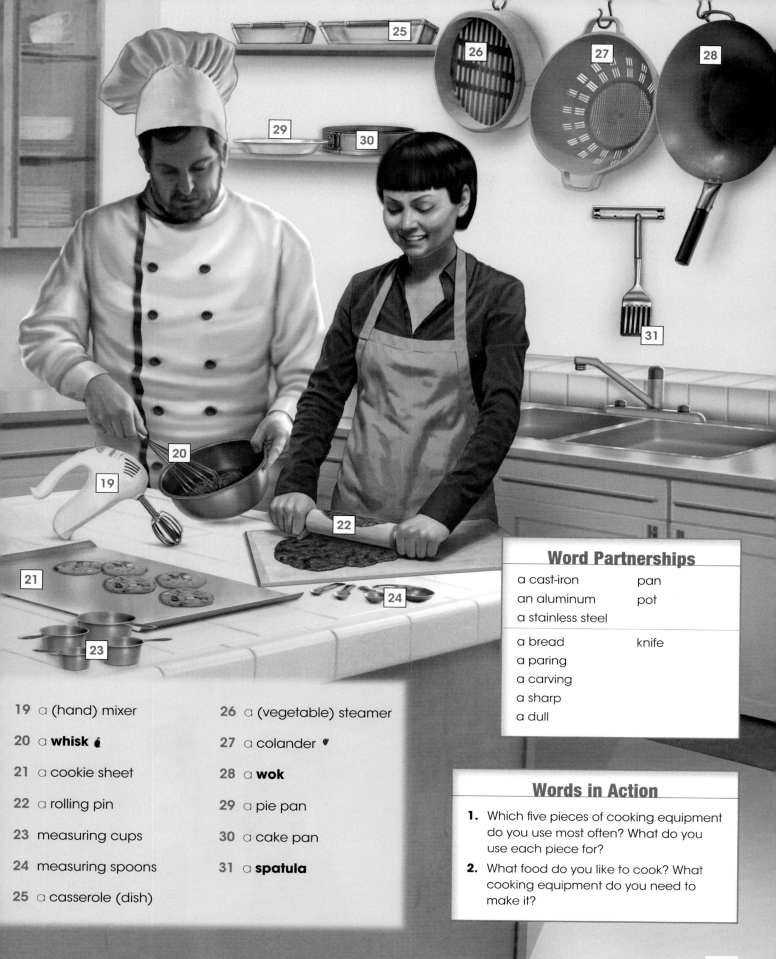

Word Partnerships

a cast-iron	pan
an aluminum	pot
a stainless steel	
a bread	knife
a paring	
a carving	
a sharp	
a dull	

19 a (hand) mixer

20 a **whisk**

21 a cookie sheet

22 a rolling pin

23 measuring cups

24 measuring spoons

25 a casserole (dish)

26 a (vegetable) steamer

27 a colander

28 a **wok**

29 a pie pan

30 a cake pan

31 a **spatula**

Words in Action

1. Which five pieces of cooking equipment do you use most often? What do you use each piece for?

2. What food do you like to cook? What cooking equipment do you need to make it?

Measurements and Containers

Abbreviations

tsp.	=	teaspoon
TBS.	=	tablespoon
c.	=	cup
oz.	=	ounce
qt.	=	quart
pt.	=	pint
gal.	=	gallon
lb.	=	pound
g.	=	gram
kg.	=	kilogram
l.	=	liter

4 qt.	=	1 gal.
3 tsp.	=	1 TBS.
1 qt.	=	.94 l.
1 oz.	=	28 g.
1 lb.	=	.45 kg.

1 a pint

2 a **cup**

3 an ounce

4 a teaspoon

5 a tablespoon

6 a **bouquet** of flowers

7 a **bottle** of olive oil

8 a **bar** of soap

9 a tube of hand cream

10 a carton of orange juice

11 a tray of pastries

12 a pot of coffee

13 a **cup** of coffee

14 a **pitcher** of lemonade

15 a piece of cake

16 a loaf of bread

17 a liter of water

18 a quart of milk

19 a **pound** of cherries

20 a **box** of strawberries

21 a gallon of cider

22 a **bag** of potatoes

23 a carton of eggs

24 a **jar** of honey

25 a container of yogurt

26 a six-pack of soda

27 a **can** of soda

28 a **pile** of tomatoes

29 a **bunch** of carrots

30 a crate of melons

31 a basket of apples

Word Partnerships

a can of	soup
	tuna
a box of	cereal
	pasta
	cookies
a cup of	tea
	sugar
	flour
a piece of	pie
	bread

Words in Action

1. Imagine you are shopping at a farmer's market. What will you buy? Why?

2. Name five containers you have at home. Tell what is in each container.

Supermarket

Words in Context

The first **supermarket** opened in France in the early 1900s. Before that, people bought **groceries** like **produce**, **dairy products**, and **canned goods** in small shops and markets. Now there are supermarkets in every country of the world. Besides food, you can find **household cleaners**, **paper products**, and **pet food** in most supermarkets.

PRODUCE

MEATS & POULTRY

DAIRY

FROZEN FOOD

1

2

3

4

8

9

10

11

12

13

14

15

16

17

18

19

20

1 **produce**

2 meats and poultry

3 dairy products

4 frozen foods

5 **bakery**

6 a deli counter

7 a **scale**

8 paper products

9 household cleaners

10 pet food

11 **beverages**

12 canned goods

13 an **aisle**

14 a paper bag

15 a checkout counter

16 a cash register

17 a shopping cart

18 a bagger

19 a barcode scanner

20 a **plastic bag**

21 a **cashier** / a checker

22 **groceries**

23 a **shopper**

24 a shopping basket

Snacks

25 a candy bar

26 pretzels

27 (potato) chips

28 **popcorn**

BAKERY

DELI

Word Partnerships

the frozen food	aisle
the produce	section
the canned goods	
the bakery	
shop for	groceries
pick up	

Words in Action

1. Where can you find the following items in the supermarket: *milk, water, bread, apples, paper towels, chicken,* and *ice cream?* Work with a partner.
   - *Milk is with the dairy products.*
   - *Water is in the beverages section.*

2. What section do you go to first in a supermarket? What do you get there?

Restaurant

1 a **chef**

2 a dishwasher

3 an apron

4 a server / a waitress

5 a busser / a busboy

6 a **server** / a waiter

7 a diner / a **customer**

8 a creamer

9 a vase

10 a sugar bowl

11 a tablecloth

12 a saltshaker

13 a pepper shaker

14 a **bowl**

15 a wine glass

16 a (water) glass

17 a high chair

18 a **cup**

19 a saucer

20 a **menu**

21 a fork

22 a napkin

23 a **plate**

24 a **knife**

25 a spoon

26 an appetizer

27 a main course

28 a dessert

29 a tray

30 a salad bar

31 a **check** / a **bill**

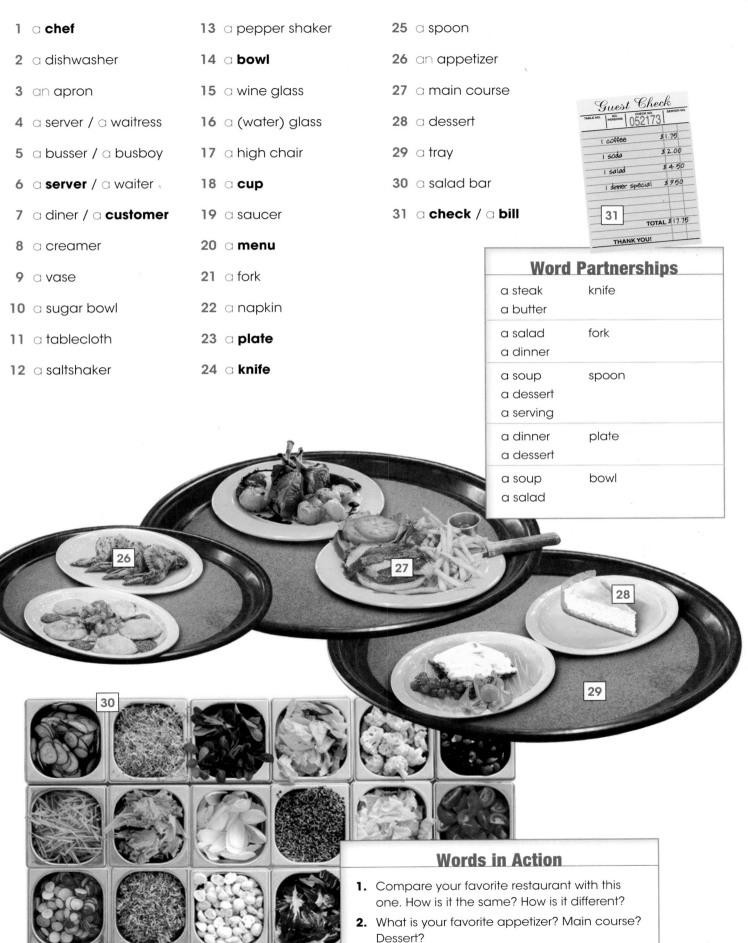

Guest Check

TABLE NO. | NO. PERSONS | CHECK NO. 052173 | SERVER NO.

1 coffee	$1.75
1 soda	$2.00
1 salad	$4.50
1 dinner special	$9.50

31

TOTAL $17.75

THANK YOU!

Word Partnerships

a steak a butter	knife
a salad a dinner	fork
a soup a dessert a serving	spoon
a dinner a dessert	plate
a soup a salad	bowl

Words in Action

1. Compare your favorite restaurant with this one. How is it the same? How is it different?

2. What is your favorite appetizer? Main course? Dessert?

101

Order, Eat, Pay

Words in Context

I'm a waitress. I **wait on** lots of customers every night. Some customers are difficult. They **order** things that aren't on the menu. They **spill** their drinks. One customer left and didn't **pay** the check! But most customers are great. Some of them **compliment** me and **leave** a big tip. They're my favorite customers!

1 **make** a reservation

2 pour water

3 light a candle

4 **carry** a tray

5 **set** the table

6 wait on someone

7 **look at** the menu

8 butter the bread

9 spill a drink

10 order

11 **take** an order

12 drink

13 compliment someone

14 refill the glass

15 eat

16 **serve** a meal

17 ask for the check

18 signal the server

19 **share** a dessert

20 **offer** a doggie bag

21 thank the server

22 wipe the table

23 **leave** a tip

24 **pay** the check

25 clear the table / bus the table

Word Partnerships

eat	out
order	breakfast
	lunch
	dinner
	supper
	a meal
	a snack

Words in Action

1. Think about the last time you ate out. Tell your class about five things you did at the restaurant.

2. Work with a partner. Act out a verb from the word list. Your partner will guess what you are doing. Take turns.

Clothes

Words in Context

The **clothes** we wear today come from around the world. For example, the **tie** is originally from Croatia. The **poncho** is from South America. The **business suit** originated in France in the 1700s. And a Bavarian immigrant named Levi Strauss made the first **blue jeans** in California in 1873.

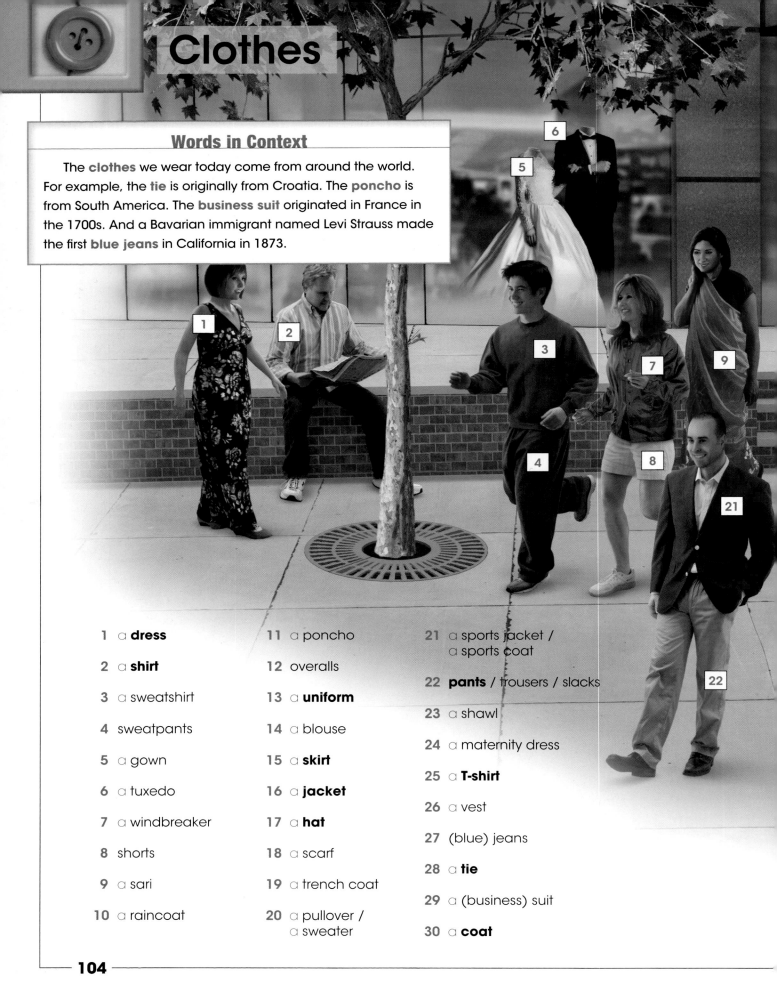

1 a **dress**

2 a **shirt**

3 a sweatshirt

4 sweatpants

5 a gown

6 a tuxedo

7 a windbreaker

8 shorts

9 a sari

10 a raincoat

11 a poncho

12 overalls

13 a **uniform**

14 a blouse

15 a **skirt**

16 a **jacket**

17 a **hat**

18 a scarf

19 a trench coat

20 a pullover / a sweater

21 a sports jacket / a sports coat

22 **pants** / trousers / slacks

23 a shawl

24 a maternity dress

25 a **T-shirt**

26 a vest

27 (blue) jeans

28 a **tie**

29 a (business) suit

30 a **coat**

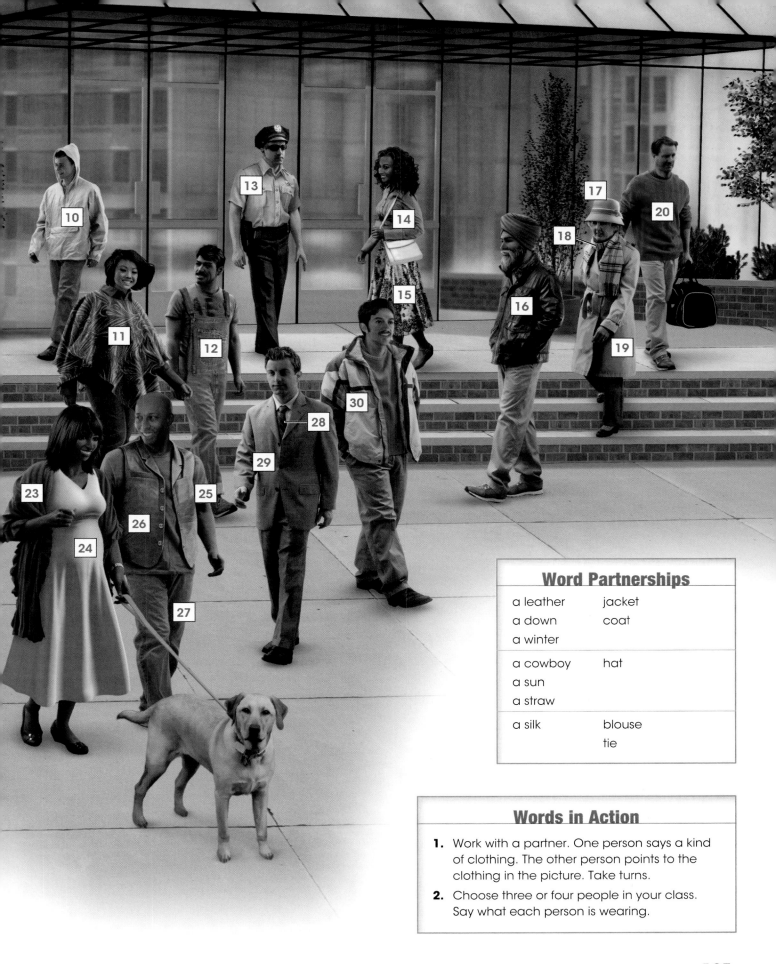

Word Partnerships

a leather	jacket
a down	coat
a winter	
a cowboy	hat
a sun	
a straw	
a silk	blouse
	tie

Words in Action

1. Work with a partner. One person says a kind of clothing. The other person points to the clothing in the picture. Take turns.

2. Choose three or four people in your class. Say what each person is wearing.

Sleepwear, Underwear, and Swimwear

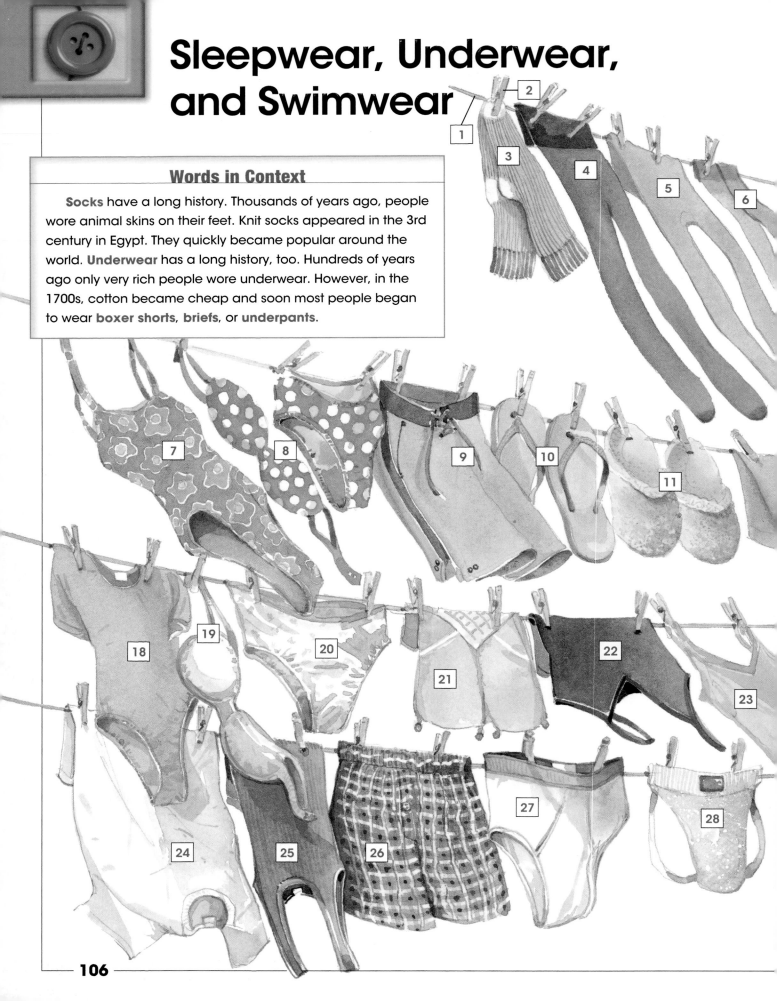

Words in Context

Socks have a long history. Thousands of years ago, people wore animal skins on their feet. Knit socks appeared in the 3rd century in Egypt. They quickly became popular around the world. **Underwear** has a long history, too. Hundreds of years ago only very rich people wore underwear. However, in the 1700s, cotton became cheap and soon most people began to wear **boxer shorts**, **briefs**, or **underpants**.

1 a clothesline
2 a clothespin
3 **socks**
4 tights
5 pantyhose / nylons
6 **stockings**
7 a **swimsuit** / a bathing suit
8 a **bikini**
9 (swimming) trunks
10 flip flops / thongs
11 **slippers**
12 a nightshirt

13 a (bath)robe
14 a **nightgown**
15 long underwear
16 a (blanket) sleeper
17 **pajamas**
18 a leotard
19 a **bra**
20 **panties** / underpants
21 a girdle
22 a camisole
23 a slip
24 an **undershirt**
25 a tank top

26 boxer shorts / boxers
27 briefs
28 an athletic supporter / a jockstrap

Word Partnerships	
a terrycloth	(bath)robe
a silk	
a flannel	
knee	socks
sweat	
ankle	
dress	
a pair of	briefs
	boxer shorts
	socks
	slippers

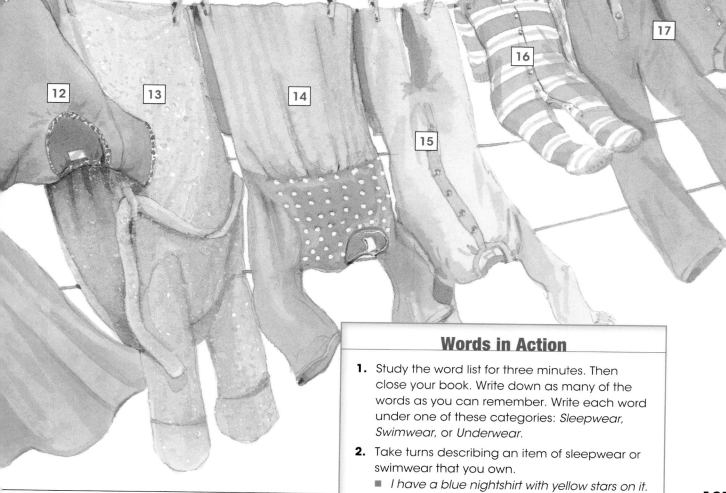

Words in Action

1. Study the word list for three minutes. Then close your book. Write down as many of the words as you can remember. Write each word under one of these categories: *Sleepwear, Swimwear,* or *Underwear.*

2. Take turns describing an item of sleepwear or swimwear that you own.
   ■ *I have a blue nightshirt with yellow stars on it.*

Shoes and Accessories

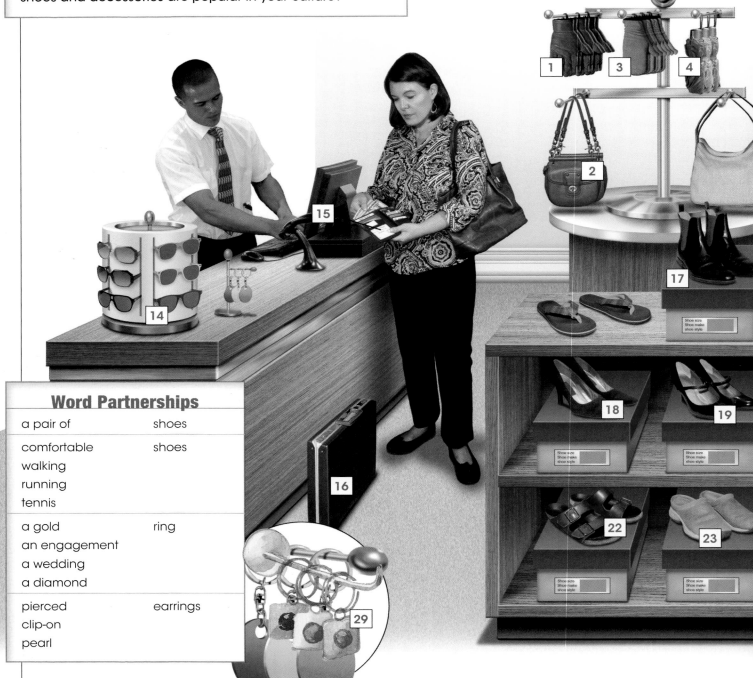

Word Partnerships

a pair of	shoes
comfortable walking running tennis	shoes
a gold an engagement a wedding a diamond	ring
pierced clip-on pearl	earrings

1 **gloves**

2 a **purse** / a handbag

3 mittens

4 an **umbrella**

5 suspenders

6 a **belt**

7 a **ring**

8 a **necklace**

9 earrings

10 a bracelet

11 a (wrist)watch

12 a **pin**

13 **jewelry**

14 sunglasses

15 a **wallet**

16 a briefcase

17 a **boot**

18 a (high) heel

19 a pump

20 a loafer

21 a hiking boot

22 a sandal

23 a clog

24 an athletic shoe

25 a sneaker

26 a (knit) hat

27 a baseball cap / a baseball hat

28 earmuffs

29 a key chain

Shoes

Words in Action

1. Name a place where you like to go. What shoes and accessories are good to wear to this place?

2. You need to buy three gifts: one for your 80-year-old grandfather, one for your 25-year-old brother, and one for your teenage sister. What shoes or accessories will you buy for each person?

Describing Clothes

Words in Context

Fashions come and go. For example, sometimes ties are **wide** and sometimes they're **narrow**. The length of **skirts** is always changing too. One year they're **long** and **straight**, and the next year they're **short** and **pleated**. It's hard to keep up with fashion!

Word Partnerships

fashionable	clothes
trendy	
designer	
work	
maternity	

7:00 Casual Clothes 24

8:00 Formal Clothes 25

1 a **light** jacket

2 a **heavy** jacket

3 a sleeveless shirt

4 a short-sleeved shirt

5 a long-sleeved shirt

6 a button-down shirt

7 a polo shirt

8 a wide tie

9 a narrow tie

10 flared jeans

11 straight leg jeans

12 baggy pants / **loose** pants

13 a V-neck sweater

14 a crew neck sweater

15 a cardigan sweater

16 a turtleneck sweater

17 a tight skirt

18 a **straight** skirt

19 a pleated skirt

20 a **short** skirt

21 a **long** skirt

22 **high** heels

23 low heels

24 **informal** clothes / **casual** clothes

25 **formal** clothes / dress clothes

Words in Action

1. Describe the clothes you and other people in class are wearing.

2. Which items of clothing in the picture are in fashion? Are any of the clothes not in fashion?

Fabrics and Patterns

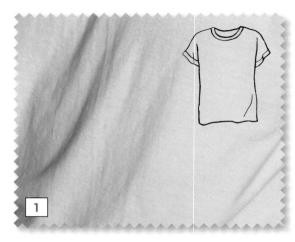

1

2

3

4

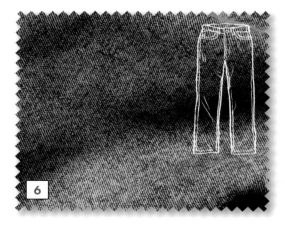

6

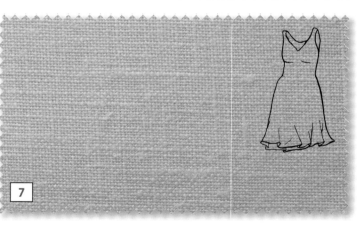

7

10

Word Partnerships

a wool	jacket
	sweater
	coat
	scarf
a silk	tie
	robe
	dress

11

Fabrics

1 **cotton**

2 corduroy

3 **velvet**

4 **silk**

5 **leather**

6 denim

7 **linen**

8 suede

9 cashmere

10 nylon

11 **lace**

12 **wool**

Patterns

13 **solid**

14 **print**

15 polka dot

16 floral

17 paisley

18 checked

19 plaid

20 **striped**

21 embroidered

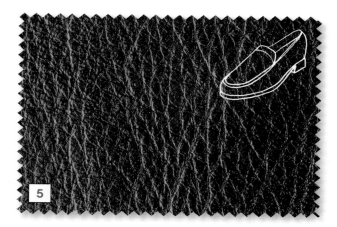

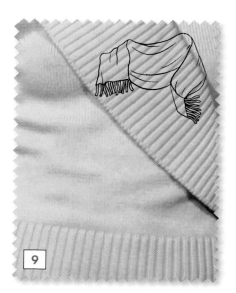

Words in Action

1. Work with a partner. Describe your partner's clothes.
   - *You're wearing brown corduroy pants and a blue and white striped cotton shirt.*

2. Design an outfit. Decide on the fabrics and patterns. Draw the outfit and describe it to your class.

Buying, Wearing, and Caring for Clothes

Words in Context

Different clothes have different care instructions. Jeans are easy. You can **wash** them in the washing machine and then **dry** them in the dryer. However, a wool shirt needs special care. You shouldn't wash a wool shirt. Instead, you should **dry clean** it. To prevent wrinkles, always **hang up** clothes.

1 go shopping

2 **look for** a jacket

3 **go into** a dressing room

4 try on

5 **buy**

6 take home

7 **cut off**

8 **put on**

9 zip

10 button

11 buckle

12 roll up

13 **wear**

14 unbutton

15 unzip

16 unbuckle

17 **take off**

18 **wash**

19 dry

20 dry clean

21 mend / **repair**

22 sew on

23 **iron** / press

24 hang (up)

Word Partnerships	
hang it	on a hook
	on a hanger
	in the closet
wash it	in cold water
	in hot water
	by hand
zip button	up

Sewing and Laundry

Words in Context

Fashion designer Josie Natori comes from the Philippines. She sells her clothes all over the world. Her company started very small. At first, Natori worked alone in her living room with a **sewing machine**, **pins**, **needles**, **buttons**, **thread**, and **scissors**. Now her company has offices in Manila, Paris, and New York.

1 an ironing board

2 an **iron**

3 fabric softener

4 (laundry) detergent

5 bleach

6 a dryer

7 a washer /
 a washing machine

8 wet clothes

9 dry clothes

10 a laundry basket

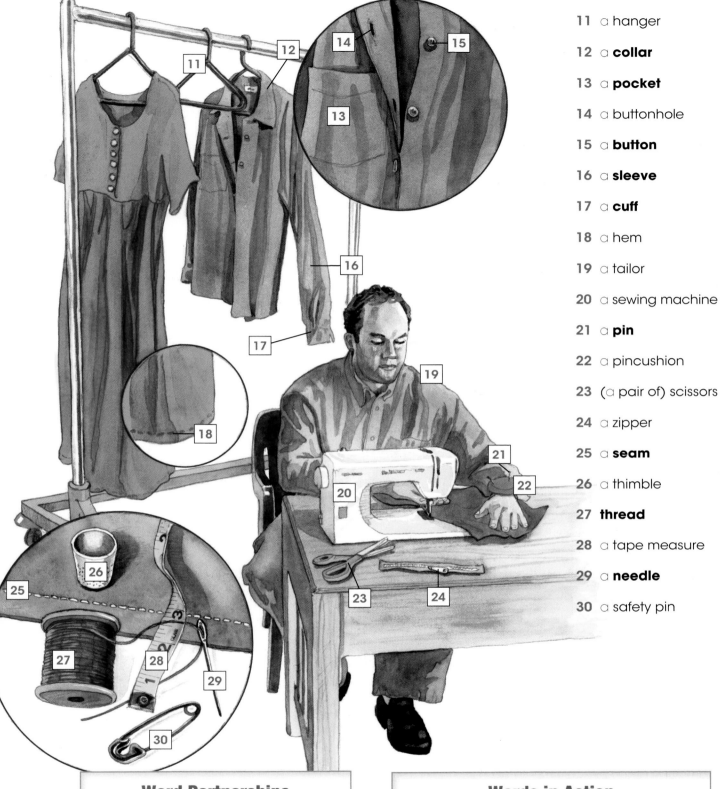

11 a hanger

12 a **collar**

13 a **pocket**

14 a buttonhole

15 a **button**

16 a **sleeve**

17 a **cuff**

18 a hem

19 a tailor

20 a sewing machine

21 a **pin**

22 a pincushion

23 (a pair of) scissors

24 a zipper

25 a **seam**

26 a thimble

27 **thread**

28 a tape measure

29 a **needle**

30 a safety pin

Word Partnerships

a wire	hanger
a plastic	
a shirt	pocket
a pants	
a jacket	
long	sleeves
short	

Words in Action

1. Find the following things on your classmates' clothes: *a buttonhole, a collar, a cuff, a pocket, a sleeve, a hem.*

2. Which of the items in the picture do you have in your home?

Vehicles and Traffic Signs

1 ONE WAY

2 STOP

3 H

4 DO NOT PASS

5 DO NOT ENTER

6 no left turn

7 RR

8 school zone

9 pedestrian crossing

10 YIELD

11 no U-turn

Signs

1 **one way**

2 **stop**

3 **hospital**

4 do not pass

5 do not enter

6 no left turn

7 railroad crossing

8 school zone

9 pedestrian crossing

10 **yield**

11 no U-turn

Vehicles

12 a school bus

13 a tow truck

14 a garbage truck

15 a pickup (truck)

16 an RV

17 a minivan

18 a limousine / a limo

19 **a sedan**

20 **a van**

21 a dump truck

22 an SUV

23 a **trailer**

24 a sports car

25 a semi / a tractor trailer

26 a police car

27 an **ambulance**

28 a fire engine

29 a station wagon

30 a compact (car)

31 a **convertible**

32 a **motorcycle**

Word Partnerships

drive	a convertible
	a truck
	an SUV
ride	a motorcycle
ride in	a limousine
ride on	a bus

Words in Action

1. Work with a partner. Make a list of the five largest vehicles in the word list. Make another list of the five smallest vehicles.

2. Imagine you have enough money to buy a new vehicle. What vehicle will you buy? Explain your choice to the class.

Parts of a Car

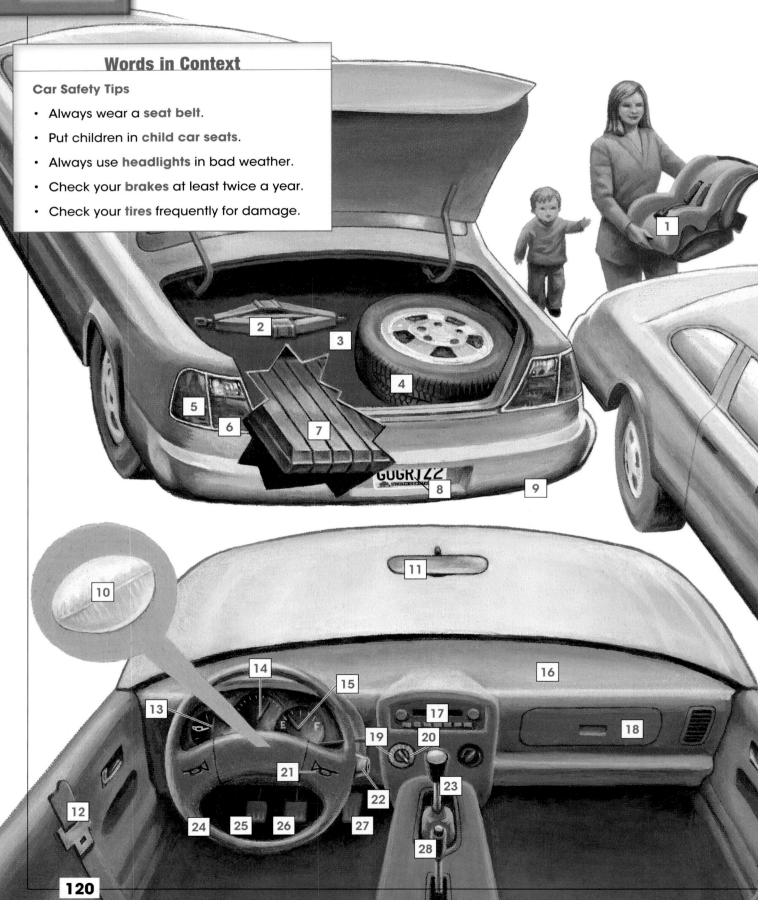

Words in Context

Car Safety Tips

- Always wear a **seat belt**.
- Put children in **child car seats**.
- Always use **headlights** in bad weather.
- Check your **brakes** at least twice a year.
- Check your **tires** frequently for damage.

1 a child car seat

2 a jack

3 a **trunk**

4 a **tire**

5 a taillight

6 a brake light

7 a gas tank

8 a license plate

9 a bumper

10 an air bag

11 a rearview mirror

12 a seat belt

13 an oil gauge

14 a speedometer

15 a gas gauge

16 a dashboard

17 a **radio**

18 a glove compartment

19 air conditioning

20 heater

21 a **horn**

22 an ignition

23 a gearshift

24 a steering wheel

25 a **clutch**

26 a brake pedal

27 an accelerator / a gas pedal

28 an emergency brake

29 a windshield wiper

30 a **hood**

31 a fender

32 an **engine** / a **motor**

33 a **battery**

34 jumper cables

35 a radiator

36 a turn signal

37 a **headlight**

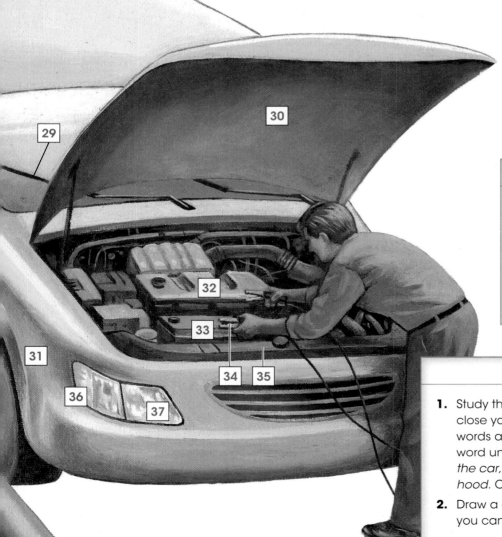

Word Partnerships

open	the hood
close	the trunk
check	the battery
	the rearview mirror
a spare	tire
a flat	

Words in Action

1. Study the word list for three minutes. Then close your book. Write down as many of the words as you can remember. Write each word under one of these categories: *Inside the car, Outside the car,* and *Under the hood.* Compare your lists with a partner.

2. Draw a car. Label as many parts of the car as you can, without looking at the word list.

Road Trip

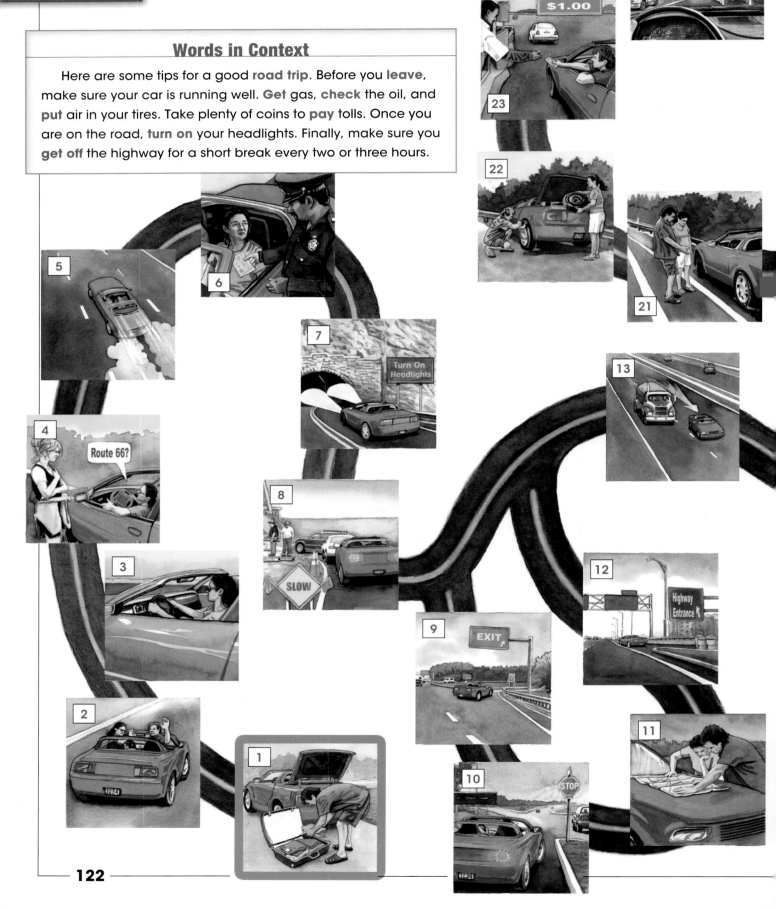

Words in Context

Here are some tips for a good **road trip**. Before you **leave**, make sure your car is running well. **Get** gas, **check** the oil, and **put** air in your tires. Take plenty of coins to **pay** tolls. Once you are on the road, **turn on** your headlights. Finally, make sure you **get off** the highway for a short break every two or three hours.

1 pack
2 **leave**
3 **drive**
4 ask for directions
5 speed up
6 get a speeding ticket
7 turn on the headlights
8 slow down

9 get off the highway
10 **stop**
11 **look at** a map
12 get on the highway
13 **pass** a truck
14 honk (the horn)
15 **get** gas
16 **check** the oil
17 **wash** the windshield
18 **put** air in the tires
19 have an accident
20 pull over
21 have a flat (tire)
22 change the tire
23 pay a toll
24 arrive at the destination
25 **park** (the car)

GAS

H-O-N-K!!!

Word Partnerships

pack	a suitcase
	a bag
stop	at a red light
	for gas
turn on	the windshield wipers
	the radio
	the air conditioning

Words in Action

1. Work with a partner. Act out a verb on the list. Your partner will guess the verb. Take turns.
2. Plan your "dream" road trip. Where will you go? What will you do on the trip?

Airport

Words in Context

Air travel is changing. **Airports** now have **automated check-in machines**. A **passenger** can quickly check in, choose a **seat**, and get a **boarding pass**. In the future, some **airplanes** will be bigger and some will fly much faster.

Airport

1 a **terminal**

2 a **ticket**

3 a photo ID

4 a ticket counter / a check-in counter

5 baggage / luggage

6 a **passenger**

7 an automated check-in machine

8 a boarding pass

9 a metal detector

10 a security checkpoint

11 arrival and departure monitors

12 a **helicopter**

13 a **runway**

14 a **gate**

15 a **pilot**

16 a carry-on bag

17 customs

18 a customs (declaration) form

19 the baggage claim (area)

20 **immigration**

21 a **line**

Airplane / Plane

22 first class

23 economy (class) / coach (class)

24 an overhead compartment

25 an emergency exit

26 a flight attendant

27 a **seat**

28 a seat belt

29 an aisle

Word Partnerships	
an aisle a middle / a center a window	seat
an electronic / an e- a paper	ticket
an arrival a departure an international	terminal

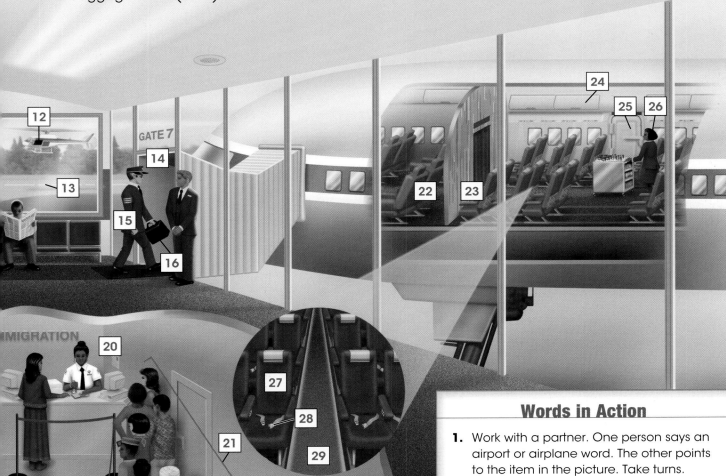

Words in Action

1. Work with a partner. One person says an airport or airplane word. The other points to the item in the picture. Take turns.

2. Make three lists: *people you see at an airport, areas you see at an airport,* and *things you see at an airport.*

Taking a Flight

1 check in
2 **show** your ID
3 **check** your baggage
4 **get** your boarding pass
5 go through security
6 **check** the monitors
7 **wait** at the gate
8 **board** the plane
9 **find** your seat
10 stow your carry-on bag
11 turn off your cell phone
12 fasten your seat belt
13 take off
14 **ask for** a pillow
15 turn on the overhead light
16 put on your headphones
17 listen to music
18 **stretch**
19 put your tray table **down**
20 **choose** a meal
21 land
22 unfasten your seat belt
23 get off the plane
24 **claim** your bags

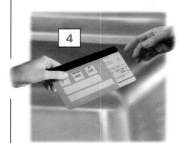

Pillow, please.

Word Partnerships	
wait	for a boarding call
	in line
go through	a metal detector
	customs
	immigration

Words in Action

1. Work with a partner. Pretend to do one of the actions on the word list. Your partner will guess what action you are doing. Take turns.

2. Make a list of things you can do on a plane to be safe. Make another list of things you can do to be comfortable.

Public Transportation

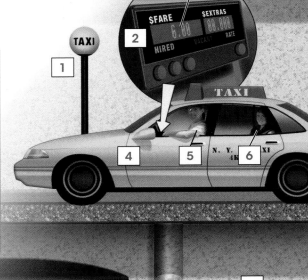

Words in Context

There are three ways to get from JFK Airport in New York to Manhattan. The first way is by **cab**. You can get a cab at the **taxi stand**. The **fare** is about $45.00. The second way is by **bus**. You can catch a bus from the **bus stop** outside the airport. The **ticket** is about $18.00. The bus will take you to a Manhattan **train station** or hotel. The third way is by **subway**. Go to the JFK Airport **subway station**. The subway will take you into Manhattan. This is the cheapest way. It costs only $2.50.

1 a taxi stand

2 a **meter**

3 the **fare**

4 a taxi / a cab

5 a taxi driver / a cab driver

6 a **passenger**

7 a bus stop

8 a bus driver

9 a **bus**

10 a ticket window

11 a **ticket**

12 a **train**

13 a conductor

14 a **track**

15 a strap

16 a (subway) line

17 a **ferry**

18 a subway (train)

19 a **platform**

20 a token

21 a fare card

22 a **schedule**

23 a turnstile

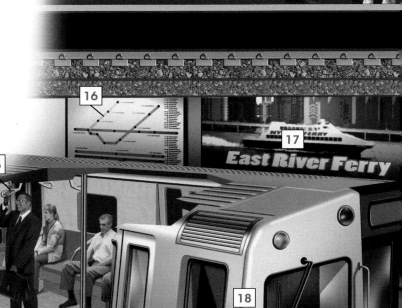

East River Ferry

TO TRAIN AND SUBWAY

7

8

9

VTA New York City Bus 827

12

13

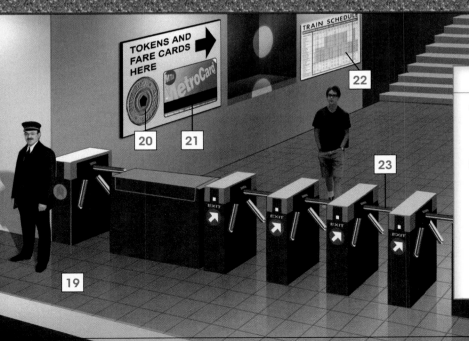

TOKENS AND FARE CARDS HERE

MTA MetroCard

TRAIN SCHEDULE

19

20

21

22

23

EXIT EXIT EXIT EXIT

Words in Action

1. What kind of public transportation do you use? Where do you get on? What is the fare?

2. One student names a form of public transportation. Other students make up sentences about that form of transportation in your town or city.
   - Student A: *the subway*
   - Student B: *You need a fare card.*
   - Student C: *There's a subway station a block from the school.*

Up, Over, Around

Words in Context

Roller-coaster rides are exciting. You go **up** a track very, very slowly. Then suddenly you go **over** the top and race **down** the track. Most roller coaster rides go **around** several sharp curves. Some even go **upside down**. But when the ride is over, people often want to do it again!

1 straight

2 **past** the house

3 **into** the tunnel

4 **through** the tunnel

5 **out of** the tunnel

6 **behind** the building

7 **toward** the rocks

8 **between** the flags

9 **around** the trees

10 **up**

11 **down**

12 upside down

13 **under** the waterfall

14 over the water

15 **left**

16 **right**

17 across the river

18 along the river

19 north

20 east

21 south

22 west

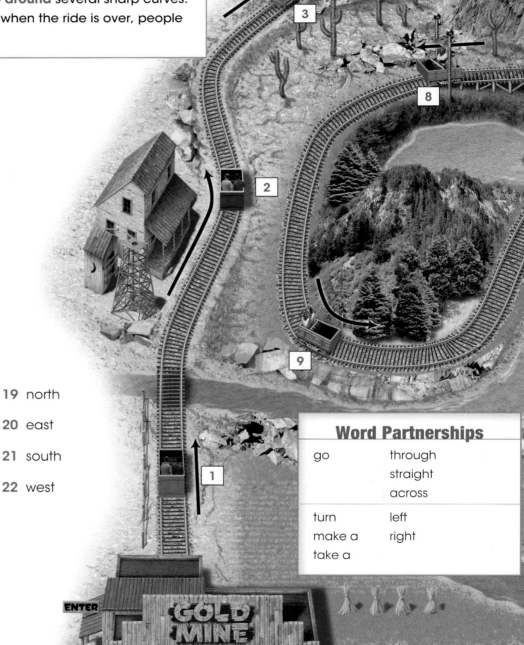

Word Partnerships

go	through
	straight
	across
turn	left
make a	right
take a	

Words in Action

1. Tell how you get to school or work every day.
   - *I go over a bridge. Then I go up a hill. After that I go past a hospital.*
2. Work in small groups to design your own roller-coaster ride. Describe it to the class.

The Human Body

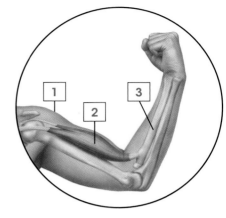

Words in Context

Always prepare for exercise. A ten-minute warm-up will stretch your **muscles** and get your **body** ready. Roll your **head** around in a circle. Move your **shoulders** up and down. Stretch your **arms** out and swing them in a circle. Bend your **knees**, and then stretch out your **legs**. Now you are ready to exercise.

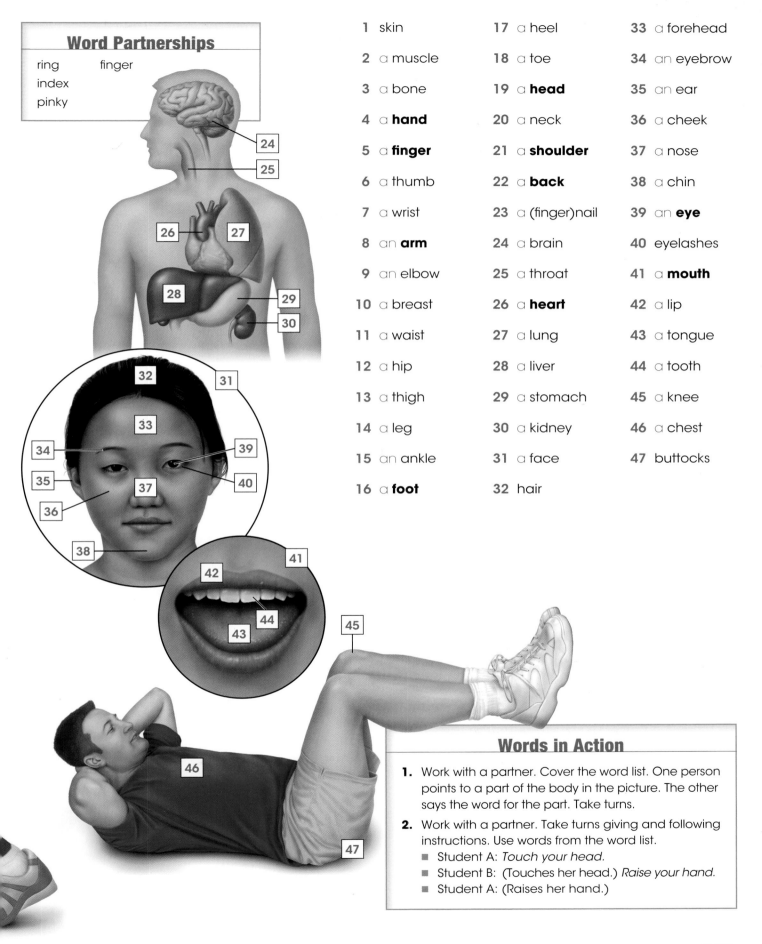

1 skin
2 a muscle
3 a bone
4 a **hand**
5 a **finger**
6 a thumb
7 a wrist
8 an **arm**
9 an elbow
10 a breast
11 a waist
12 a hip
13 a thigh
14 a leg
15 an ankle
16 a **foot**

17 a heel
18 a toe
19 a **head**
20 a neck
21 a **shoulder**
22 a **back**
23 a (finger)nail
24 a brain
25 a throat
26 a **heart**
27 a lung
28 a liver
29 a stomach
30 a kidney
31 a face
32 hair

33 a forehead
34 an eyebrow
35 an ear
36 a cheek
37 a nose
38 a chin
39 an **eye**
40 eyelashes
41 a **mouth**
42 a lip
43 a tongue
44 a tooth
45 a knee
46 a chest
47 buttocks

Words in Action

1. Work with a partner. Cover the word list. One person points to a part of the body in the picture. The other says the word for the part. Take turns.

2. Work with a partner. Take turns giving and following instructions. Use words from the word list.
   - Student A: *Touch your head.*
   - Student B: (Touches her head.) *Raise your hand.*
   - Student A: (Raises her hand.)

133

Illnesses, Injuries, Symptoms, and Disabilities

Words in Context

There are many reasons people visit the doctor's office. In winter, many people get a **sore throat**, a **cough**, or the **flu**. In summer, bad **sunburns** are common. **Earaches**, **stomachaches**, and **backaches** are common problems all year round.

Word Partnerships

a head	cold
a bad	
catch	a cold
have	a cold
	the flu
	a sore throat
feel	dizzy
	nauseous

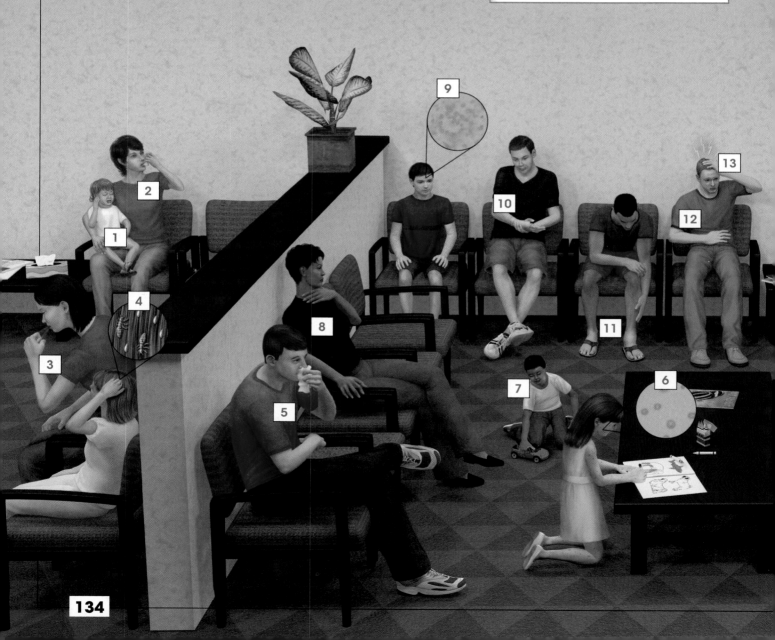

1 an earache
2 asthma
3 a **cough**
4 lice
5 a **cold**
6 chicken pox
7 mumps
8 a sore throat
9 measles
10 a sprained wrist
11 a swollen ankle
12 a stomachache

13 a **headache**
14 the **flu**
15 a **fever** /
   a **temperature**
16 **arthritis**
17 a backache
18 **blind**
19 nauseous
20 dizzy
21 deaf
22 acne
23 a **cut**
24 a burn

25 a blister
26 a rash
27 a sunburn

28 a bee sting
29 a bloody nose
30 a **bruise**

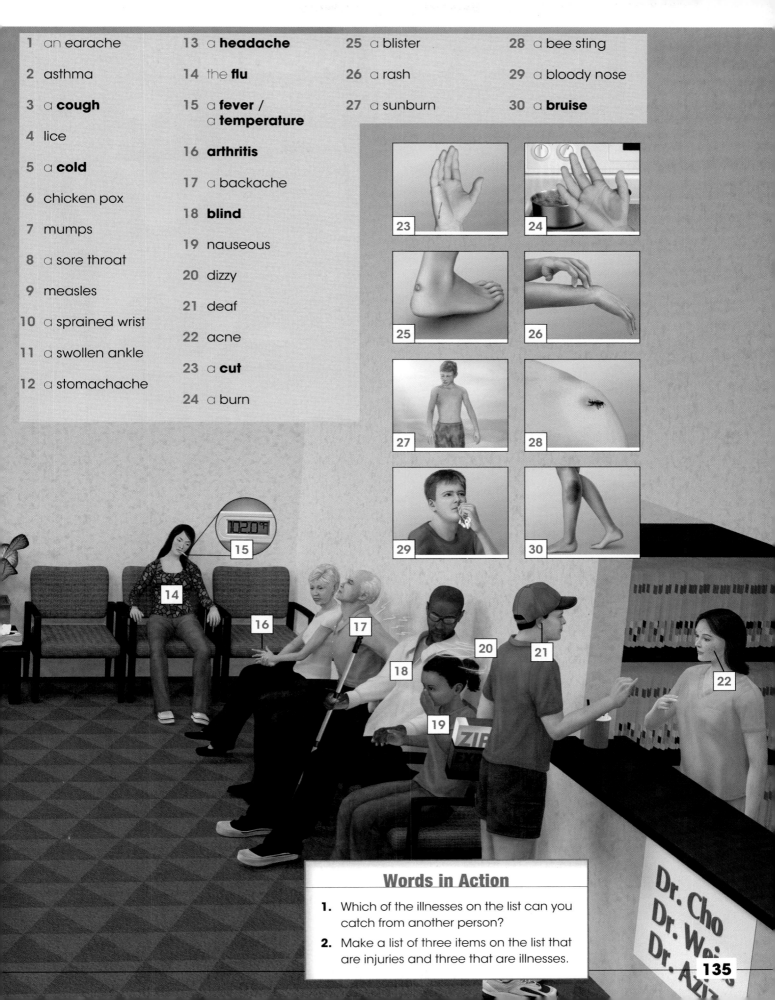

Words in Action

1. Which of the illnesses on the list can you catch from another person?
2. Make a list of three items on the list that are injuries and three that are illnesses.

Dr. Cho
Dr. We
Dr. Azi

Hurting and Healing

Are you **coughing** and **sneezing**? You probably have a cold. **Drink** plenty of fluids and **rest** as much as possible. Do you feel hot? **Take** your temperature. You might have the flu. **Make** an appointment with your doctor. He will **examine** you. You may need to **take** pills or get a shot. Follow your doctor's instructions. You will soon **feel** better.

1 **be** in pain

2 **be** unconscious

3 bleed

4 **be** in shock

5 **break** a leg

6 burn yourself

7 choke

8 cut yourself

9 drown

10 swallow poison

11 overdose (on drugs)

12 **have** an allergic reaction

13 **have** a heart attack

14 **get** a(n electric) shock

15 **fall**

Word Partnerships

be	injured	
	hurt	
feel	much	better
	a little	

136

16 cough	23 check his blood pressure	
17 sneeze	24 draw his blood	
18 vomit / throw up	25 **give** him a shot	
19 **take** your temperature	26 rest	
20 **call** the doctor	27 take a pill	
21 **make** an appointment	28 drink fluids	
22 examine the patient	29 **feel** better	

Words in Action

1. Look at page 136. Which things on the list are more likely to happen to adults? Which are more likely to happen to children?

2. Work with a partner. One person pretends to have one of the medical problems on the list. The other guesses the problem. Take turns.

Hospital

1 a nurses' station

2 a **nurse**

3 an intensive care unit

4 an IV / an intravenous drip

5 an operating room

6 an X-ray

7 an anesthesiologist

8 an operating table

9 **blood**

Words in Context

Here are some things to look for in a **hospital**:

- Are the **doctors** and **nurses** friendly and helpful?
- Are there plenty of nurses at each **nurses' station**?
- Are the **patients** happy with the hospital?

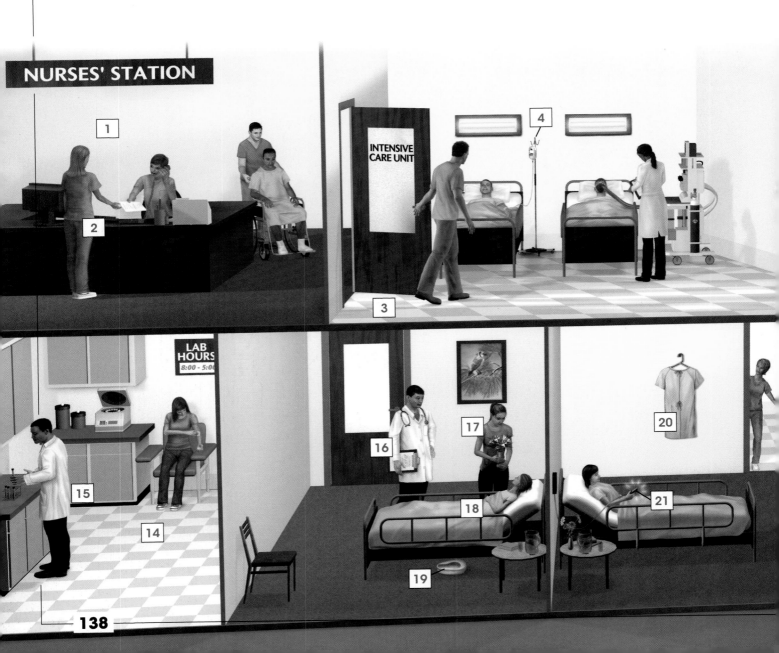

NURSES' STATION

INTENSIVE CARE UNIT

LAB HOURS 8:00 - 5:00

138

10 a **surgeon**

11 an **operation**

12 latex gloves

13 a (surgical) mask

14 a **lab** / a **laboratory**

15 a lab technician

16 a **doctor**

17 a **visitor**

18 a **patient**

19 a bedpan

20 a hospital gown

21 a call button

22 an orderly

23 a wheelchair

24 CPR / cardiopulmonary resuscitation

25 an emergency room

26 a paramedic / an EMT

27 a stretcher

28 stitches

29 an **ambulance**

Word Partnerships

an in- an out-	patient
a blood	test type donor
give donate	blood

OPERATING ROOM

EMERGENCY

Words in Action

1. Make three lists: *People in a Hospital, Places in a Hospital,* and *Things in a Hospital.*

2. What things would you see in a patient's room? What things would you see in an operating room?

Medical Center

Words in Context

During a **physical**, a doctor does several tests. She listens to the patient's heart and lungs with a **stethoscope**. She checks the patient's blood pressure with a **blood pressure monitor**. For patients over 40, the doctor may also give the patient an **EKG**.

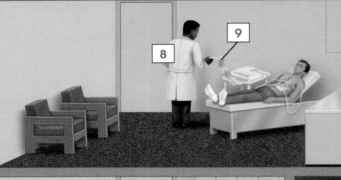

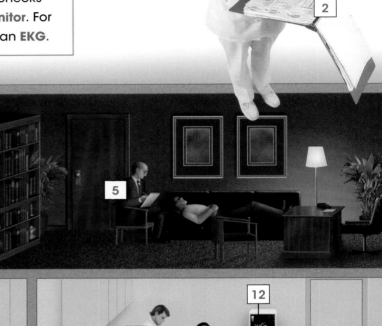

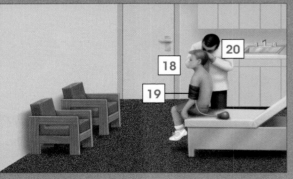

Word Partnerships

hard	contacts / contact lenses
soft	
disposable	
a leg	cast
an arm	
an annual	physical
a dental	checkup

1 a stethoscope

2 a medical chart

3 acupuncture

4 an acupuncturist

5 a **psychologist**

6 a waiting room

7 a **pediatrician**

8 a cardiologist

9 an EKG / an electrocardiogram

10 an obstetrician

11 a **pregnant woman**

12 a sonogram / an ultrasound

13 a **sling**

14 a **crutch**

15 a **cast**

16 a receptionist

17 an orthopedist

18 a physical (exam) / a checkup

19 a blood pressure monitor

20 a GP / a general practitioner

21 an eye chart

22 a contact (lens)

23 an optometrist

24 (eye)glasses

25 a (dental) hygienist

26 a **dentist**

27 a filling

28 a **tooth**

29 braces

30 gums

31 a **drill**

32 a **cavity**

Words in Action

1. Work with a partner. Cover the word list. One person points to a person or object in the picture. The other says the word for the person or object. Take turns.

2. Work with a group. Make three lists. Who in your group has had a cast? Who has had a sling? Who has had crutches?

Pharmacy

1 a **tablet**

2 a **capsule**

3 a **pill**

4 prescription medicine

5 a **pharmacist**

6 over-the-counter medication

7 cough syrup

8 an antacid

9 (throat) lozenges

10 cough drops

11 an inhaler

12 a nasal (decongestant) spray

13 eyedrops

14 antihistamine

15 a **prescription**

16 a warning label

17 a **cane**

18 a knee brace

19 an elastic bandage

20 **vitamins**

21 a heating pad

22 hydrogen peroxide

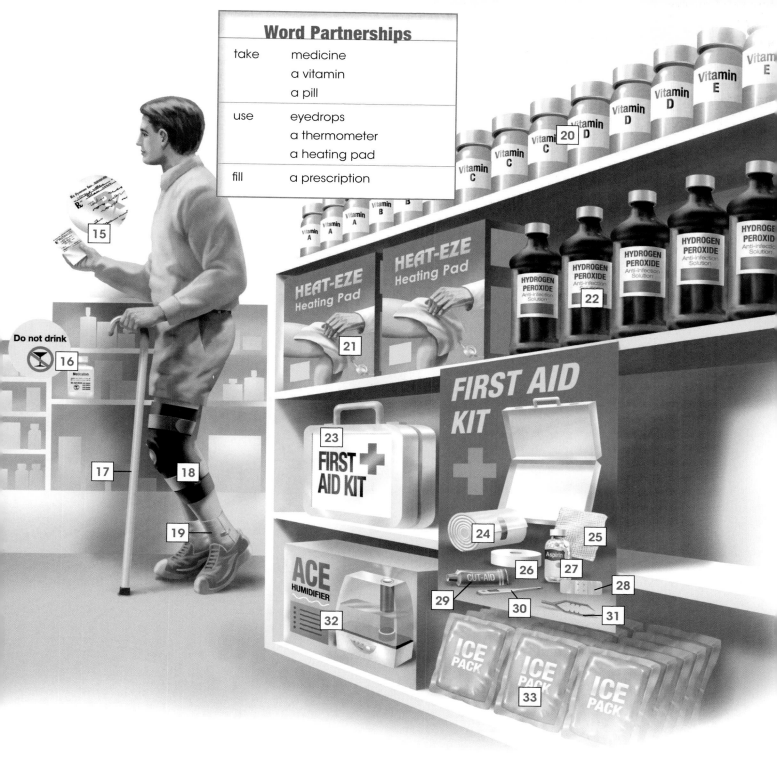

Word Partnerships

take	medicine
	a vitamin
	a pill
use	eyedrops
	a thermometer
	a heating pad
fill	a prescription

23 a first-aid kit

24 gauze

25 a sterile pad

26 sterile tape

27 aspirin

28 an adhesive bandage

29 antibacterial ointment / antibacterial cream

30 a **thermometer**

31 tweezers

32 a humidifier

33 an ice pack

Words in Action

1. Which pharmacy items on the word list do you have in your home?

2. Which pharmacy items are good for a cold? Which are good for a cut? Which are good for a sprain? Discuss with a partner.

143

Soap, Comb, and Floss

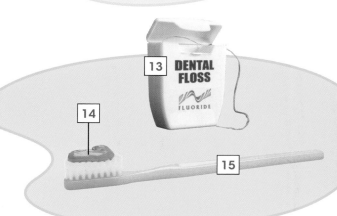

1 hairspray

2 **shampoo**

3 **conditioner**

4 hair gel

5 a curling iron

6 a blow dryer / a hair dryer

7 a barrette

8 a **comb**

9 rollers / curlers

10 a (hair)brush

11 nail polish

12 a nail clipper

13 dental floss

14 toothpaste

15 a **toothbrush**

16 shaving cream

17 aftershave

18 a **razor**

19 an electric shaver / an electric razor

20 deodorant

21 **perfume**

22 sunscreen

23 **lotion**

24 **soap**

25 **tissues**

Makeup

26 face powder

27 **lipstick**

28 blush / rouge

29 eye shadow

30 mascara

31 eyeliner

Verbs

32 wash

33 rinse

34 comb

35 (blow) dry

36 brush

37 cut

Word Partnerships

a disposable	razor
a dull	
nail polish	remover
hand	soap
face	
antibacterial	
hand	lotion
body	
put on	aftershave
wear	mascara
	lipstick

Words in Action

1. What things from the list do you use every day?
2. Work with a partner. One person pretends to use one of the items from the list. The other guesses what it is. Take turns.

Jobs 1

Words in Context

What kind of work is right for you? Do you like to work with your hands? You could be a **carpenter**, an **assembler**, or a **construction worker**. Do you want to help people? You could be a **babysitter**, a **home health aide**, or a **doctor**. Are you creative? You could be a **hairstylist**, a **florist**, or an **architect**. Are you good with numbers? You could be an **accountant** or an **engineer**.

1 an accountant	9 a delivery person	17 a barber
2 a dentist	10 a computer technician	18 an assembler
3 an **artist**	11 a janitor / a custodian	19 an **architect**
4 a **cook**	12 a **doctor**	20 a butcher
5 a hairstylist / a hairdresser	13 a homemaker	21 a (home) health aide / a (home) attendant
6 a construction worker	14 a florist	22 an **engineer**
7 a graphic artist	15 a housekeeper	23 a **businessman** / a businesswoman
8 a gardener	16 an **editor**	

3

4

5

6

2

12

7

Word Partnerships

a	part-time	job
	well-paid	
	blue-collar	
	white-collar	
look for	a job	
apply for		
get		
lose		

13

14

21

22

23

24

24 a cashier

25 an **actor**

26 a **carpenter**

27 an electrician

27

29

28 a **firefighter**

29 a garment worker

30 a babysitter

28

30

Words in Action

1. Look at the list. What are the best five jobs to have? Why?

2. Which jobs are done in offices? Which are done in shops? Which are done outdoors? Make three lists.

Jobs 2

Words in Context

There are many **jobs** in my family. I'm a **reporter** for a newspaper. My sister is a **musician**. My brother likes to work with animals, so he is a **veterinarian**. My other brother travels a lot. He's a **truck driver**. Our parents are **teachers**. They taught us to love work.

1 a **reporter**

2 a manicurist

3 a **lawyer**

4 a **soldier**

5 a receptionist

6 a physical therapist

7 a locksmith

8 a security guard

9 a **teacher** / an instructor

10 a mechanic

11 a **police officer**

12 a photographer

13 a stockbroker

14 a (house) painter

15 a plumber

16 a **scientist**

17 a taxi driver

18 a **server**

19 a **nurse**

20 a real estate agent

21 a salesperson

22 a tour guide

23 a **pilot**

24 a musician

25 a **writer**

26 a truck driver

27 a travel agent

28 a veterinarian / vet

Word Partnerships

a fashion	photographer
a wedding	
a registered	nurse
a school	
a commercial	pilot
a private	
a fighter	

3

6

5

4

8

SECURITY

HOMEWORK PAGE 98

9

10

11

16

TAXI

17

18

24

Book
Signing
TODAY

25

26

27

ISLAND FUN

28

Words in Action

1. Look at the list. Which are the five most difficult jobs? Why? Which are the five easiest? Why?

2. Look at the list. Which people use vehicles in their jobs? What vehicles do they use? Which people use equipment in their jobs? What equipment do they use?

Working

Words in Context

Needed: Office Assistant

Can you answer phones, **take** messages, **schedule** appointments, and **file**? Can you **use** a computer and a fax machine? Can you **type** 50 words per minute? You may be the right person for this job. Call 555-9389 to schedule an appointment for an interview.

1 cook
2 examine
3 **speak**
4 **arrest**
5 open mail
6 load
7 deliver
8 **type**

9 take care of
10 act / **perform**
11 sing
12 take a message
13 hire
14 **sell**
15 repair / fix
16 **plan**

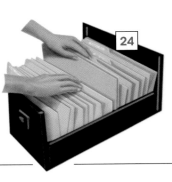

150

17 staple

18 **manage**

19 **design**

20 make copies

21 use a computer

22 call in sick

23 manufacture

24 **file**

25 **drive**

26 make a decision

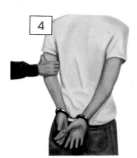

... and then ...

Words in Action

1. Which of the things on the list can you do?

2. Choose five verbs on the list. Look at the jobs on pages 146–149. Can you find one or more jobs that match the verb?

Farm

Words in Context

Jimmy Carter was the 39th president of the U.S. He grew up on a **farm** full of animals. There were **dogs**, **turkeys**, **horses**, and **cows** on the farm. Carter did many jobs around the farm. He **milked** the cows each day after school. He also **picked** cotton and peanuts in the **fields**.

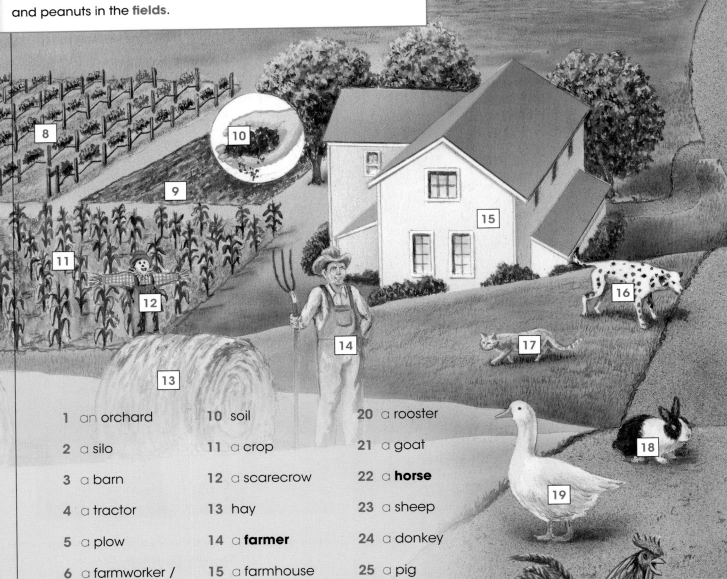

1 an orchard	10 soil	20 a rooster
2 a silo	11 a crop	21 a goat
3 a barn	12 a scarecrow	22 a **horse**
4 a tractor	13 hay	23 a sheep
5 a plow	14 a **farmer**	24 a donkey
6 a farmworker / a farmhand	15 a farmhouse	25 a pig
7 a bull	16 a **dog**	26 a **cow**
8 a vineyard	17 a **cat**	27 a **turkey**
9 a **field**	18 a rabbit	28 a **chicken**
	19 a goose	

Verbs

29 plant

30 water

31 **pick**

32 milk

33 **feed**

Animal	Baby Animal
dog	puppy
cat	kitten
chicken	chick
pig	piglet
sheep	lamb
cow	calf
goat	kid

Words in Action

1. Study the word list for three minutes. Then close your book. Write down as many of the words as you can remember. Write each word under one of these categories: *People and animals on a farm, Things on a farm, Places on a farm.*

2. Choose a word and draw a picture of it on the board. The first classmate to guess the word gets a point and draws the next picture on the board.

Office

Words in Context

Offices are very different today than they were 100 years ago. Back then there were no **computers**, **fax machines**, or **photocopiers**. People used **typewriters** to write letters. However, some things are the same. Most offices still have **file cabinets** and use supplies like **staplers**, **paper clips**, and **rubber bands**.

Employee of the Month

1

2

3

4

5

6

7

8

9

10

11

12

13

14

15

16

JOHN LOPEZ
45 Lawrence Street • Brooklyn, New York 11203 • (718) 555-0303

Executive Assistant

QUALIFICATIONS

• A highly organized and detail-oriented Executive Assistant providing skillful administrative support.
• Able to prioritize tasks and achieve goals.
• A self-motivated professional.
• Excellent research and writing skills.
• Computer skills include: MS Word, PowerPoint, Excel

EXPERIENCE

KEMCORP, New York, N.Y.

• Executive Assistant to the CEO, 2011-present
• Coordinated conference calls.
• Created effective filing systems, including quick indexing, fili...
• Conducted exhaustive research on competitors.
• Updated and maintained CEO's calendar.
• ...duled appointments with important clients and...
• ...systems and procedures which...

1 a binder

2 a fax machine

3 a (photo)copier / a copy machine

4 a (photo)copy

5 an office manager

6 a **desk**

7 a **computer**

8 **tape**

9 a stapler

10 a **calculator**

11 a **telephone**

12 letterhead

13 an appointment book / a date book

14 a business card file

15 a (paper) shredder

16 a resume

17 a file cabinet

18 an office assistant / a **secretary**

19 a (file) folder

20 an (electric) pencil sharpener

21 a supply cabinet

22 a thumbtack

23 a rubber band

24 **glue**

25 sticky notes

26 **staples**

27 correction fluid

28 a paper clip

29 a hole punch

30 a **pad**

31 a **label**

Word Partnerships

double sided	tape
packing	
hook up	a fax machine
turn on	a computer
turn off	

Words in Action

1. Which items on the list do you have at home?
2. Work with a partner. One student describes an office item. The other student guesses the item.
   - Student A: *You use this to add numbers.*
   - Student B: *A calculator.*

Factory

1 a **designer**
2 a **front office**
3 an **assembly line**
4 a **worker**
5 a **robot**
6 a conveyor belt
7 a **packer**

8 a hard hat
9 a **supervisor**
10 a forklift
11 a time card
12 a time clock
13 **parts**
14 a machine operator

Words in Context

Making a chair is a process. There are many steps. The **designer** creates a design. **Parts** for the chair arrive at the **factory's loading dock**. Then **assembly line workers** put the chair together. It travels down a **conveyor belt** and gets a new part at each area. At the end of the assembly line, **packers** put the chair into a box. It goes into a **warehouse**. Then a **shipping clerk** sends it to a store near you!

FRONT OFFICE

PARTS

30 biohazard
31 electrical hazard
32 explosive materials
33 flammable materials
34 poisonous materials
35 radioactive materials

15 a **warehouse**

16 a shipping clerk

17 a fire extinguisher

18 a loading dock

19 a hand truck / a dolly

20 a hairnet

21 a safety visor

22 a **respirator**

23 safety goggles

24 earplugs

25 safety glasses

26 a particle mask

27 a safety vest

28 safety boots

29 safety earmuffs

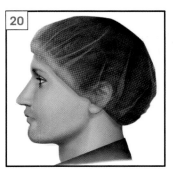

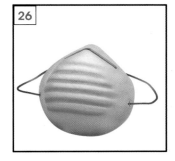

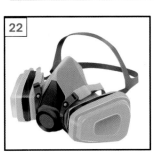

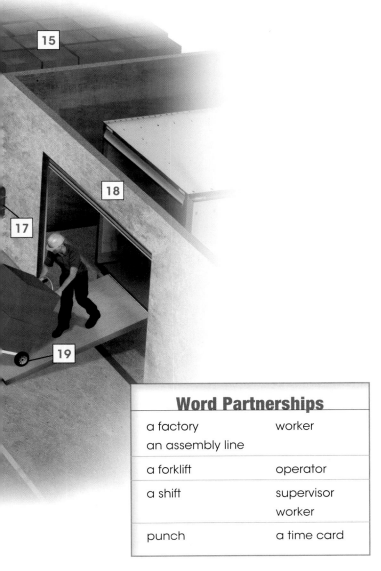

Word Partnerships

a factory	worker
an assembly line	
a forklift	operator
a shift	supervisor
	worker
punch	a time card

Words in Action

1. Make a list of the people in this factory. Which job is the most interesting to you? Which is the least interesting? Why?

2. What part of the body do each of these pieces of safety equipment protect: earplugs, a hard hat, safety boots, safety goggles, a safety visor, safety earmuffs, safety glasses, a particle mask, a hairnet.

Hotel

Words in Context

There's a **hotel** in Sweden made completely of ice! You **check in** at the ice **lobby**. All the **rooms** and **suites** are made of ice, too. **Room service** brings you a hot drink in the morning. You can go to the **sauna** to warm up. Room rates are high, but the Ice Hotel is very popular. Be sure to **make** a reservation before you go!

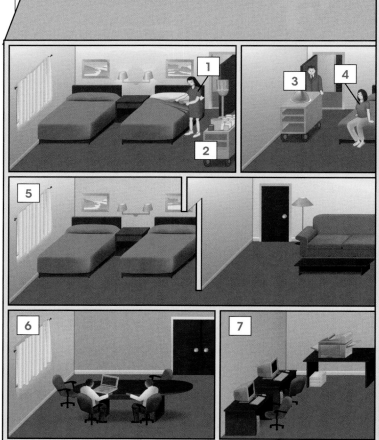

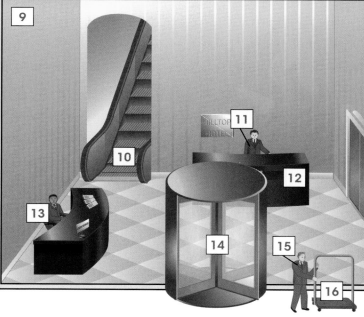

Verbs

24 make a reservation

25 check in

26 order room service

27 check out

1 a **housekeeper**

2 a housekeeping cart

3 room service

4 a (hotel) guest

5 a **suite**

6 a meeting room

7 a business center

8 a **ballroom**

9 a **lobby**

10 an escalator

11 a desk clerk

12 a registration desk

13 a concierge

14 a revolving door

15 a bellhop

16 a luggage cart

17 a (double) room

18 a (single) room

19 a fitness center

20 a sauna

21 a (swimming) **pool**

22 a **gift shop**

23 valet parking

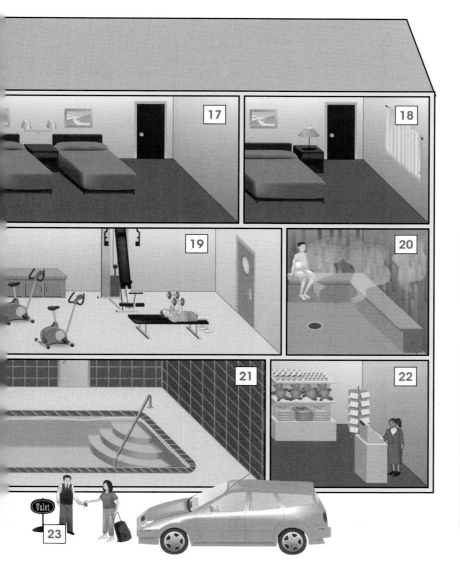

Word Partnerships	
a luxury	hotel
a budget	
room	rates
an indoor	(swimming) pool
an outdoor	
a heated	

Words in Action

1. Make three lists: *People in a hotel, Places in a hotel,* and *Things in a hotel.*

2. Role-play with a partner. One of you is the desk clerk at a hotel. The other is calling with questions about the hotel.

- Student A: *How much is a double room?*
- Student B: *It's $50 a night for a double.*
- Student A: *Is there a swimming pool?*

Tools and Supplies 1

Words in Context

I go to hardware stores a lot because I work in construction. I keep my **wrench**, my **hammer**, and my **screwdriver** in my **tool belt**. Those are the **tools** I use the most.

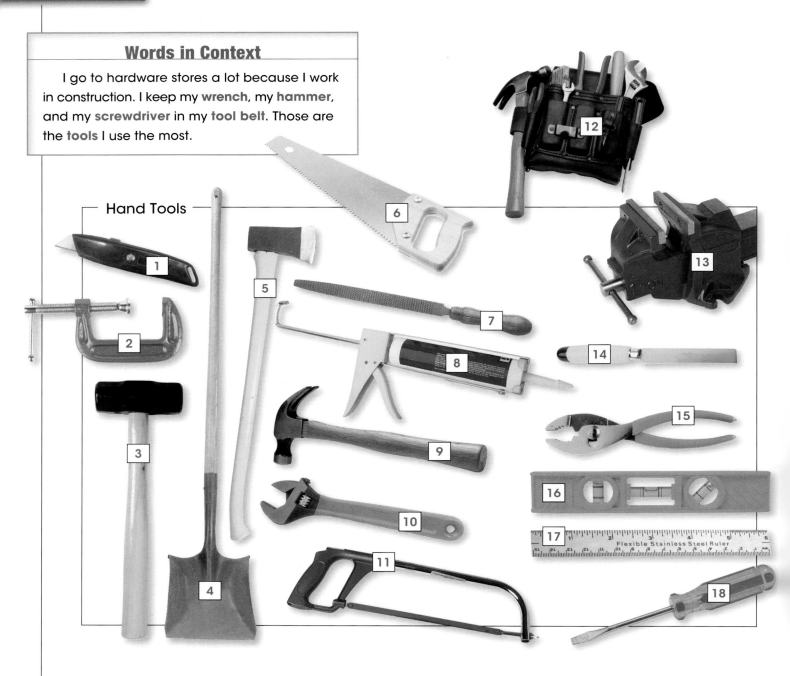

Hand Tools

1 a utility knife	7 a **file**	13 a vise	19 electrical tape
2 a C-clamp	8 a caulking gun	14 a chisel	20 an extension cord
3 a sledgehammer	9 a **hammer**	15 pliers	21 **wire**
4 a **shovel**	10 a **wrench**	16 a level	22 a lightbulb
5 an **ax**	11 a hacksaw	17 a **ruler**	23 a wire stripper
6 a handsaw	12 a tool belt	18 a screwdriver	24 (pipe) fittings

Electrical

Plumbing

Power Tools

25 a pipe wrench

26 a **pipe**

27 a router

28 a **drill**

29 a drill bit

30 a **blade**

31 a circular saw

32 a power sander

Word Partnerships	
a tool	bench
	box
a Phillips	screwdriver
a flathead	
an electric	drill
a cordless	

Words in Action

1. Which items on the list have you used? What job did you do with each item?

2. Which tools would you use to:
   - build a bookcase?
   - wire a house?
   - install a sink?

161

Tools and Supplies 2

Words in Context

How to Hang a Picture on a Wall

- With a **tape measure** or ruler, measure **66 to 68 inches** above the floor.
- Put a small piece of **masking tape** on the wall.
- Put a **nail** through a picture **hook**, and pound it in through the masking tape.
- Hang your picture.

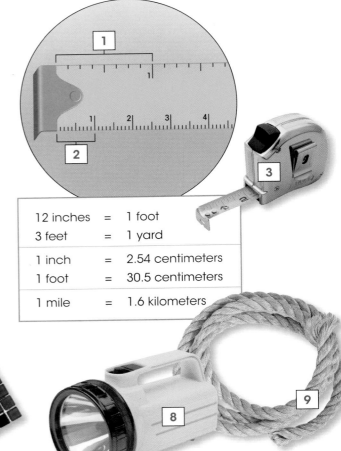

12 inches	=	1 foot
3 feet	=	1 yard
1 inch	=	2.54 centimeters
1 foot	=	30.5 centimeters
1 mile	=	1.6 kilometers

Building Material

Paint Supplies

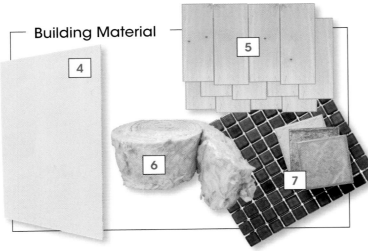

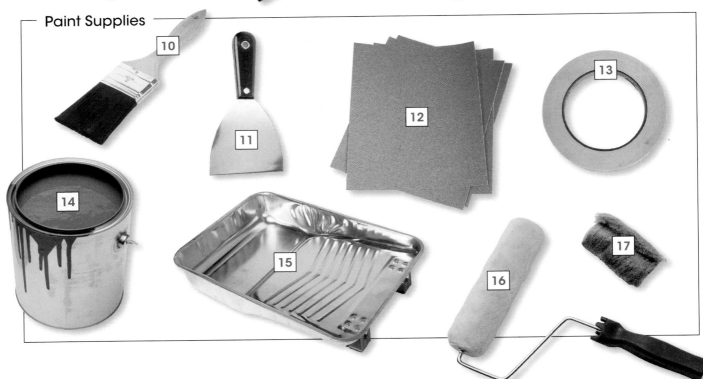

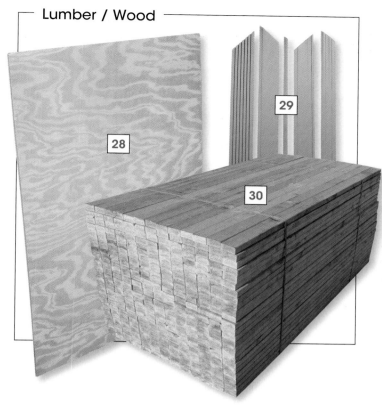

1	an **inch**	14	**paint**	27	a **hook**
2	a centimeter	15	a paint tray	28	plywood
3	a tape measure	16	a (paint) roller	29	molding
4	drywall	17	steel wool	30	board lumber
5	shingles	18	an anchor	31	duct tape
6	insulation	19	an eye hook	32	a **chain**
7	tile	20	a **nail**	33	a **battery**
8	a flashlight	21	a **bolt**	34	a padlock
9	a **rope**	22	a **screw**		
10	a paintbrush	23	a **nut**		
11	a scraper	24	a wing nut		
12	sandpaper	25	a hinge		
13	masking tape	26	a washer		

Word Partnerships

a hardware	store
	section
a sheet of	plywood
	drywall
spray	paint
latex	
acrylic	

Words in Action

1. Name one of the items on the list, then think of as many uses for the item as you can.

2. Imagine you need to paint some windows in an old house. Which items will you need to prepare the windows and paint them?

Drill, Sand, Paint

Words in Context

In 1980, Edouard Arsenault, a Canadian fisherman, began to make buildings with old glass bottles. He used thousands of bottles. He **mixed** cement. Then, instead of **laying** bricks, he laid rows of bottles in the wet cement. After he **put up** the glass walls, he **installed** skylights. Many people visit these buildings each year.

Word Partnerships

paint	a wall
	a room
	a house
install	a phone line
	a water heater
shovel	gravel
	snow

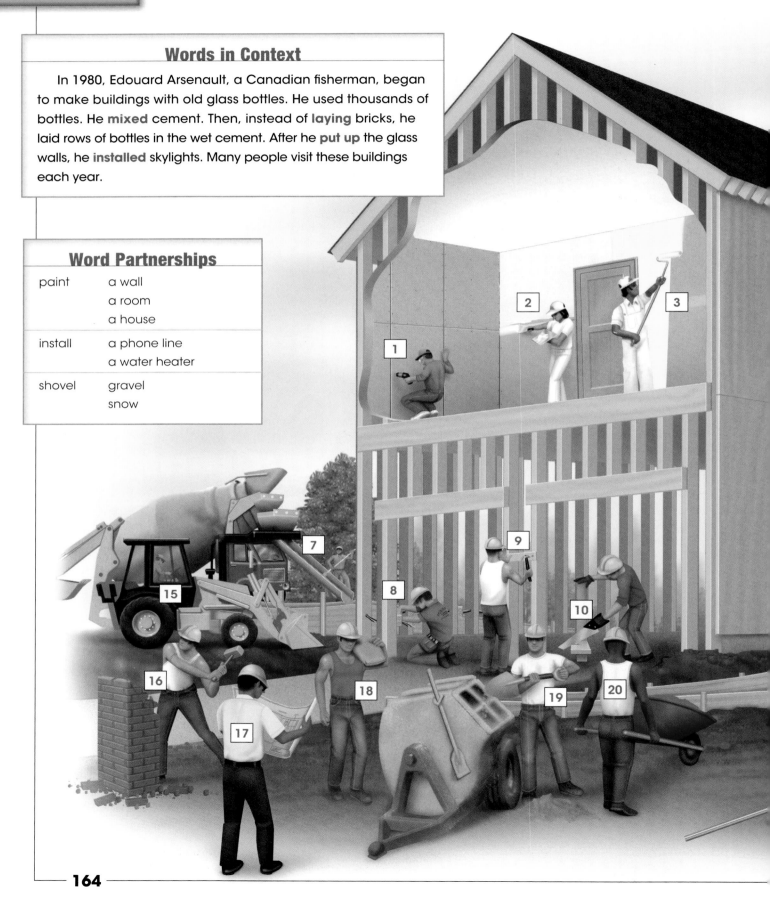

1 put up drywall

2 plaster a wall

3 **paint** a wall

4 drill a hole

5 **lay** bricks

6 **pull** a rope

7 **pour** concrete

8 wire a house

9 hammer a nail

10 saw wood

11 **measure**

12 weld

13 install a window

14 **climb** a ladder

15 **operate** a backhoe

16 tear down a wall

17 **read** blueprints

18 **carry** a bag

19 shovel sand

20 **push** a wheelbarrow

21 **cut** a pipe

22 dig a trench

23 plane wood

24 glue wood

25 sand wood

Words in Action

1. Check off the things on the list you have done.

2. Pretend to be doing one of the actions on the word list. Your partner will guess what you are doing.

Weather

Words in Context

Today's **weather**:

Don't expect **sunshine** today. The morning will be **cold** and **windy** with a good chance of **rain**. This afternoon the temperature will drop, and we will see five to seven inches of **snow** tonight!

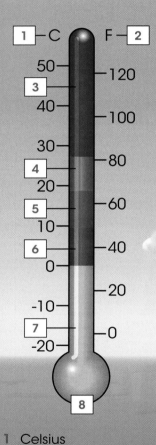

1 Celsius	9 the **sun**	17 **wind**
2 Fahrenheit	10 the **sky**	18 hail
3 **hot**	11 a rainbow	19 snow
4 **warm**	12 a cloud	20 **rain**
5 **cool**	13 sunshine	21 a hailstone
6 **cold**	14 a **storm**	22 a snowflake
7 freezing	15 lightning	23 a raindrop
8 a thermometer	16 fog	24 **ice**

25 It's sunny.

26 It's cloudy.

27 It's windy.

28 It's snowing.

29 It's foggy.

30 It's raining.

Word Partnerships		
25	degrees	Celsius
77		Fahrenheit
a cold	wind	
a bitter		
a heavy	rain	
a light		
a blue	sky	
a gray		
a cloudless		

Words in Action

1. Describe the weather today. Then describe yesterday's weather.

- *It's rainy and cool today. Yesterday was sunny and warm.*

2. What is your favorite kind of weather? Why?

- *I like sunny weather because I can go to the beach.*

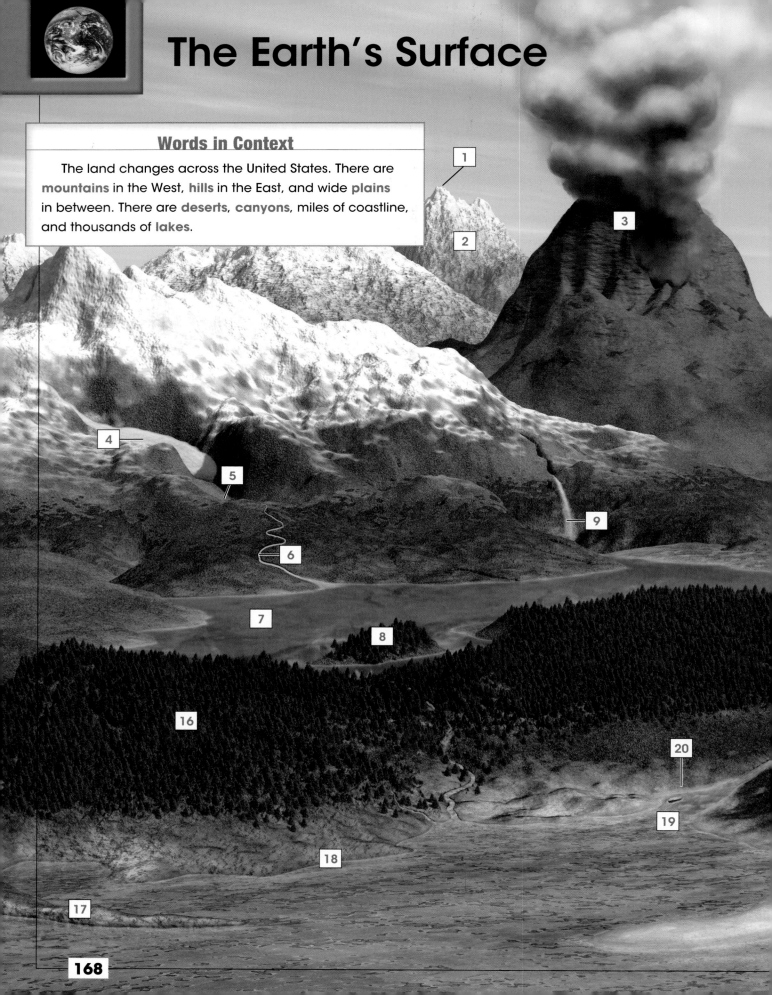

The Earth's Surface

Words in Context

The land changes across the United States. There are **mountains** in the West, **hills** in the East, and wide **plains** in between. There are **deserts**, **canyons**, miles of coastline, and thousands of **lakes**.

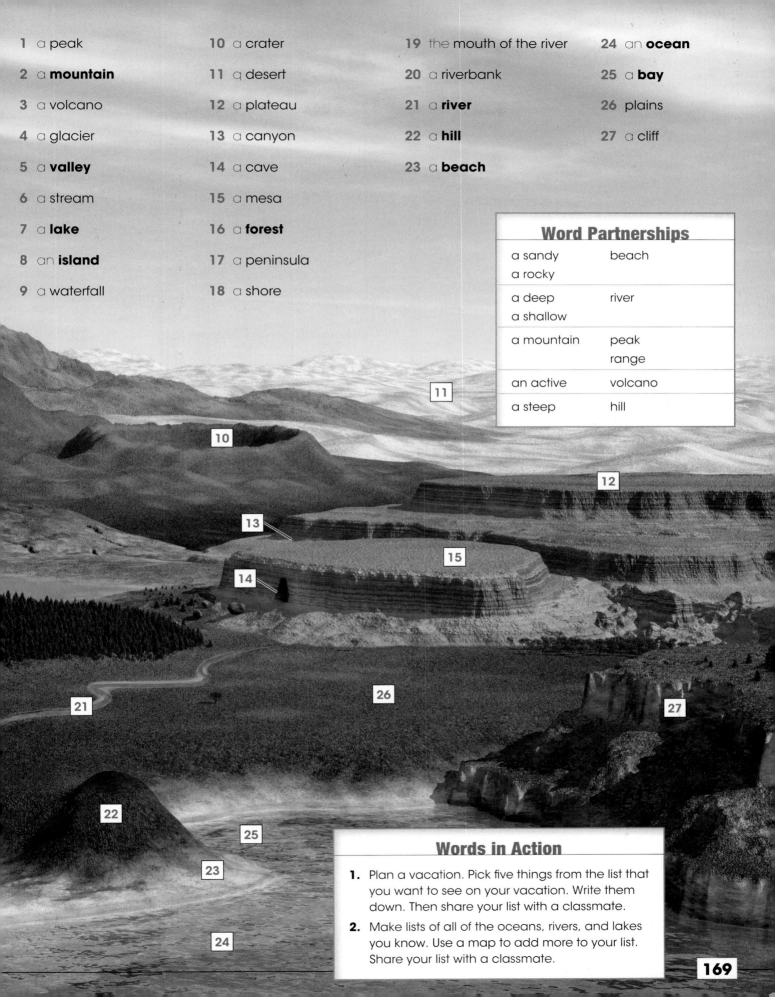

1 a peak
2 a **mountain**
3 a volcano
4 a glacier
5 a **valley**
6 a stream
7 a **lake**
8 an **island**
9 a waterfall

10 a crater
11 a desert
12 a plateau
13 a canyon
14 a cave
15 a mesa
16 a **forest**
17 a peninsula
18 a shore

19 the mouth of the river
20 a riverbank
21 a **river**
22 a **hill**
23 a **beach**

24 an **ocean**
25 a **bay**
26 plains
27 a cliff

Word Partnerships

a sandy a rocky	beach
a deep a shallow	river
a mountain	peak range
an active	volcano
a steep	hill

Words in Action

1. Plan a vacation. Pick five things from the list that you want to see on your vacation. Write them down. Then share your list with a classmate.

2. Make lists of all of the oceans, rivers, and lakes you know. Use a map to add more to your list. Share your list with a classmate.

Energy, Pollution, and Natural Disasters

Words in Context

Automobile exhaust creates air pollution. Air pollution can turn into acid rain. Acid rain kills plants and animals. Some new cars run on solar energy. These cars don't create air pollution.

1

2

3

4

5

6

7

8

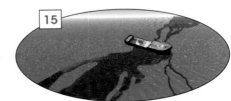
9

10

11

12

13

14

15

16

17

18

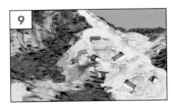
19

20

21

Natural Disasters

1 a forest fire

2 a blizzard

3 a **drought**

4 a famine

5 an **earthquake**

6 a **flood**

7 an avalanche

8 a **hurricane**

9 a mudslide

10 a **tsunami** / a tidal wave

11 a **tornado**

12 a volcanic eruption

Pollution

13 air pollution / smog

14 acid rain

15 an oil spill

16 pesticide poisoning

17 **radiation**

18 hazardous waste

19 water pollution

20 automobile exhaust

21 litter

Energy

22 natural gas

23 **oil** / petroleum

24 **wind**

25 geothermal energy

26 **coal**

27 solar energy

28 nuclear energy

29 hydroelectric power

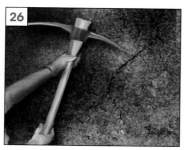

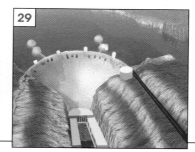

Word Partnerships	
a long a severe	drought
a flash	flood
a minor a major	earthquake
environmental	disasters pollution

Words in Action

1. Work with a group. Choose two or three natural disasters. In what parts of the world has each disaster happened? Make a list for each disaster.

2. Which kind of energy source do you use to heat your home? Which do you use to cook? Which do you use to dry your clothes? Discuss with a group.

The United States and Canada

Words in Context

There are fifty states in the **United States**. The capital is **Washington, D.C.** The U.S. city with the most people is **New York City**. **Canada** is much larger than the U.S., but it has far fewer people. The capital of Canada is **Ottawa** and the city with the most people is **Toronto**.

Regions of Canada

1. Northern Canada
2. **British Columbia**
3. the Prairie Provinces
4. **Ontario**
5. **Quebec**
6. the Atlantic Provinces

Regions of the United States

7. the **West Coast**
8. the **Rocky Mountain States**
9. the **Midwest**
10. the **Mid-Atlantic States**
11. **New England**
12. the **Southwest**
13. the **South**

ARC
OC

ALASKA
(United States)

YUKON

NORTHW

★Whitehorse

TERRIT

Juneau★

2

**BRITISH
COLUMBIA**

ALBE

★

Victoria★

Olympia★ WASH.

Salem★

★H
MO

OREGON

★Boise

IDAHO

PACIFIC
OCEAN

7

8

Carson
City★

V

Sacramento★

Salt
Lake
City

NEVADA

CALIFORNIA

UTAH

ARIZONA

★Phoenix

Honolulu

HAWAI'I

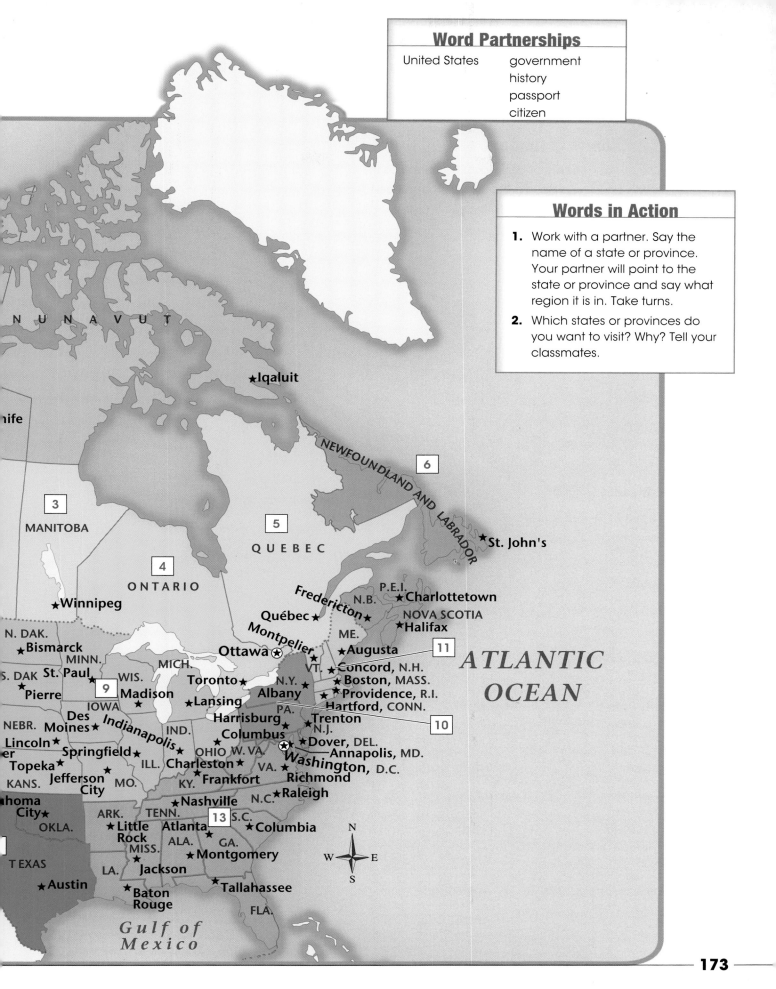

Words in Action

1. Work with a partner. Say the name of a state or province. Your partner will point to the state or province and say what region it is in. Take turns.

2. Which states or provinces do you want to visit? Why? Tell your classmates.

N U N A V U T

★Iqaluit

6

NEWFOUNDLAND AND LABRADOR

3

MANITOBA

5

★St. John's

QUEBEC

4

ONTARIO

P.E.I.

Fredericton
N.B. ★Charlottetown

★Winnipeg

Québec★
Montpelier

NOVA SCOTIA
★Halifax

N. DAK.
★Bismarck

ME.

Ottawa ✪

★Augusta

11

MINN.

MICH.

VT.

★Concord, N.H.

ATLANTIC
OCEAN

S. DAK
St. Paul
★Pierre

WIS.

Toronto★

N.Y.

★Boston, MASS.

9

★Madison

Albany
★

★Providence, R.I.
Hartford, CONN.

IOWA

★Lansing

10

NEBR. Des
★Moines
★Lincoln

Indianapolis

PA.

★Trenton

IND.

Harrisburg
★

N.J.

★Springfield

★Columbus

★Dover, DEL.

Topeka★

OHIO W. VA.

✪Washington, ━Annapolis, MD.
D.C.

ILL. ★Charleston

KANS.
Jefferson
City
MO.

KY. ★Frankfort

VA.

★Richmond

homa
City★

★Nashville

N.C. ★Raleigh

13

OKLA.

ARK.

TENN.

S.C.

★Little
Rock

Atlanta
★

★Columbia

TEXAS

ALA.

GA.

N

MISS.

★Montgomery

W

E

LA.

★
Jackson

S

★Austin

★Baton
Rouge

★Tallahassee

FLA.

Gulf of
Mexico

The World

Words in Context

There are seven **continents** and almost 200 countries in the **world**. **Russia** and **Canada** are the biggest countries. **China** and **India** are the countries with the most people.

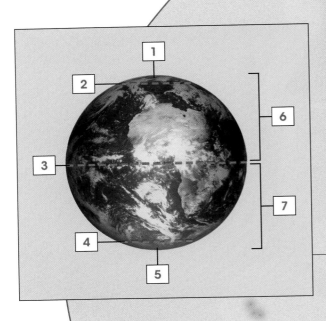

CANADA

8 **NORTH AMERICA**

UNITED STATES

ATLANTIC OCEAN

MEXICO

BAHAMAS

CUBA
JAMAICA **HAITI** **DOM. REP.** **PUERTO RICO (U.S.)**
BELIZE
GUATEMALA **HONDURAS** **ST. KITTS AND NEVIS**
EL SALVADOR **NICARAGUA** **ANTIGUA AND BARBUDA**
COSTA RICA **ST. LUCIA** **DOMINICA**
GRENADA **BARBADOS**
PANAMA **VENEZUELA** **ST. VINCENT AND THE GREN.**
COLOMBIA **GUYANA** **TRINIDAD AND TOBAGO**
SURINAME
FRENCH GUIANA (France)

ECUADOR

BRAZIL
9 **SOUTH AMERICA**
PERU
BOLIVIA
PARAGUAY

SAMOA
AMERICAN SAMOA (U.S.)
FRENCH POLYNESIA (France)
TONGA

CHILE
URUGUAY
ARGENTINA

N
W   E
S

1 the **North Pole**

2 the Arctic Circle

3 the **Equator**

4 the Antarctic Circle

5 the **South Pole**

6 the Northern Hemisphere

7 the Southern Hemisphere

Continents

8 **North America**

9 **South America**

10 **Europe**

11 **Asia**

12 **Africa**

13 **Australia**

14 **Antarctica**

Words in Action

1. Go around the room saying the name of a country for each letter of the alphabet. (There are no countries that start with the letter *x*.)

2. Work with a partner. Say the name of a country. Your partner will point to the country on the map and say the name of the continent it is in. Take turns.

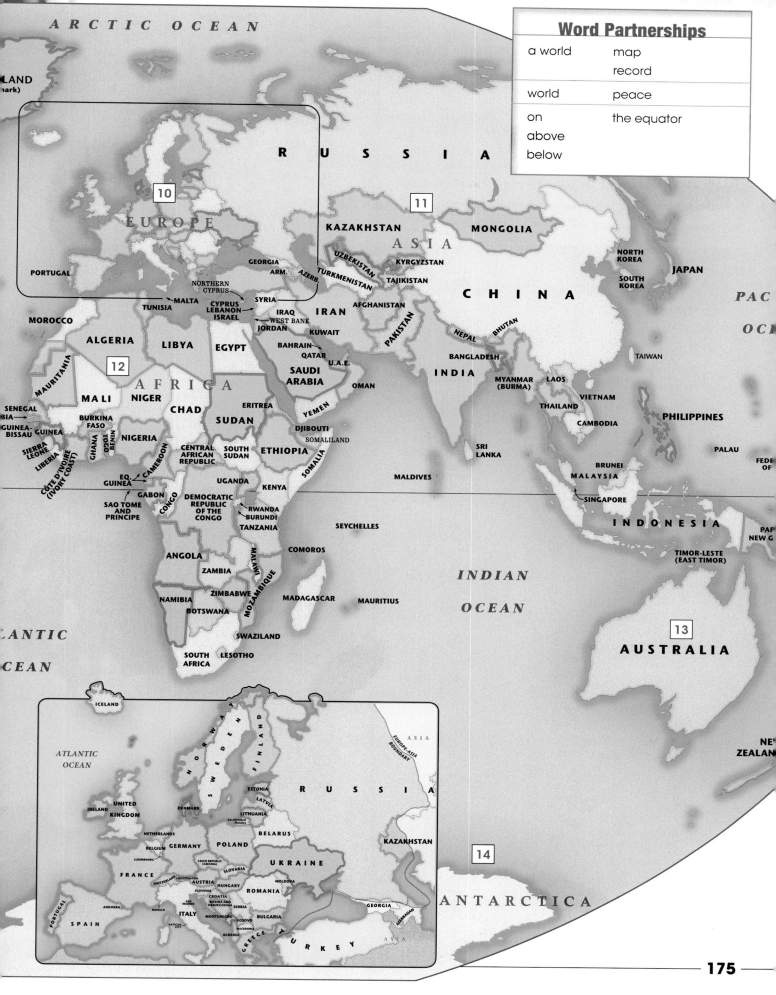

ARCTIC OCEAN

Word Partnerships

a world	map
	record
world	peace
on	the equator
above	
below	

LAND
(mark)

RUSSIA

10

EUROPE

PORTUGAL

11

KAZAKHSTAN

ASIA

MONGOLIA

GEORGIA
ARM.
AZERB.

TURKMENISTAN

UZBEKISTAN

KYRGYZSTAN

TAJIKISTAN

NORTH
KOREA

JAPAN

SOUTH
KOREA

CHINA

PAC

OC

NORTHERN
CYPRUS

MALTA

TUNISIA

CYPRUS
LEBANON
ISRAEL

SYRIA

WEST BANK
JORDAN

IRAQ

IRAN

AFGHANISTAN

PAKISTAN

NEPAL

BHUTAN

MOROCCO

ALGERIA

LIBYA

EGYPT

12

AFRICA

MAURITANIA

MALI

NIGER

CHAD

BAHRAIN
QATAR
U.A.E.

KUWAIT

SAUDI
ARABIA

OMAN

BANGLADESH

INDIA

TAIWAN

MYANMAR
(BURMA)

LAOS

THAILAND

VIETNAM

CAMBODIA

PHILIPPINES

PALAU

FEDE
OF

SENEGAL
BIA
GUINEA-
BISSAU

GUINEA

BURKINA
FASO

GHANA

TOGO
BENIN

NIGERIA

CENTRAL
AFRICAN
REPUBLIC

SUDAN

ERITREA

SOUTH
SUDAN

DJIBOUTI

SOMALILAND

ETHIOPIA

YEMEN

SOMALIA

SRI
LANKA

MALDIVES

BRUNEI

MALAYSIA

SIERRA
LEONE

LIBERIA

CÔTE D'IVOIRE
(IVORY COAST)

EQ.
GUINEA

CAMEROON

GABON

SAO TOME
AND
PRINCIPE

CONGO

UGANDA

DEMOCRATIC
REPUBLIC
OF THE
CONGO

RWANDA
BURUNDI

KENYA

TANZANIA

SEYCHELLES

SINGAPORE

INDONESIA

PAP
NEW G

TIMOR-LESTE
(EAST TIMOR)

ANGOLA

ZAMBIA

MALAWI

COMOROS

INDIAN

OCEAN

13

AUSTRALIA

NAMIBIA

BOTSWANA

ZIMBABWE

MOZAMBIQUE

MADAGASCAR

MAURITIUS

LANTIC

CEAN

SOUTH
AFRICA

LESOTHO

SWAZILAND

ICELAND

ATLANTIC
OCEAN

NORWAY

SWEDEN

FINLAND

ESTONIA

ASIA

EUROPE-ASIA
BOUNDARY

NEW
ZEALAN

IRELAND

UNITED
KINGDOM

DENMARK

LATVIA

LITHUANIA

KALININGRAD
(Russia)

RUSSIA

NETHERLANDS

BELGIUM

GERMANY

POLAND

BELARUS

KAZAKHSTAN

14

LUXEMBOURG

CZECH REPUBLIC
(CZECHIA)

SLOVAKIA

UKRAINE

FRANCE

SWITZERLAND
LIECHTENSTEIN

AUSTRIA

HUNGARY

MOLDOVA

ROMANIA

SLOVENIA

CROATIA

ANDORRA

MONACO

SAN MARINO

BOSNIA AND
HERZEGOVINA

SERBIA

PORTUGAL

SPAIN

ITALY

VATICAN
CITY

MONTENEGRO

KOSOVO

BULGARIA

GEORGIA

AZERBAIJAN

ANTARCTICA

ALBANIA

MACEDONIA

GREECE

TURKEY

ASIA

The Universe

The first **satellite** went into **space** in 1957. The first human went into space in 1961. In 1969 an **astronaut** walked on the **moon** for the first time. Today some astronauts even live on a **space station** for a few months at a time!

1 a space station

2 a constellation

3 a **star**

4 a **rocket**

5 an eclipse

6 an **orbit**

7 a galaxy

8 an observatory

9 a telescope

10 an astronomer

11 **space**

12 the **moon**

13 a **satellite**

14 an astronaut

15 **Earth's** atmosphere

16 a meteor

17 a space shuttle

18 the **sun**

19 a comet

The Planets

20 Neptune

21 Uranus

22 Saturn

23 Jupiter

24 **Mars**

25 **Earth**

26 Venus

27 **Mercury**

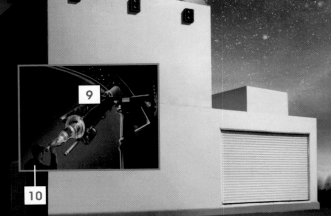

176

28 a new moon   **29** a crescent moon   **30** a quarter moon   **31** a full moon

Word Partnerships

space	travel
	exploration
a distant	star
a shooting	
a bright	
a solar	eclipse
a lunar	

Words in Action

1. Imagine you are an astronaut. You can go to any one place in the solar system. Where will you go? Why? Share your answer with the class.

2. Look at the sky tonight and report back to your class. Was it a new moon, a crescent moon, a quarter moon, or a full moon? Does everyone in the class agree?

Garden

Words in Context

There are 350,000 kinds of plants. Most plants grow from a **seed**. First **roots** grow from seeds, then **stems**, and then **leaves**. In **pine trees**, seeds come from the **pinecones**. In **lilacs**, **poppies**, **sunflowers**, and many other plants, seeds come from inside the **flowers**.

1

2

3

4

10

11

13

12

Parts of a Tree

14

15

16

17

18

Parts of a Flower

19

20

21

22

23

24

25

26

178

1 a pine (tree)
2 a willow (tree)
3 a birch (tree)
4 a maple (tree)
5 an oak (tree)
6 an elm (tree)
7 a lilac bush
8 a greenhouse
9 a pinecone
10 a **branch**
11 a **trunk**

12 **roots**
13 a **leaf**
14 a **flower**
15 a **stem**
16 a petal
17 a **bud**
18 a bulb
19 irises
20 lilies
21 chrysanthemums
22 daffodils

23 violets
24 a **seed**
25 tulips
26 marigolds
27 **ivy**
28 **roses**
29 sunflowers
30 geraniums
31 daisies
32 poppies

Word Partnerships

a shade	tree
an evergreen	
send	flowers
give	
get / receive	
a bouquet of	roses
a dozen	
long-stem	

Words in Action

1. Which of the flowers and trees grow in your area? Make a list with your class.
2. Describe a flower or tree to a partner. Your partner will guess the flower or tree. Take turns.
   - Student A: *It has a yellow center and white petals. It doesn't really have a smell.*
   - Student B: *It's a daisy.*

Desert

Words in Context

Fourteen percent of the earth's surface is **desert**. Deserts contain mostly sand and **rocks**. They get very little rain. Many animals and **insects**, like **camels**, **lizards**, **snakes**, **ants**, and **spiders**, live in the desert. The largest desert in the world is the Sahara in North Africa. It has an area of about nine million square kilometers.

Word Partnerships

a red	ant
a black	
a fire	
a carpenter	
a swarm of	ants
	flies
a poisonous	snake
	spider

1 a **hawk**

2 an **owl**

3 a **boulder**

4 a coyote

5 a mountain lion

6 a sand dune

7 a palm tree

8 a **camel**

9 a vulture

10 a lizard

11 a **rock**

12 a tortoise

13 a **rat**

14 a **snake**

15 an oasis

16 a cactus

17 a pebble

Insects / Bugs

18 a **spider**

19 a grasshopper

20 a **fly**

21 a moth

22 a cricket

23 a scorpion

24 an **ant**

Words in Action

1. One student chooses a word from the word list. The other students ask "Yes / No" questions to gather information and try to guess the word.
   - Student A: *Is it an animal?*
     Student B: *No.*
   - Student C: *Is it an insect?*
     Student B: *Yes.*
   - Student D: *Does it have wings?*
     Student B: *Yes.*
   - Student D: *Is it a fly?*
     Student B: *Yes!*

2. Imagine you are taking a trip to the desert. What things do you want to see? Discuss this with your class.

181

Rain Forest

Words in Context

Many plants and animals live in **rain forests**. Colorful **parrots** and playful **monkeys** live there. Beautiful **orchids** and long **vines** grow there. At night, **tigers** and **panthers** hunt in the rain forest.

1	a parakeet	14	an aardvark
2	a **vine**	15	a flamingo
3	a chimpanzee	16	a fern
4	a **bat**	17	a panther
5	a parrot	18	an alligator
6	a **monkey**	19	a crocodile
7	a **gorilla**	20	a caterpillar
8	a peacock	21	a **butterfly**
9	a **tiger**	22	a snail
10	a hummingbird	23	a wasp
11	an orchid	24	a beetle
12	a **frog**	25	a tarantula
13	an orangutan		

Word Partnerships

frogs	hop
wasps	sting
tigers	leap
monkeys	swing

26 swing

27 hop

28 hang

4

5

6

10

11

9

12

17

16

15

19

20

21

22

23

24

25

Words in Action

1. Work with a partner. Put the words into groups of plants, animals, and insects.

2. Choose one of the animals on the list that makes a noise. Make that animal's noise. Your partner will guess the animal. Take turns.

Grasslands

Animals in the **grasslands** have different sources of food. **Giraffes** and **elephants** graze on the tallest trees. **Buffalo** and **gazelles** graze on grasses. The large cats, like **lions**, **leopards**, and **cheetahs**, feed on other animals.

184

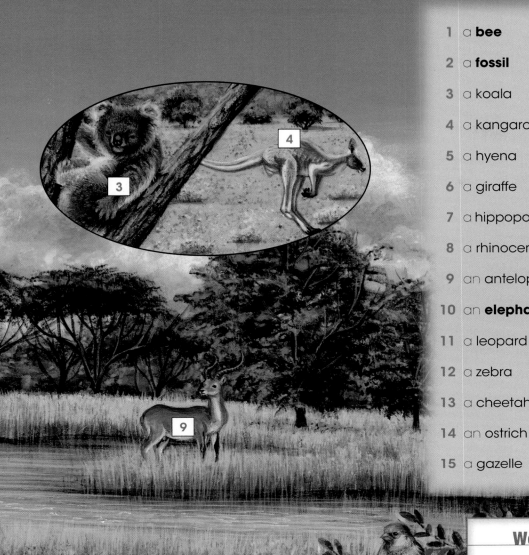

1	a **bee**	16	a **shrub** / a **bush**
2	a **fossil**	17	a buffalo
3	a koala	18	a sparrow
4	a kangaroo	19	a gopher
5	a hyena	20	a **lion**
6	a giraffe	21	an antler
7	a hippopotamus	22	a hoof
8	a rhinoceros	23	a **horn**
9	an antelope	24	a tusk
10	an **elephant**	25	a **trunk**
11	a leopard	26	a mane
12	a zebra	27	a paw
13	a cheetah	28	**fur**
14	an ostrich	29	a **tail**
15	a gazelle		

Word Partnerships

a herd of	antelope
	buffalo
	elephants
lions	roar
bees	buzz
hyenas	laugh

Words in Action

1. Which animals on the list have fur? Which have a tail? Which have paws? Make lists with a partner.

2. Describe an animal to a partner. Your partner says the name and points to the correct picture.
   - Student A: *It's big and it has two horns on its head.*
   - Student B: (pointing to the rhinoceros) *It's a rhinoceros.*

Polar Lands

1

2

3

6

7

8

9

11

10

Word Partnerships

a humpback a blue	whale
a Canada a wild	goose
a pack of	wolves
a flock of	birds

186

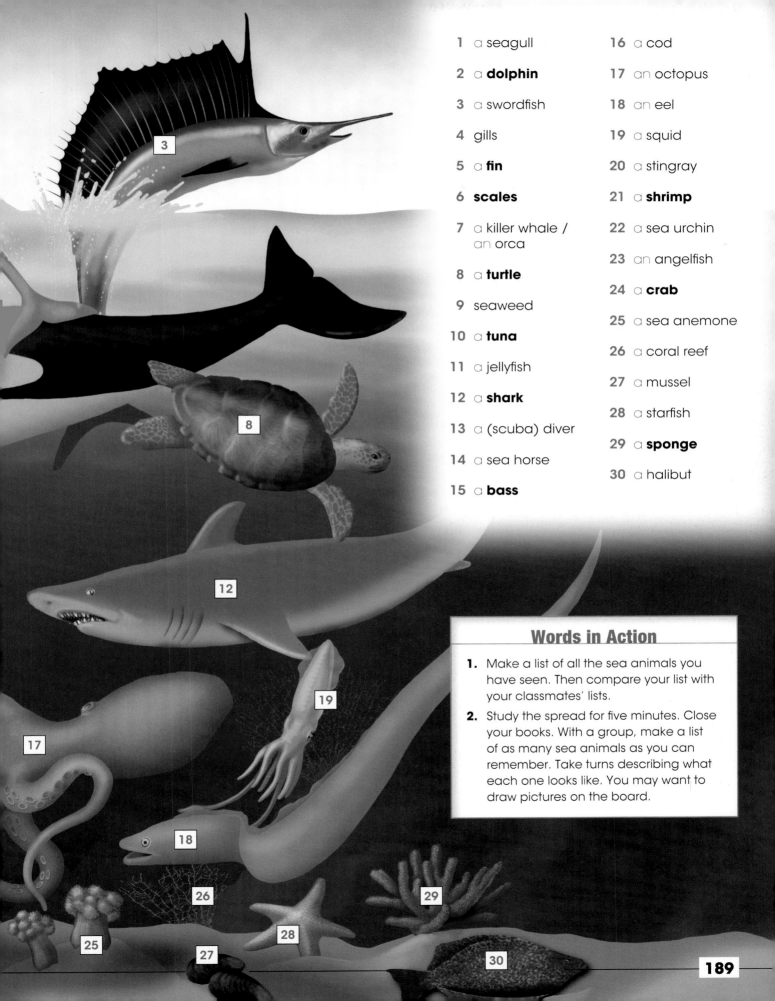

1 a seagull
2 a **dolphin**
3 a swordfish
4 gills
5 a **fin**
6 **scales**
7 a killer whale / an orca
8 a **turtle**
9 seaweed
10 a **tuna**
11 a jellyfish
12 a **shark**
13 a (scuba) diver
14 a sea horse
15 a **bass**

16 a cod
17 an octopus
18 an eel
19 a squid
20 a stingray
21 a **shrimp**
22 a sea urchin
23 an angelfish
24 a **crab**
25 a sea anemone
26 a coral reef
27 a mussel
28 a starfish
29 a **sponge**
30 a halibut

Words in Action

1. Make a list of all the sea animals you have seen. Then compare your list with your classmates' lists.

2. Study the spread for five minutes. Close your books. With a group, make a list of as many sea animals as you can remember. Take turns describing what each one looks like. You may want to draw pictures on the board.

Woodlands

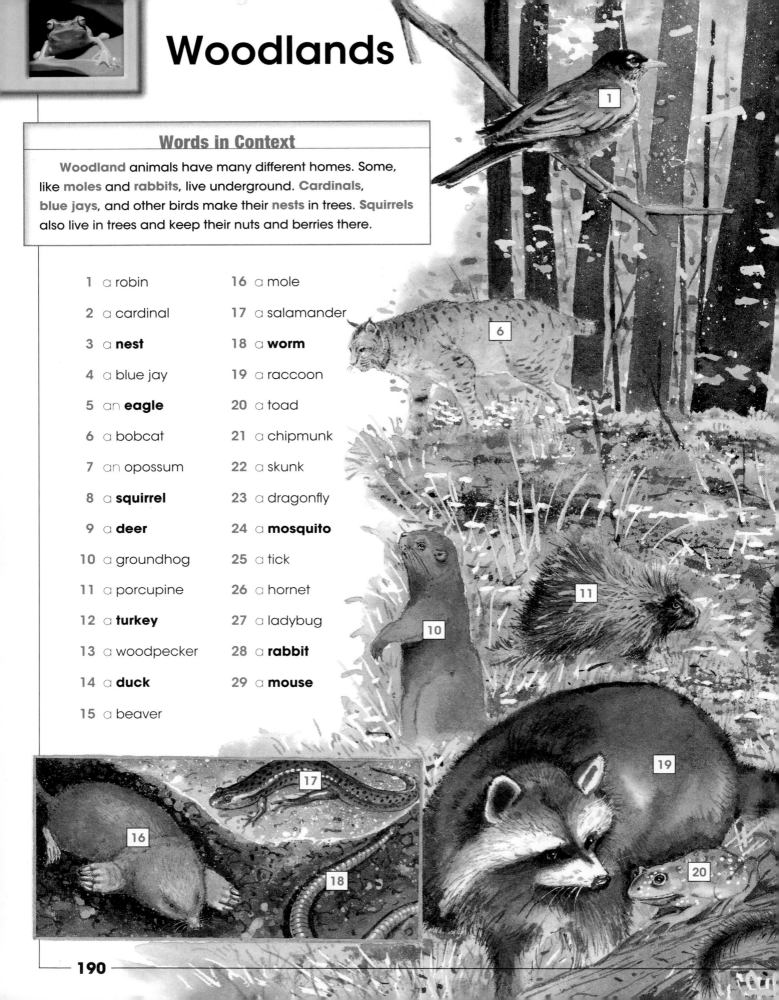

Words in Context

Woodland animals have many different homes. Some, like moles and rabbits, live underground. Cardinals, blue jays, and other birds make their nests in trees. Squirrels also live in trees and keep their nuts and berries there.

1 a robin
2 a cardinal
3 a **nest**
4 a blue jay
5 an **eagle**
6 a bobcat
7 an opossum
8 a **squirrel**
9 a **deer**
10 a groundhog
11 a porcupine
12 a **turkey**
13 a woodpecker
14 a **duck**
15 a beaver

16 a mole
17 a salamander
18 a **worm**
19 a raccoon
20 a toad
21 a chipmunk
22 a skunk
23 a dragonfly
24 a **mosquito**
25 a tick
26 a hornet
27 a ladybug
28 a **rabbit**
29 a **mouse**

Word Partnerships

as quiet as a mouse

as busy as a beaver

as prickly as a porcupine

as scared as a rabbit

Words in Action

1. What animals live on or near water? What animals live on land? Make lists with a partner.

2. Choose three animals on the list. Write a list of at least three things you know about each of the animals.
   Ducks
   1. They have wings.
   2. They live on water.
   3. Baby ducks follow their mother.

Math

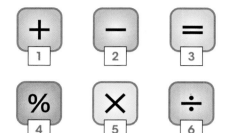

+ 1
− 2
= 3
% 4
× 5
÷ 6

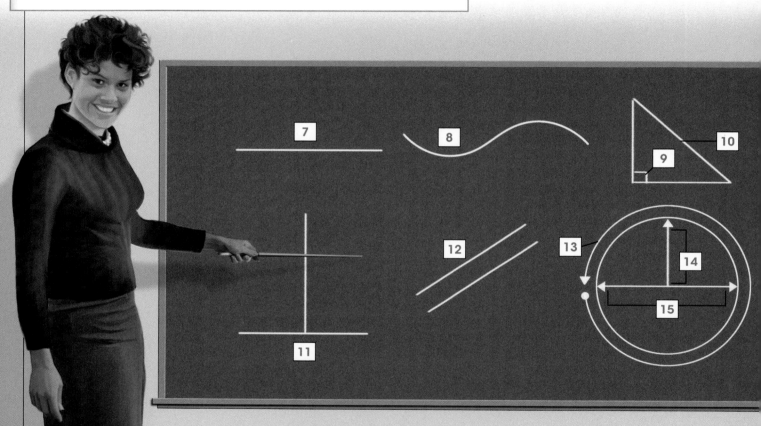

7
8
10
9
12
13
14
15
11

26	$6 + 3 = 9$
27	$6 - 3 = 3$
28	$6 \times 3 = 18$
29	$3 \div 6 = \frac{1}{2}$
30	

Word Families

Noun	Verb
addition	add
subtraction	subtract
multiplication	multiply
division	divide

1 **plus**	9 an **angle**	17 an oval	25 a cylinder
2 minus	10 a **side**	18 a rectangle	26 **addition**
3 equals	11 perpendicular lines	19 a triangle	27 subtraction
4 **percent**	12 parallel lines	20 a **square**	28 multiplication
5 multiplied by / times	13 the circumference	21 a pyramid	29 **division**
6 divided by	14 the radius	22 a cube	30 a **fraction**
7 a straight line	15 the diameter	23 a **sphere**	31 geometry
8 a curved line	16 a **circle**	24 a cone	32 algebra

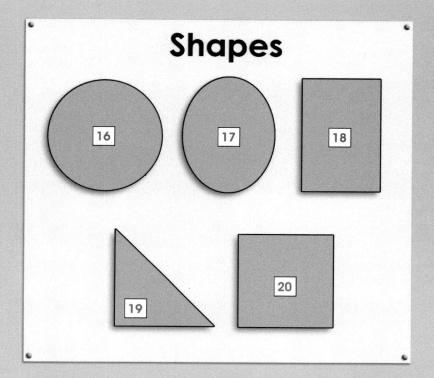

Shapes

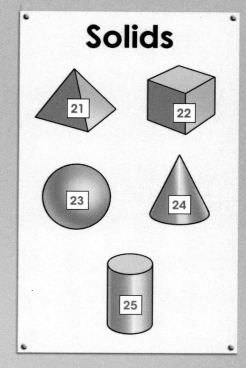

Solids

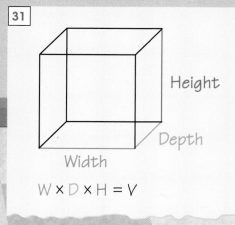

31

Height

Depth

Width

$W \times D \times H = V$

32

$ax^2 + bx + c = 0$

Words in Action

1. Look around your classroom. Find an example of each of the shapes on the list. Share your ideas with the class.
   - *My desk is a rectangle and the clock is a circle.*

2. Work with a partner. One student writes down a math problem. The other student figures out the answer, then reads the problem and the answer out loud.
   - Student A: (writes: *3 + 3*)
   - Student B: *Three plus three equals six.*

Science

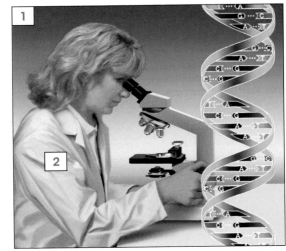

Words in Context

The famous **physicist** Albert Einstein won the Nobel Prize in **Physics** for his ideas about space and time. He is also famous for his **formula** $E = mc^2$. There is even an **element** in the **periodic table** named after Einstein. It's called *einsteinium*.

1 **biology**

2 a biologist

3 **chemistry**

4 a chemist

5 **physics**

6 a physicist

7 a prism

8 forceps

9 a balance

10 a **solid**

11 a **liquid**

12 a **gas**

13 a test tube

14 a Bunsen burner

15 the periodic table

16 an **element**

17 an **atom**

18 a **molecule**

19 a **formula**

20 a graduated cylinder

21 a dropper

22 a stopper

23 a beaker

24 a flask

25 a microscope

26 a magnifying glass

27 a funnel

28 a slide

29 a petri dish

30 a magnet

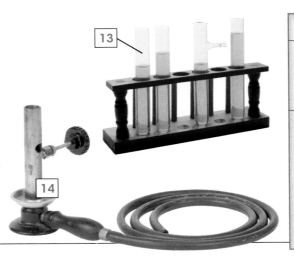

Word Partnerships

| a biology | class |
| a chemistry | lab / laboratory |

Word Families

Noun	Adjective
atom	atomic
magnet	magnetic
microscope	microscopic
liquid	liquid
solid	solid

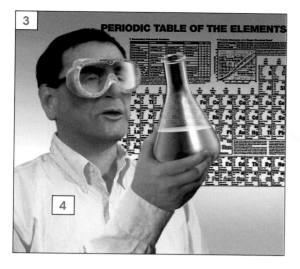

PERIODIC TABLE OF THE ELEMENTS

3

4

5

6

$E=mc^2$

17

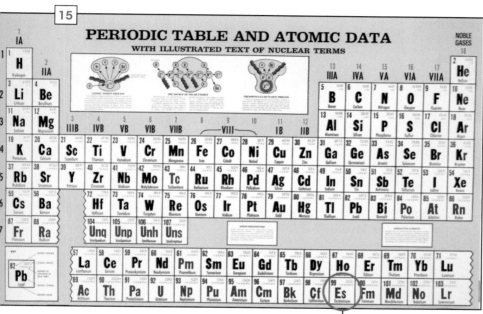

15

PERIODIC TABLE AND ATOMIC DATA
WITH ILLUSTRATED TEXT OF NUCLEAR TERMS

16

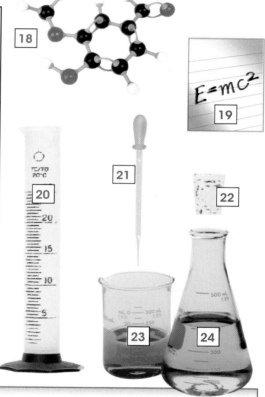

18

19

$E=mc^2$

20

21

22

23

24

26

27

25

28

29

30

Writing

Words in Context

Writing an **essay** is a process. First you **brainstorm** ideas. Next you **write** an outline, and then you write a draft. Before you **edit**, you **get** feedback. Are you ready to write the final draft? Before you do, make sure the **punctuation** is correct. Have you used **capital letters** for the first letter of each **word** in the **title**? Have you indented each **paragraph**? If so, now you are ready to write the final draft.

1 a **letter**

2 a **word**

3 a **sentence**

4 a **paragraph**

5 a **paper** / an **essay**

6 an indentation

7 a **margin**

8 a **title**

9 punctuation

10 a **period**

11 a **comma**

12 a question mark

13 an exclamation point / an exclamation mark

14 an apostrophe

15 parentheses

16 quotation marks

17 a colon

18 a semicolon

19 a hyphen

Verbs

20 brainstorm ideas

21 write an outline

22 write a draft

23 get feedback

24 edit your essay

25 type your final draft

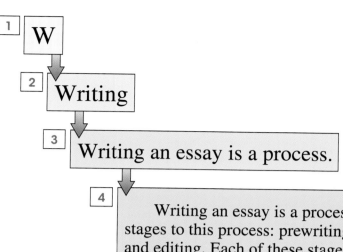

1	W
2	Writing
3	Writing an essay is a process.

4 Writing an essay is a process. There are four stages to this process: prewriting, drafting, revising, and editing. Each of these stages is an important part in the process that leads a writer to create a well thought out and well organized paper.

5

Megan Purdum
English 1A

8 The Writing Process

6

Writing an essay is a process. There are four stages to this process: prewriting, drafting, revising, and editing. Each of these stages is an important part in the process that leads a writer to create a well thought out and well organized paper.

7

Prewriting consists of things the writer does before writing a draft of a paper. This is the stage in which the writer gathers and organizes ideas for the paper. This stage can include thinking, talking to others, gathering information, brainstorming, and making an outline of the paper.

In the next stage, the writer writes a draft. While writing a draft, the writer puts ideas into sentences and paragraphs. Each paragraph must have a topic sentence. The topic sentence is what that paragraph is about. The rest of the paragraph should explain and support the topic sentence. It is not important to focus on things like grammar and spelling at this stage.

9

10 •

11 ,

12 ?

13 !

14 '

15 ( )

16 " "

17 :

18 ;

19 −

Words in Action

1. Look at a magazine or newspaper article. Find and circle the following:
   - a comma
   - an apostrophe
   - a sentence
   - a paragraph
2. What are the steps in writing a paper? Discuss with a partner.

Explore, Rule, Invent

Words in Context

Humans have achieved amazing things. We have **composed** operas and poetry. We have **discovered** cures for diseases. We have **sailed** the world's oceans and **explored** the continents. We have **launched** rockets into space and **reached** the moon.

1 Humans **migrate** from Asia to the Americas.

2 Mesopotamians **produce** the first wheel.

3 The Egyptians **build / construct** pyramids.

4 The Vikings **sail** to present-day Canada.

5 The Chinese **grow** tea.

6 Joan of Arc **defends** France.

7 Montezuma I **rules** the Aztecs.

8 Amerigo Vespucci **explores** the Amazon.

9 Sir Isaac Newton **discovers** gravity.

10 Ludwig van Beethoven **composes** his first symphony.

11 The Suez Canal **opens**.

12 Thomas Edison **invents** the lightbulb.

13 The Wright brothers **fly** the first plane.

14 World War II **ends**.

15 The Soviet Union **launches** the first satellite.

16 Martin Luther King Jr. **wins** the Nobel Peace Prize.

17 Japan **introduces** the high-speed "bullet" train.

18 Apollo 11 astronauts **reach** the moon.

19 The Berlin Wall **falls**.

20 The United States **elects** Barack Obama president.

21 Deepsea Challenger **dives** to the bottom of the ocean.

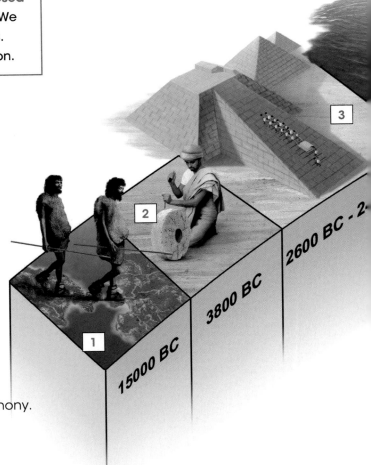

Word Partnerships

win	a war
	a contest
compose	a song
	a letter
elect	a prime minister
	a president
	a mayor
build	a road
	a bridge

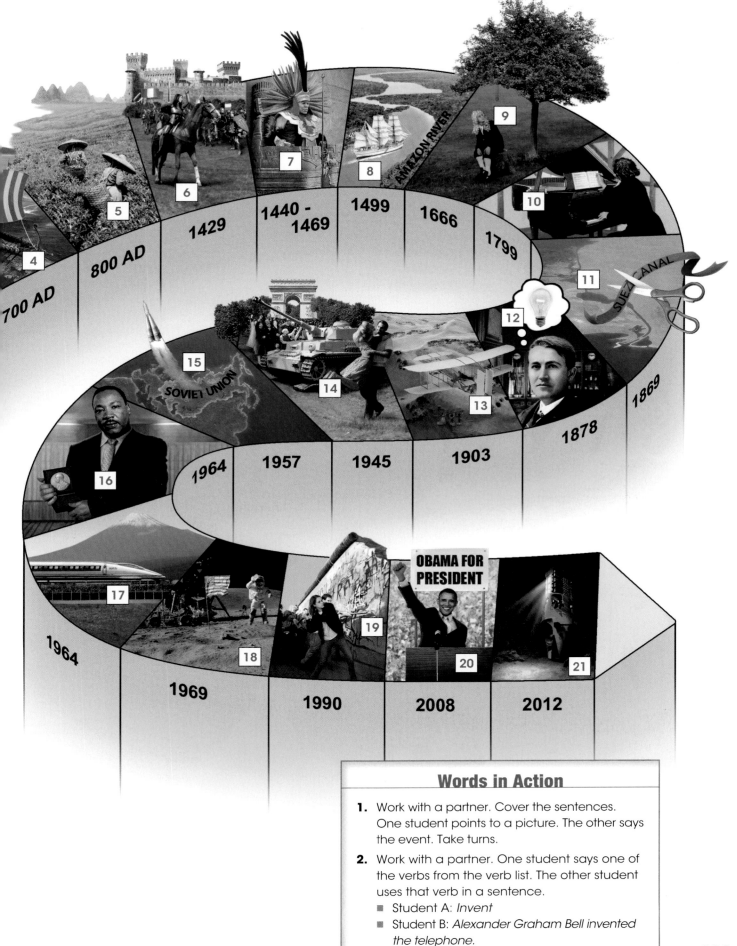

700 AD

800 AD

1429

1440 – 1469

1499

AMAZON RIVER

1666

1799

SUEZ CANAL

1869

1878

1903

1945

1957

SOVIET UNION

1964

1964

1969

1990

2008

2012

OBAMA FOR PRESIDENT

Words in Action

1. Work with a partner. Cover the sentences. One student points to a picture. The other says the event. Take turns.

2. Work with a partner. One student says one of the verbs from the verb list. The other student uses that verb in a sentence.
   - Student A: *Invent*
   - Student B: *Alexander Graham Bell invented the telephone.*

U.S. Government and Citizenship

Words in Context

The U.S. **government** has three parts. These parts are called *branches.* The executive branch includes the **president** and the **vice president**. The legislative branch includes the **House of Representatives** and the **Senate**. There are 100 **senators** in the Senate and 435 **congressmen** and **congresswomen** in the House of Representatives. The judicial branch includes nine **Supreme Court justices**.

1 a (political) candidate

2 a **ballot**

3 a voting booth

4 a **citizen**

5 the U.S. Constitution

6 the Capitol (Building)

7 the **White House**

8 the **Supreme Court**

9 a **congresswoman** / a **congressman**

10 a **senator**

11 the **president**

12 the **vice president**

13 the **justices**

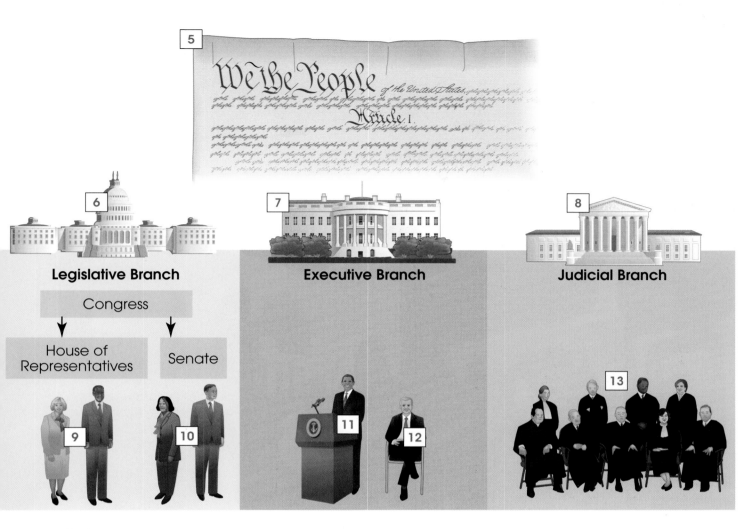

5 We the People

6 Legislative Branch

Congress

House of Representatives

Senate

9 **10**

7 Executive Branch

11 **12**

8 Judicial Branch

13

Verbs

14 vote

15 obey the law

16 pay taxes

17 serve on a jury

18 protest / demonstrate

19 serve in the military

Words in Action

1. Compare the U.S. government with the government of another country. How are they similar? How are they different?

2. Discuss which branch of the U.S. government you think is most important. Explain your reasons.

Fine Arts

Words in Context

Pablo Picasso is probably the most famous artist of the last 100 years. His **portraits** and **still lifes** hang in the world's great museums. Picasso worked as a **painter**, **sculptor**, and **potter**. He **painted** with oils and watercolors, and he sculpted in **clay**.

1 a **frame**

2 a still life

3 a **portrait**

4 a **landscape**

5 a **model**

6 a palette

7 a **painting**

8 a paintbrush

9 a painter

10 **paint**

11 an easel

12 a canvas

13 a sketchpad

14 a sketch

15 a **mural**

16 a sculpture

17 a sculptor

18 pottery

19 a potter

20 a potter's wheel

21 clay

22 a **photograph**

23 a photographer

Verbs

24 **draw**

25 **paint**

26 photograph /
take a photograph

Word Partnerships

modern	art
a work of	
oil	paint
acrylic	
watercolor	
a watercolor	painting
an oil	

Words in Action

1. Work with a group. Make a list of famous artists. Answer the following questions about each:
   - What kind of artist is he/she?
   - What materials did/does this artist use?
   - Do you know the names of any of the artist's works?

2. What is your favorite kind of art? Why? Discuss with a partner.

Performing Arts

Words in Context

Different **performing arts** began in different countries around the world. For example, theater began in ancient Greece. The **actors** wore **masks** and performed **plays** in large outdoor theaters. **Opera** began in Italy at the end of the 16th century, and soon became popular in France and Germany. **Ballet** also began in Italy at the end of the 16th century, and it became very popular in France while Louis XIV was king.

1 a ballet
2 a balcony
3 a dancer
4 **a mask**
5 a costume

6 **a stage**
7 a conductor
8 an orchestra
9 an **audience**

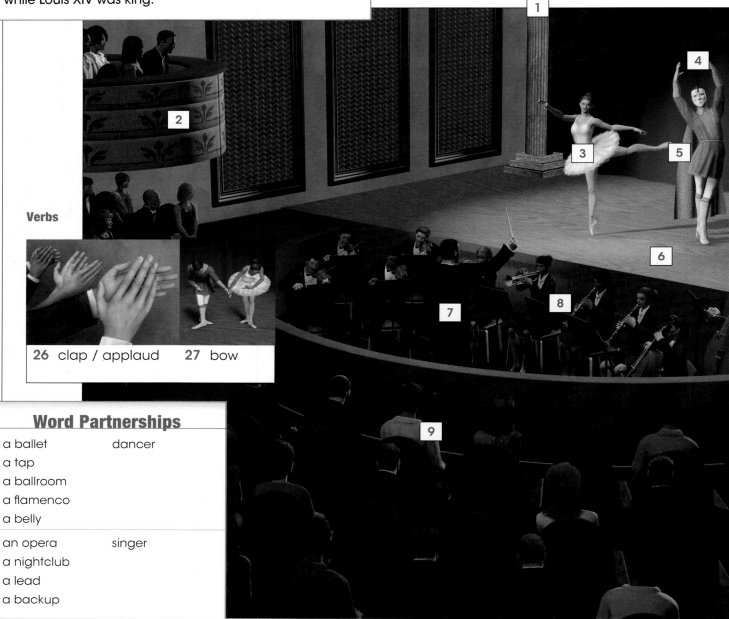

Verbs

26 clap / applaud   27 bow

Word Partnerships

a ballet	dancer
a tap	
a ballroom	
a flamenco	
a belly	
an opera	singer
a nightclub	
a lead	
a backup	

10 a (rock) concert

11 a spotlight

12 a drummer

13 a microphone

14 **a singer**

15 a guitarist

16 backup singers

17 **a play**

18 an **actor**

19 a set

20 a **seat**

21 an usher

22 a **ticket**

23 a **program**

24 a box office

25 an **opera**

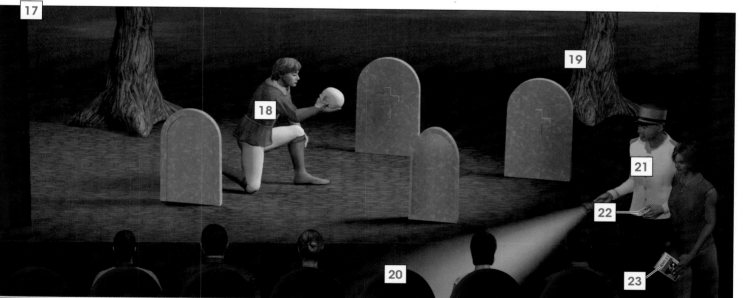

Words in Action

1. Have you ever seen a ballet? An opera? A play? Choose your favorite and tell a partner about it.

2. Imagine you are the directors of a new arts center. What kinds of concerts, plays, and other performances will you present this year? Discuss with your group.

Instruments

Words in Context

Percussion instruments are thousands of years old. **Drums** are one of the oldest percussion instruments. They were part of African culture as early as **6000** B.C. The **tambourine** is also thousands of years old. Many countries, from Japan to Morocco to England, use tambourines in their music. Other percussion instruments include **maracas**, from Latin America, and **cymbals**, from China.

Word Partnerships

play tune	an instrument
practice	the piano the violin the cello
an acoustic an electric a bass	guitar

206

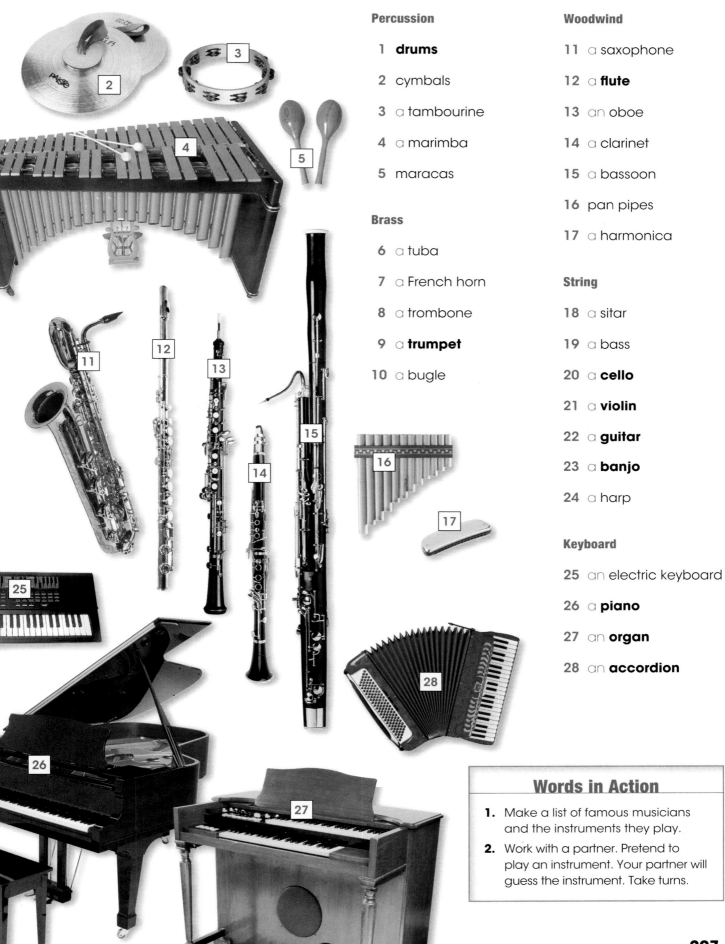

Percussion

1 **drums**

2 cymbals

3 a tambourine

4 a marimba

5 maracas

Brass

6 a tuba

7 a French horn

8 a trombone

9 a **trumpet**

10 a bugle

Woodwind

11 a saxophone

12 a **flute**

13 an oboe

14 a clarinet

15 a bassoon

16 pan pipes

17 a harmonica

String

18 a sitar

19 a bass

20 a **cello**

21 a **violin**

22 a **guitar**

23 a **banjo**

24 a harp

Keyboard

25 an electric keyboard

26 a **piano**

27 an **organ**

28 an **accordion**

Words in Action

1. Make a list of famous musicians and the instruments they play.

2. Work with a partner. Pretend to play an instrument. Your partner will guess the instrument. Take turns.

207

Film, TV, and Music

Words in Context

My husband and I never agree on **films**. For example, my husband always wants to see **action** films or **horror movies**. I usually prefer **dramas** or **comedies**. But we have children, so we usually end up at **animated** films!

1

OFFICER BABY

2

THE RAMIREZ FILES

4

A CLUE

3

Love in Paris

5

STARDATE 2075

6

AGENT 009

COWBOY

7

Dragon Story

8

MIDNIGHT

9

A FISH Story

11

HISTORY OF THE PYRAMIDS

10

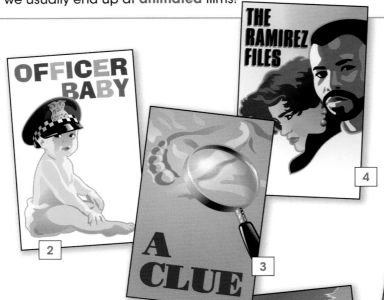

Films / Movies

1 action / adventure

2 **comedy**

3 **mystery** / suspense

4 **drama**

5 romance

6 science fiction

7 **western**

8 **fantasy**

9 **horror**

10 **documentary**

11 animated

Word Partnerships

an independent a foreign	film
a funny a scary	movie
satellite cable	TV
a TV	station commercial
loud soft	music

TV programs

12 **news**

13 sitcom

14 cartoon

15 game show

16 soap opera

17 talk show

18 nature program

19 children's program

20 **sports**

21 reality show

Music

22 pop

23 **jazz**

24 rock

25 blues

26 R&B / soul

27 hip hop

28 classical

29 country and western

Words in Action

1. With your class, make a list of:
   - action films
   - comedy films
   - sitcoms
   - game shows

2. What is your favorite kind of music? Why? Tell your partner.

Beach

Verbs

30 surf

31 dive

32 swim

33 float

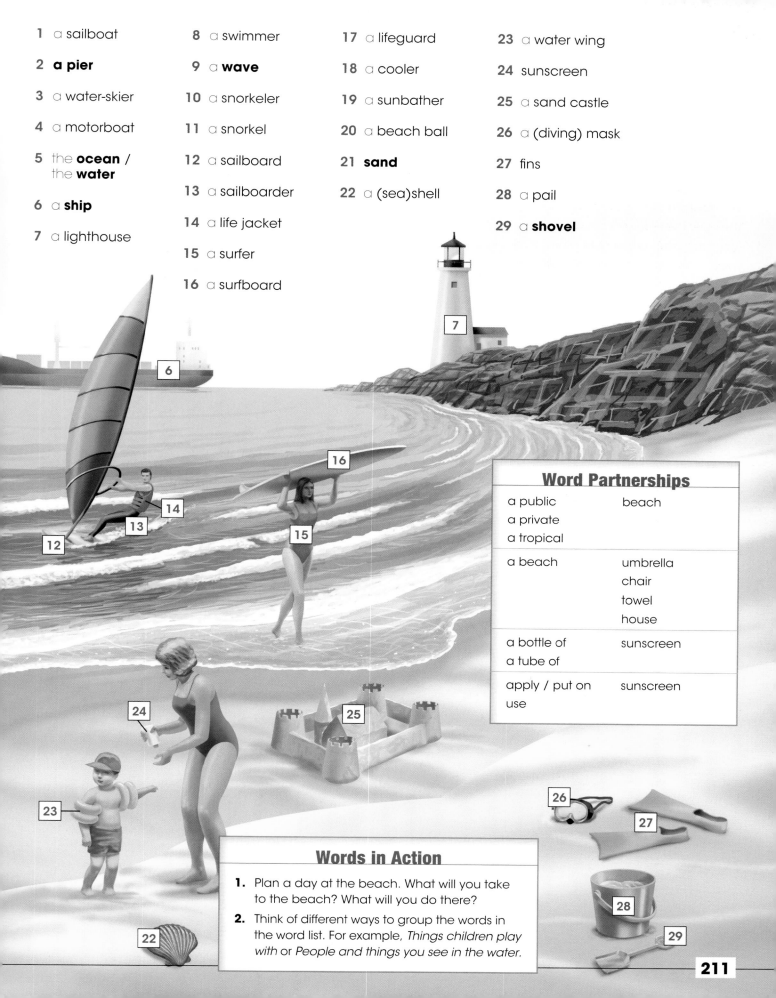

1 a sailboat
2 **a pier**
3 a water-skier
4 a motorboat
5 the **ocean** / the **water**
6 **a ship**
7 a lighthouse

8 a swimmer
9 **a wave**
10 a snorkeler
11 a snorkel
12 a sailboard
13 a sailboarder
14 a life jacket
15 a surfer
16 a surfboard

17 a lifeguard
18 a cooler
19 a sunbather
20 a beach ball
21 **sand**
22 a (sea)shell

23 a water wing
24 sunscreen
25 a sand castle
26 a (diving) mask
27 fins
28 a pail
29 **a shovel**

Word Partnerships

a public a private a tropical	beach
a beach	umbrella chair towel house
a bottle of a tube of	sunscreen
apply / put on use	sunscreen

Words in Action

1. Plan a day at the beach. What will you take to the beach? What will you do there?

2. Think of different ways to group the words in the word list. For example, *Things children play with* or *People and things you see in the water.*

211

Camping

Words in Context

The Appalachian Trail is a 2,174-mile* **trail** in the U.S. It starts in Maine and goes all the way to Georgia. Some people **hike** a small part of the trail for a day. Others hike longer portions of the trail. These **hikers** usually bring a **backpack**, a **tent**, and a **sleeping bag**, along with other camping equipment like a **trail map**, a **compass**, a **water bottle**, and a **pocket knife**. Hiking the whole trail takes an entire season!

*3,478.4 kilometers

Word Partnerships

a camping	trip
	site
a fishing	boat
a ski	
a street	map
a city	
a road	

212

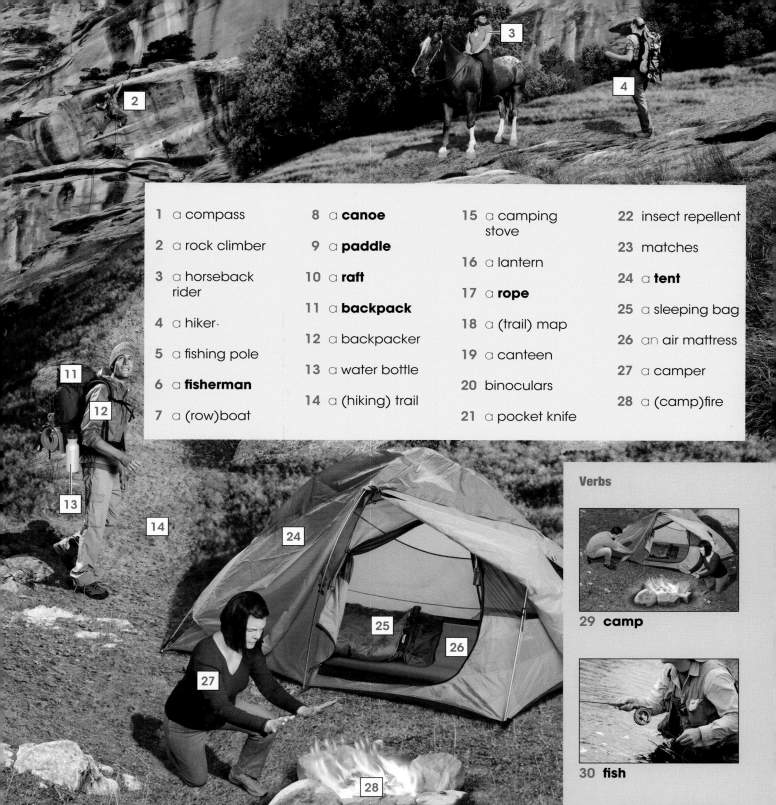

1 a compass
2 a rock climber
3 a horseback rider
4 a hiker
5 a fishing pole
6 a **fisherman**
7 a (row)boat
8 a **canoe**
9 a **paddle**
10 a **raft**
11 a **backpack**
12 a backpacker
13 a water bottle
14 a (hiking) trail
15 a camping stove
16 a lantern
17 a **rope**
18 a (trail) map
19 a canteen
20 binoculars
21 a pocket knife
22 insect repellent
23 matches
24 a **tent**
25 a sleeping bag
26 an air mattress
27 a camper
28 a (camp)fire

Verbs

29 **camp**

30 **fish**

31 **hike**

Words in Action

1. Imagine you are going on a camping trip. What will you do? What will you take?

2. You are lost on a hiking trail. You can only bring five of the items on the list. Which items will you bring? Explain why you need each one.

City Park

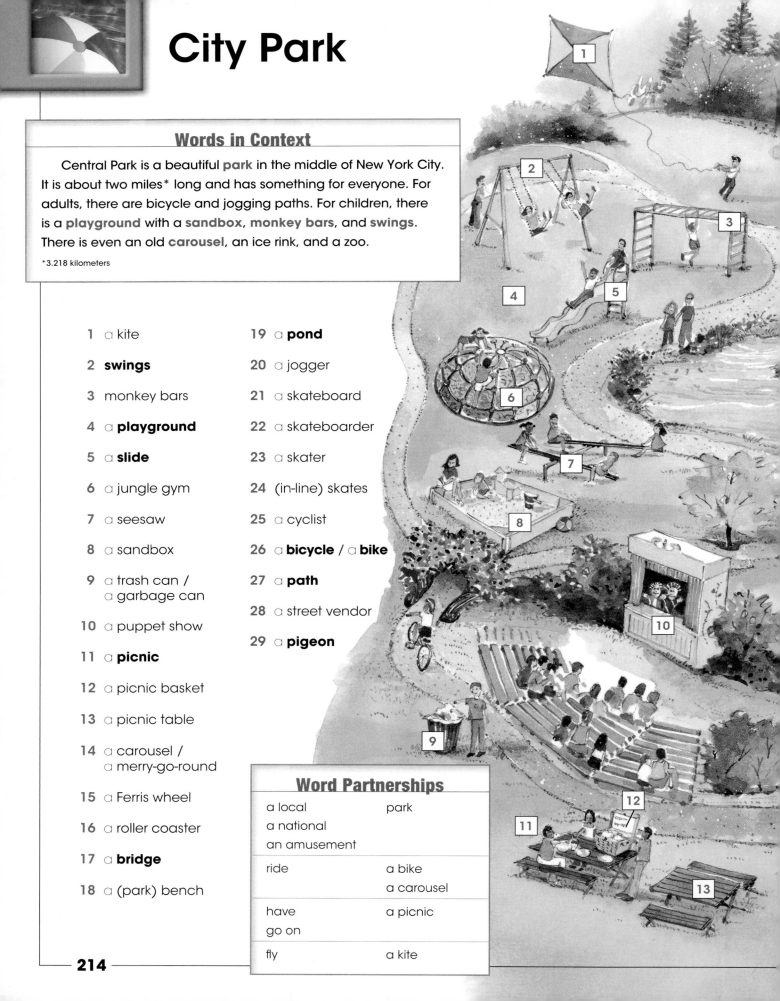

Words in Context

Central Park is a beautiful **park** in the middle of New York City. It is about two miles* long and has something for everyone. For adults, there are bicycle and jogging paths. For children, there is a **playground** with a **sandbox**, **monkey bars**, and **swings**. There is even an old **carousel**, an ice rink, and a zoo.

*3.218 kilometers

1 a kite

2 **swings**

3 monkey bars

4 a **playground**

5 a **slide**

6 a jungle gym

7 a seesaw

8 a sandbox

9 a trash can / a garbage can

10 a puppet show

11 a **picnic**

12 a picnic basket

13 a picnic table

14 a carousel / a merry-go-round

15 a Ferris wheel

16 a roller coaster

17 a **bridge**

18 a (park) bench

19 a **pond**

20 a jogger

21 a skateboard

22 a skateboarder

23 a skater

24 (in-line) skates

25 a cyclist

26 a **bicycle** / a **bike**

27 a **path**

28 a street vendor

29 a **pigeon**

Word Partnerships

a local a national an amusement	park
ride	a bike a carousel
have go on	a picnic
fly	a kite

Words in Action

1. Work with your class. Discuss your dream park. Draw a picture of the park on the board. Each student adds an item to the park and labels this item.

2. When did you last go to a park? What did you do? What did you see? Tell a partner.

Places to Visit

Words in Context

Try a new activity this weekend. Do you like shopping? You could go to a flea market or a **garage sale**. Do you enjoy nature? You could walk on a **hiking trail** or ride your bicycle on a **bicycle path**. Do you like animals? You could go to a **zoo** or an **aquarium**.

1 a **café**

2 a **zoo**

3 a planetarium

4 a **nursery**

5 a bowling alley

6 a sporting event

7 a pool hall

8 an **aquarium**

9 a garage sale

10 an amusement park

11 a (hiking) trail

12 a **lecture**

13 a botanical garden

14 a **gym**

15 a **circus**

16 miniature golf

17 a bicycle path

18 a **carnival**

19 a **museum**

20 a water park

21 a **movie theater**

22 a rodeo

216

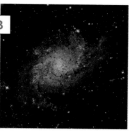

Word Partnerships	
a petting	zoo
a traveling a three-ring	circus
an outdoor a sidewalk an internet	café

Words in Action

1. What are your five favorite places to visit from this list? Compare your favorite places with your classmates'. Can you find another student with the same favorite places?

2. Work with a group. Make a list of famous:
   - zoos
   - amusement parks
   - museums

Indoor Sports and Fitness

1 martial arts
2 **yoga**
3 **basketball**
4 a **referee**
5 a basketball court
6 a (basketball) player
7 a basketball
8 ping-pong
9 a ping-pong paddle
10 a ping-pong table
11 a chin-up
12 a push-up
13 a sit-up
14 a (stationary) bike
15 a treadmill
16 **boxing**
17 a **boxer**
18 a boxing glove
19 a boxing ring
20 a punching bag

21 **wrestling**
22 a wrestler
23 gymnastics
24 a gymnast
25 weightlifting
26 a weightlifter
27 a **bench**
28 a barbell
29 a dartboard
30 darts
31 a fitness class
32 a diving board
33 a **diver**
34 a **(swimming) pool**
35 a **locker room**

Word Partnerships

sports	club
	team
	equipment
	injury
a yoga	instructor
a fitness	class
a martial arts	

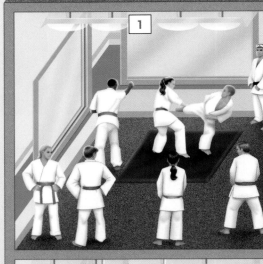

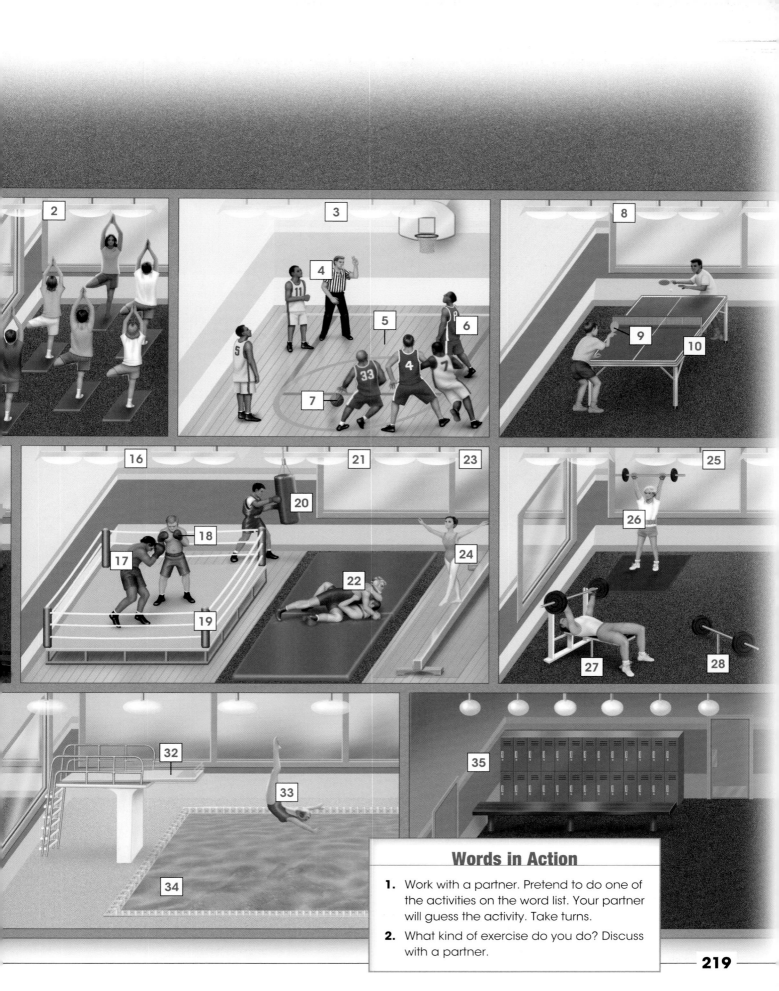

Words in Action

1. Work with a partner. Pretend to do one of the activities on the word list. Your partner will guess the activity. Take turns.

2. What kind of exercise do you do? Discuss with a partner.

Outdoor Sports and Fitness

Words in Context

Tennis is one of the most popular sports in the world. The rules are simple. A player uses a racket to hit a tennis ball over the net. The other player tries to hit the ball back. The first player to win four points wins the game.

1 **tennis**

2 a (tennis) racket

3 a (tennis) ball

4 **baseball**

5 a **baseball**

6 a batter

7 a bat

8 a catcher

9 volleyball

10 a volleyball

11 a (volleyball) net

12 **golf**

13 a (golf) club

14 a golfer

15 a golf course

16 track

17 a runner

18 a **track**

19 **soccer**

20 a **fan**

21 a soccer field

22 a **uniform**

23 **football**

24 a goalpost

25 a (football) helmet

26 a cheerleader

27 a **football**

Words in Action

1. Which of these sports do you like to play? Which do you like to watch? Discuss with a partner.

2. Work with a partner. One person pretends to play one of these sports. The other guesses the sport. Take turns.

Winter Sports

Word Partnerships

a hockey	team
	game
	arena
	rink
a skiing	injury
	lesson

Words in Context

Skiing began in Norway in the 1700s. Early **skiers** used long wooden cross-country **skis** and wooden **ski poles**. Today there is a new kind of **winter sport** called **snowboarding**. **Snowboarders** don't use ski poles. They slide down the slopes with both feet on a **snowboard**.

1 a **snowmobile**	6 ski poles	11 (cross-country) skiing
2 snowshoes	7 a toboggan	12 (downhill) skiing
3 a **sled**	8 a chairlift	13 a **skier**
4 **skis**	9 ice skating	14 snowboarding
5 ski boots	10 an ice skater	15 a snowboarder

16 a snowboard

17 (ice) hockey

18 a **scoreboard**

19 a **score**

20 an ice (skating) rink

21 a **goal**

22 a **(hockey) player**

23 a hockey stick

24 a **(hockey) puck**

25 **(ice) skates**

Words in Action

1. Which winter sports are the most fun? Which are the most dangerous? Discuss with your class.

2. One student names a winter sport. The other students take turns naming clothing and equipment for that sport.
   - Student A: *Hockey.*
   - Student B: *Ice skates.*
   - Student C: *A hockey stick.*

Games, Toys, and Hobbies

Words in Context

Playing **cards** are popular in countries around the world. The French style deck is the most common. This deck has 52 cards and four suits—**spades**, **hearts**, **diamonds**, and **clubs**. There are 13 cards in each suit: **ace**, **king**, **queen**, **jack**, and numbers 2 through 10. People use these cards to play different **games** around the world, like *bridge* and *gin rummy* in the U.S., *king* in Brazil, and *dai hin min* in Japan.

1

7 8 9 10

3 4 5 6
2

1 **cards**

2 an **ace**

3 a **king**

4 a **queen**

5 a **jack**

6 a joker

7 a spade

8 a diamond

9 a club

10 a heart

11 backgammon

12 chess

13 mah-jongg

14 dominoes

15 checkers

16 a **puzzle**

17 **dice**

18 crayons

19 a **doll**

20 knitting needles

21 yarn

22 a crochet hook

23 (embroidery) thread

24 a **needle**

Verbs

25 knit

26 crochet

27 embroider

28 **build** a model

20 21 22

Word Partnerships

a board	game
a card	
a chess	board
a checker	piece
a deck of	cards
a hand of	
play	cards
	a game
king of	hearts
nine of	spades

Words in Action

1. Make a list of your three favorite games from the list. Put the list in order, with the game you like best at the top. Share your list with a partner.

2. Take a poll to find out the favorite games of the students in your class.
   - Which is the most popular game?
   - Which is the least popular game?

Camera, Stereo, and DVD

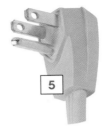

1 a **camera**

2 a zoom lens

3 a camcorder

4 a tripod

5 a **plug**

6 an adapter (plug)

7 an **MP3 player**

8 a dock

9 **headphones**

10 a **CD player**

11 a **CD** / a compact disc

12 a **speaker**

13 a stereo (system)

14 a boom box

15 a satellite dish

16 a **television / TV**

17 a (video) game system

18 a (video game) controller

19 a remote control

20 a **DVD player**

21 a **DVD**

Word Partnerships

a digital a disposable	camera
play	a DVD a CD
turn up turn down	the TV the stereo

227

Words in Action

1. Which three items on the list would you most like to get as gifts? Why? Discuss with a partner.

2. Which items on the list could help you learn English? How? Discuss with your class.

Holidays and Celebrations

Words in Context

People celebrate the **New Year** in different ways around the world. In Brazil, many people have **parties**. They often go to the beach after midnight and watch **fireworks**. It is also traditional to throw **flowers** into the sea. The Chinese New Year happens between January 17 and February 19. Chinese people all over the world celebrate with **parades** and **firecrackers**.

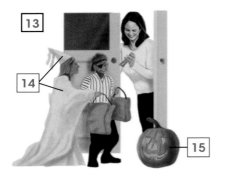

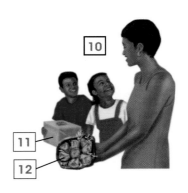

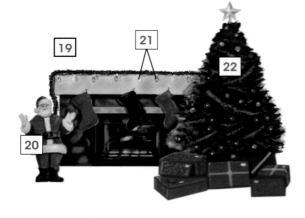

1 New Year	8 fireworks
2 a firecracker	9 a barbeque
3 a parade	10 Mother's Day
4 Valentine's Day	11 a **gift** / a **present**
5 chocolates	12 flowers
6 a **card**	13 Halloween
7 Independence Day	14 a costume

Verbs

29 wrap
a present

30 light
candles

31 blow out
candles

32 open
a present

3

23

24

25

26

27

28

Word Partnerships

a birthday	party
a retirement	
a New Year's Eve	
a birthday	gift
a wedding	cake
a birthday	card
a Valentine's Day	
a Mother's Day	

15 a jack-o-lantern

16 Thanksgiving

17 **a turkey**

18 a pumpkin pie

19 **Christmas**

20 Santa Claus

21 **lights**

22 a (Christmas) tree

23 a **birthday**

24 a balloon

25 a cake

26 an **anniversary**

27 a **baby shower**

28 a **retirement**

Words in Action

1. Work with a group. Choose a holiday on the list. What are the different ways the people in your group celebrate this holiday? Discuss with your group.

2. Plan a birthday party for a friend.
   - What will you eat?
   - How will you decorate?
   - What gift will you give?

Index

Index Guide

All entries in the index are followed by a phonetic listing. Following the phonetic listing, most entries have two numbers. The first number, in bold type, is the page number on which the entry item is found. The second number corresponds to the item's number in the word list. See the example below.

Some entries have two numbers in bold type. In this case, the entry is a topic covered in a two-page lesson, and the numbers indicate the page numbers of this lesson.

If the entry is in capital letters, it is a unit title, and the two numbers in bold type indicate the pages on which this unit begins and ends.

If an entry is followed by only a single number in bold type, then the entry appears on this page number as a subhead in the word list, or it appears somewhere else on the page.

Verb and verb phrase entries appear in bold type in the index. Some entries appear twice in the index—once in bold and once in regular type. In these cases, the bold type entry is a verb, and the regular type entry is a noun.

Guide to Pronunciation Symbols

Vowels

Symbol	Key Word	Pronunciation
/ɑ/	hot	/hɑt/
	far	/fɑr/
/æ/	cat	/kæt/
/aɪ/	fine	/faɪn/
/aʊ/	house	/haʊs/
/ɛ/	bed	/bɛd/
/eɪ/	name	/neɪm/
/i/	need	/nid/
/ɪ/	sit	/sɪt/
/oʊ/	go	/goʊ/
/ʊ/	book	/bʊk/
/u/	boot	/but/
/ɔ/	dog	/dɔg/
	four	/fɔr/
/ɔɪ/	toy	/tɔɪ/
/ʌ/	cup	/kʌp/
/ɛr/	bird	/bɛrd/
/ə/	about	/əˈbaʊt/
	after	/ˈæftər/

Consonants

Symbol	Key Word	Pronunciation
/b/	boy	/bɔɪ/
/d/	day	/deɪ/
/ʤ/	just	/ʤʌst/
/f/	face	/feɪs/
/g/	get	/gɛt/
/h/	hat	/hæt/
/k/	car	/kɑr/
/l/	light	/laɪt/
/m/	my	/maɪ/
/n/	nine	/naɪn/
/ŋ/	sing	/sɪŋ/
/p/	pen	/pɛn/
/r/	right	/raɪt/
/s/	see	/si/
/t/	tea	/ti/
/ʧ/	cheap	/ʧip/
/v/	vote	/voʊt/
/w/	west	/wɛst/
/y/	yes	/yɛs/
/z/	zoo	/zu/
/ð/	they	/ðeɪ/
/θ/	think	/θɪŋk/
/ʃ/	shoe	/ʃu/
/ʒ/	vision	/ˈvɪʒən/

Stress

/ˈ/	city	/ˈsɪti/	used before a syllable to show primary (main) stress
/ˌ/	dictionary	/ˈdɪkʃəˌnɛri/	used before a syllable to show secondary stress

aardvark /ˈɑrdˌvɑrk/ **182**–14
above /əˈbʌv/ **13**–10
absence note /ˈæbsəns noʊt/ **23**–27
accelerator /ɪkˈsɛləˌreɪtər/ **121**–27
accessories /ɪkˈsɛsəriz/ **108–109**
accident /ˈæksədənt/
      have an... /hæv ən/ **123**–19
accordion /æˈkɔrdiən/ **207**–28
accountant /əˈkaʊntnt/ **146**–1
ace /eɪs/ **224**–2
acid rain /ˈæsɪd reɪn/ **171**–14
acne /ˈækni/ **135**–22
across /əˈkrɔs/ **130**–17
act /ækt/ **150**–10
action /ˈækʃən/ **208**–1
actor /ˈæktər/ **147**–25, **205**–18
acupuncture /ˈækyəˌpʌŋktʃər/ **141**–3
acupuncturist /ˈækyəˌpʌŋktʃərɪst/ **141**–4
adapter (plug) /əˈdæptər (plʌg)/ **226**–6
add /æd/ **92**–4
addition /əˈdɪʃən/ **193**–26
address /əˈdrɛs/ **53**–21
address /əˈdrɛs/ **42**
    mailing... /ˈmeɪlɪŋ/ **52**–6
    return... /rɪˈtɜrn/ **52**–4
adhesive bandage /ədˈhisɪv ˈbændɪdʒ/ **143**–28
adult /əˈdʌlt/ **30**
adventure /ədˈvɛntʃər/ **208**–1
afraid /əˈfreɪd/ **39**–19
Africa /ˈæfrɪkə/ **174**–12
afternoon /ˌæftərˈnun/ **5**
aftershave /ˈæftərʃeɪv/ **144**–17
agree /əˈgri/ **40**–11
air bag /ɛr bæg/ **121**–10
air conditioner /ɛr kənˈdɪʃənər/ **67**–14
air conditioning /ɛr kənˈdɪʃənɪŋ/ **121**–19
air mattress /ɛr ˈmætrɪs/ **213**–26
airplane /ˈɛrpleɪn/ **125**
air pollution /ɛr pəˈluʃən/ **171**–13
airport /ˈɛrpɔrt/ **124–125**
aisle /aɪl/ **99**–13, **125**–29
alarm clock /əˈlɑrm klɑk/ **74**–9
algebra /ˈældʒəbrə/ **193**–32
alive /əˈlaɪv/ **14**–11
allergic reaction /əˈlɜrdʒɪk riˈækʃən/
    have an... /hæv ən/ **136**–12
alligator /ˈæləˌgeɪtər/ **182**–18
almonds /ˈɑməndz/ **83**–31
along /əˈlɔŋ/ **130**–18
alphabet /ˈælfəˌbɛt/ **19**–1
ambulance /ˈæmbyələns/ **118**–27, **139**–29
American /əˈmɛrɪkən/ **44**–2
amusement park /əˈmyuzmənt pɑrk/ **216**–10
anchor /ˈæŋkər/ **163**–18
anesthesiologist /ænəsθiziˈɑlədʒɪst/ **138**–7
angelfish /ˈeɪndʒəlfɪʃ/ **189**–23
angle /ˈæŋgəl/ **193**–9
angry /ˈæŋgri/ **38**–3
animals /ˈænəməlz/ **153**
ANIMALS, PLANTS, AND HABITATS
   /ˈænəməlz, plænts, ənd ˈhæbəˌtæts/ **178–191**
animated /ˈænəmeɪtəd/ **208**–11
ankle /ˈæŋkəl/ **133**–15
    swollen... /ˈswoʊlən/ **135**–11
anniversary /ˌænəˈvɜrsəri/ **229**–26
answer /ˈænsər/ **17**–25
ant /ænt/ **181**–24
antacid /æntˈæsɪd/ **142**–8
Antarctica /æntˈɑrktɪkə/ **174**–14
Antarctic Circle /æntˈɑrktɪk ˈsɜrkəl/ **174**–4

antelope /ˈæntlˌoʊp/ **185**–9
antibacterial cream /æntibækˈtɪriəl krim/ **143**–29
antibacterial ointment /æntibækˈtɪriəl ˈɔɪntmənt/ **143**–29
antihistamine /ˌæntiˈhɪstəˌmin/ **142**–14
antler /ˈæntlər/ **185**–21
ants /ˈænts/ **76**–23
apartment /əˈpɑrtmənt/ **63**–9
    decorate the... /ˈdɛkəˌreɪt ði/ **64**–13
    look for an... /lʊk fər ən/ **64**–1
    rent an... /rɛnt ən/ **31**–7
    studio... /ˈstudioʊ/ **67**–9
    see the... /si ði/ **64**–4
apartment building /əˈpɑrtmənt ˈbɪldɪŋ/ **66–67**
apologize /əˈpɑləˌdʒaɪz/ **40**–9
apostrophe /əˈpɑstrəfi/ **196**–14
app / æp/ **16**–2
appetizer /ˈæpəˌtaɪzər/ **101**–26
applaud /əˈplɔd/ **204**–26
apple /ˈæpəl/ **83**–11
apple juice /ˈæpəl dʒus/ **88**–28
apples /ˈæpəlz/
    basket of... /ˈbæskɪt ʌv/ **97**–31
application / æplɪˈkeɪʃən/ **16**–2
apply for /əˈplaɪ fər/ **65**–22
appointment /əˈpɔɪntmənt/
    make an... /meɪk ən/ **64**–2, **137**–21
appointment book /əˈpɔɪntmənt bʊk/ **155**–13
apricot /ˈæprɪˌkɑt/ **83**–16
April /ˈeɪprəl/ **7**–19
apron /ˈeɪprən/ **101**–3
aquarium /əˈkwɛriəm/ **216**–8
architect /ˈɑrkəˌtɛkt/ **146**–19
Arctic Circle /ˈɑrktɪk ˈsɜrkəl/ **174**–2
area code /ˈɛriə koʊd/ **16**–20
Argentine /ˈɑrdʒəntin/ **44**–9
Argentinean /ɑrdʒənˈtiniən/ **44**–9
argue /ˈɑrgyu/ **40**–1
arm /ɑrm/ **133**–8
armchair /ˈɑrmˌtʃɛr/ **72**–3
armed robbery /ɑrmd ˈrɑbəri/ **61**–15
around /əˈraʊnd/ **13**–12, **130**–9
arrange /əˈreɪndʒ/ **64**–12
arrest /əˈrɛst/ **150**–4
arrest /əˈrɛst/ **61**–16
arrival and departure monitors
   /əˈraɪvəl ənd dɪˈpɑrtʃər ˈmɑnətərz/ **125**–11
arrive at /əˈraɪv/ **123**–24
arson /ˈɑrsən/ **61**–8
art gallery /ɑrt ˈgæləri/ **58**–3
arthritis /ɑrˈθraɪtɪs/ **135**–16
artichoke /ˈɑrtəˌtʃoʊk/ **84**–13
artist /ˈɑrtɪst/ **146**–3
    graphic... /ˈgræfɪk/ **146**–7
THE ARTS /ðə ɑrts/ **202–209**
Asia /ˈeɪʒə/ **174**–11
ask /æsk/ **64**–5
ask for /æsk fər/
    ...a pillow /ə ˈpɪloʊ/ **126**–14
    ...directions /dəˈrɛkʃənz/ **123**–4
    ...the check /ðə tʃɛk/ **102**–17
asparagus /əˈspærəgəs/ **84**–3
aspirin /ˈæsprɪn/ **143**–27
assembler /əˈsɛmblər/ **146**–18
assembly line /əˈsɛmbli laɪn/ **156**–3
asthma /ˈæzmə/ **135**–2
astronaut /ˈæstrəˌnɔt/ **176**–14
astronomer /əˈstrɑnəmər/ **176**–10
athletic shoe /æθˈlɛtɪk ʃu/ **109**–24
athletic supporter /æθˈlɛtɪk səˈpɔrtər/ **107**–28
Atlantic Provinces /ətˈlæntɪk ˈprɑvɪnsəz/ **172**–6

atlas /ˈætləs/ **55**-14
ATM /ˈeɪtiɛm/ **51**-20
ATM card /ˈeɪtiɛm kɑrd/ **51**-22
    insert your... /ɪnˌsɛrt yər/ **51**-24
atmosphere /ˈætməsˌfɪr/
    Earth's... /ɜrθs/ **176**-15
atom /ˈætəm/ **194**-17
attendant /əˈtɛndənt/ **146**-21
attic /ˈætɪk/ **69**-2
attorney /əˈtɜrni/ **61**-25
audience /ˈɔdiəns/ **204**-9
auditorium /ˌɔdəˈtɔriəm/ **23**-11
August /ˈɔɡəst/ **7**-23
aunt /ænt/ **27**-3
Australia /ɔsˈtreɪlyə/ **174**-13
Australian /ɔsˈtreɪlyən/ **44**-30
author /ˈɔθər/ **55**-20
autobiography /ˌɔtəbaɪˈɑɡrəfi/ **55**-23
automated check-in machine /ˈɔtoʊmeɪtəd tʃɛk-ɪn məˈʃin/ **124**-7
automobile exhaust /ˌɔtəməˈbil ɪɡˈzɔst/ **171**-20
auto theft /ˈɔtoʊ θɛft/ **61**-2
autumn /ˈɔtəm/ **7**-14
avalanche /ˈævəˌlænʧ/ **171**-7
avocado /ˌavəˈkadoʊ/ **83**-10
ax /æks/ **160**-5
baby /ˈbeɪbi/ **30, 56**-32
baby animals /ˈbeɪbi ˈænəməlz/ **153**
baby carrier /ˈbeɪbi ˈkæriər/ **57**-9
baby lotion /ˈbeɪbi ˈloʊʃən/ **57**-23
baby powder /ˈbeɪbi ˈpaʊdər/ **57**-22
baby shower /ˈbeɪbi ˈʃaʊər/ **229**-27
babysitter /ˈbeɪbiˌsɪtər/ **147**-30
baby swing /ˈbeɪbi swɪŋ/ **57**-6
baby wipes /ˈbeɪbi waɪps/ **57**-24
back /bæk/ **133**-22
backache /ˈbækeɪk/ **135**-17
backgammon /ˈbækˌɡæmən/ **224**-11
backhoe /ˈbækhoʊ/
    operate a... /ˈɑpəˌreɪt ə/ **165**-15
backpack /ˈbækˌpæk/ **23**-10, **213**-11
backpacker /ˈbækˌpækər/ **213**-12
backup singers /ˈbækˌʌp ˈsɪŋərz/ **205**-16
bacon /ˈbeɪkən/ **88**-20
    broil... /brɔɪl/ **92**-9
bag /bæɡ/
    carry a... /ˈkæri ə/ **165**-18
    ...of potatoes /ʌv pəˈteɪtoʊz/ **97**-22
bagel /ˈbeɪɡəl/ **90**-5
baggage /ˈbæɡɪʤ/ **124**-5
    check your... /ʧɛk yər/ **126**-3
baggage claim (area) /ˈbæɡɪʤ kleɪm (ˈɛriə)/ **125**-19
bagger /ˈbæɡər/ **99**-18
baggy /ˈbæɡi/
    ...pants /pænts/ **111**-12
bags /bæɡz/
    claim your... /kleɪm yər/ **126**-24
bake /beɪk/ **93**-31
baked potato /beɪkd pəˈteɪtoʊ/ **90**-9
bakery /ˈbeɪkəri/ **48**-21, **99**-5
balance /ˈbæləns/ **51**-18, **194**-9
balcony /ˈbælkəni/ **67**-16, **204**-2
bald /bɔld/ **33**-14
ball /bɔl/
    tennis... /ˈtɛnɪs/ **220**-3
ballet /bælˈeɪ/ **204**-1
balloon /bəˈlun/ **229**-24
ballot /ˈbælət/ **200**-2
ballroom /ˈbɔlˌrum/ **159**-8
banana /bəˈnænə/ **83**-29
bandage /ˈbændɪʤ/
    adhesive... /ədˈhisɪv/ **143**-28

bangs /bæŋz/ **33**-23
banjo /ˈbænʤoʊ/ **207**-23
bank /bæŋk/ **50-51, 58**-2
bankcard /ˈbæŋkˌkard/ **51**-22
bank manager /ˈbæŋk ˈmænɪʤər/ **51**-8
bar /bar/
    ...of soap /ʌv soʊp/ **97**-8
barbecue /ˈbarbɪˌkyu/ **69**-6
barbell /ˈbarˌbɛl/ **218**-28
barbeque /ˈbarbɪˌkyu/ **228**-9
barber /ˈbarbər/ **146**-17
barbershop /ˈbarbərˌʃap/ **48**-12
bar code /bar koʊd/ **9**-23
barcode scanner /ˈbarkoʊd ˈskænər/ **99**-19
barn /barn/ **152**-3
barrette /bəˈrɛt/ **144**-7
baseball /ˈbeɪsˌbɔl/ **220**-4
baseball /ˈbeɪsˌbɔl/ **220**-5
baseball cap /ˈbeɪsˌbɔl kæp/ **109**-27
baseball hat /ˈbeɪsˌbɔl hæt/ **109**-27
basement /ˈbeɪsmənt/ **67**-7, **77**-9
BASIC WORDS /ˈbeɪsɪk wɜrdz/ **2-27**
basket /ˈbæskɪt/ **97**-31
basketball /ˈbæskɪtˌbɔl/ **218**-3, **218**-7
basketball court /ˈbæskɪtˌbɔl kɔrt/ **218**-5
basketball player /ˈbæskɪtˌbɔl ˈpleɪər/ **218**-6
bass (fish) /bæs/ **189**-15
bass (instrument) /beɪs/ **207**-19
bassoon /bəˈsun/ **207**-15
baste /beɪst/ **92**-16
bat /bæt/ **182**-4, **220**-7
bath /bæθ/
    take a... /teɪk ə/ **34**-22
bathe /beɪð/ **29**-7
bathing suit /ˈbeɪðɪŋ sut/ **107**-7
bathrobe /ˈbæθˌroʊb/ **107**-13
bathroom /ˈbæθˌrum/ **23**-8, **74-75**
bathtub /ˈbæθˌtʌb/ **75**-22
batter /ˈbætər/ **220**-6
battery /ˈbætəri/ **121**-33, **163**-33
bay /beɪ/ **169**-25
be /bi/
    ...a single mother
        /ə ˈsɪŋɡəl ˈmʌðər/ **27**-29
    ...divorced /dɪˈvɔrsd/ **26**-28
    ...in pain /ɪn peɪn/ **136**-1
    ...in shock /ɪn ʃak/ **136**-4
    ...married /ˈmærɪd/ **26**-27
    ...online /ˌanˈlaɪn/ **24**-30
    ...pregnant /ˈprɛɡnənt/ **31**-14
    ...remarried /riˈmærɪd/ **27**-30
    ...unconscious /ʌnˈkanʃəs/ **136**-2
beach /ˈbiʧ/ **169**-23, **210-211**
beach ball /ˈbiʧ bɔl/ **211**-20
beak /bik/ **187**-20
beaker /ˈbikər/ **194**-23
beans /binz/ **91**-28
bean sprouts /bin spraʊts/ **84**-20
bear /bɛr/
    grizzly... /ˈɡrɪzli/ **187**-5
    polar... /ˈpoʊlər/ **187**-8
bear cub /bɛr kʌb/ **187**-9
beard /bɪrd/ **33**-16
beat /bit/ **93**-27
beautiful /ˈbyutəfəl/ **14**-14
beauty salon /ˈbyuti səˈlan/ **48**-11
beaver /ˈbivər/ **190**-15
be born /bi bɔrn/ **31**-1
become /bɪˈkʌm/
    ...a grandparent
        /ə ˈɡrænˌpɛrənt/ **31**-21

bed /bɛd/ **74**-14
  go to... /goʊ tə/ **34**-23
  make the... /meɪk ðə/ **79**-1
bedpan /ˈbɛdˌpæn/ **139**-19
bedroom /ˈbɛdˌrum/ **74-75**
bedspread /ˈbɛdˌsprɛd/ **74**-17
bee /bi/ **185**-1
beef /bif/ **86**
bee sting /bi stɪŋ/ **135**-28
beetle /ˈbɪtl/ **182**-24
beets /ˈbits/ **84**-2
behave /bɪˈheɪv/ **29**-24
behind /bɪˈhaɪnd/ **13**-14, **130**-6
beige /beɪʒ/ **10**-17
bellhop /ˈbɛlˌhɑp/ **159**-15
bell pepper /bɛl ˈpɛpər/ **84**-23
below /bɪˈloʊ/ **13**-13
belt /bɛlt/ **109**-6
  tool... /tul/ **160**-12
bench /bɛntʃ/ **72**-1, **218**-27
  park... /park/ **214**-18
beside /bɪˈsaɪd/ **13**-11
between /bɪˈtwin/ **13**-4, **130**-8
beverages /ˈbɛvrɪʤəz/ **99**-11
bib /bɪb/ **57**-16
bicycle /ˈbaɪsɪkəl/ **214**-26
bicycle path /ˈbaɪsɪkəl pæθ/ **216**-17
big /ˈbɪg/ **14**-2
bike /baɪk/ **214**-26
  stationary... /ˈsteɪʃəˌneri/ **218**-14
bikini /bɪˈkini/ **107**-8
bill /bɪl/ **52**-1, **101**-31
billboard /ˈbɪlˌbɔrd/ **58**-9
bills /ˈbɪlz/ **8**
  pay the... /peɪ ðə/ **79**-6
binder /ˈbaɪndər/ **155**-1
binoculars /bəˈnɑkyələrz/ **213**-20
biography /baɪˈɑgrəfi/ **55**-22
biohazard /ˌbaɪoʊˈhæzərd/ **156**-30
biologist /baɪˈɑləʤɪst/ **194**-2
biology /baɪˈɑləʤi/ **194**-1
birch (tree) /bɜrtʃ (tri)/ **179**-3
birth certificate /bɜrθ sərˈtɪfɪkɪt/ **43**-24
birthday /ˈbɜrθˌdeɪ/ **229**-23
  celebrate a... /ˈsɛləˌbreɪt ə/ **31**-20
black /blæk/ **10**-22
blackboard /ˈblækˌbɔrd/ **19**-14
blackboard eraser /ˈblækˌbɔrd ɪˈreɪsər/ **19**-4
black hair /blæk hɛr/ **33**-3
blade /bleɪd/ **161**-30
blanket /ˈblæŋkɪt/ **74**-2
blanket sleeper /ˈblæŋkɪt ˈslipər/ **107**-16
bleach /blitʃ/ **116**-5
bleachers /ˈblitʃərz/ **23**-5
bleed /blid/ **136**-3
blender /ˈblɛndər/ **70**-12
blind /blaɪnd/ **135**-18
blinds /blaɪndz/ **72**-19
blister /ˈblɪstər/ **135**-25
blizzard /ˈblɪzərd/ **171**-2
blond hair /blɑnd hɛr/ **33**-4
blood /blʌd/ **138**-9
  draw... /drɔ/ **137**-24
blood pressure /blʌd ˈprɛʃər/
  check... /tʃɛk/ **137**-23
blood pressure monitor /blʌd ˈprɛʃər ˈmɑnətər/ **141**-19
bloody nose /ˈblʌdi noʊz/ **135**-29
blouse /blaʊs/ **104**-14
blow dryer /ˈbloʊˌdraɪər/ **144**-6
blow out /ˈbloʊ aʊt/
  ...candles /ˈkændls/ **229**-31

blue /blu/ **10**-9
  ...navy /ˈneɪvi/ **10**-11
blueberries /ˈbluˌbɛriz/ **83**-17
blue jay /blu ʤeɪ/ **190**-4
blue jeans /blu ʤinz/ **104**-27
blueprints /ˈbluˌprɪntz/
  read... /rid/ **165**-17
blues /bluz/ **209**-25
blush /blʌʃ/ **144**-28
board /bɔrd/ **126**-8
board /bɔrd/
  black... /blæk/ **19**-6
  bulletin... /ˈbʊlətn/ **19**-7
  erase the... /ɪˈreɪs ðə/ **20**-17
  go to... /goʊ tu/ **20**-16
  white... /waɪt/ **19**-14
boarding pass /ˈbɔrdɪŋ pæs/ **124**-8
board lumber /bɔrd ˈlʌmbər/ **163**-30
boat /boʊt/ **213**-7
bobcat /ˈbɑbˌkæt/ **190**-6
boil /bɔɪl/ **92**-17
bolt /boʊlt/ **163**-21
bone /boʊn/ **133**-3
book /bʊk/ **19**-12
  appointment... /əˈpɔɪntmənt/ **155**-13
  close your... /kloʊz yər/ **20**-9
  date... /deɪt/ **155**-13
  look for a... /lʊk fər ə/ **54**-25
  open your... /ˈoʊpən yər/ **20**-10
  share a... /ʃɛr ə/ **21**-21
bookcase /ˈbʊkˌkeɪs/ **72**-22
books /bʊks/
  check out... /tʃɛk aʊt/ **54**-26
  return... /rɪˈtɜrn/ **55**-28
bookshelf /ˈbʊkʃɛlf/ **19**-11
bookstore /ˈbʊkstɔr/ **48**-9
boom box /bum bɑks/ **226**-14
boot /but/ **109**-17
boots /buts/
  safety... /ˈseɪfti/ **157**-28
bored /bɔrd/ **39**-13
botanical garden /bəˈtænəkal ˈgardn/ **216**-13
bottle /ˈbɑtl/ **57**-2
  ...of olive oil /ʌv ˈɑlɪv ɔɪl/ **97**-7
bottled water /ˈbɑtld ˈwɔtər/ **88**-15
bottle opener /ˈbɑtl ˈoʊpənər/ **94**-15
boulder /ˈboʊldər/ **181**-3
bouquet /boʊˈkeɪ/ **97**-6
bow /boʊ/ **40**-14, **204**-27
bowl /ˈboʊl/ **70**-24, **101**-14
bowling alley /ˈboʊlɪŋ ˈæli/ **216**-5
box /bɑks/ **97**-20
boxer /ˈbɑksər/ **218**-17
boxers /ˈbɑksərz/ **107**-26
boxer shorts /ˈbɑksər ʃɔrts/ **107**-26
boxing /ˈbɑksɪŋ/ **218**-16
boxing glove /ˈbɑksɪŋ ˈglʌv/ **218**-18
boxing ring /ˈbɑksɪŋ rɪŋ/ **218**-19
box office /ˈbɑks ˈɔfɪs/ **205**-24
boy /bɔɪ/ **57**-14
bra /brɑ/ **107**-19
bracelet /ˈbreɪslɪt/ **109**-10
braces /ˈbreɪsəz/ **141**-29
braids /breɪdz/ **33**-21
brain /breɪn/ **133**-24
brainstorm /ˈbreɪnˌstɔrm/ **196**-20
brake light /breɪk laɪt/ **121**-6
brake pedal /breɪk ˈpɛdl/ **121**-26
branch /bræntʃ/ **179**-10
brass /bræs/ **207**
Brazilian /brəˈzɪlyən/ **44**-7

bread /brɛd/
    butter the... /ˈbʌtər ðə/ **102**–8
    loaf of... /louf ʌv/ **97**–16
break /breɪk/
    ...a leg /ə lɛg/ **136**–5
break /breɪk/
    take a... /teɪk ə/ **20**–14
breaker panel /ˈbreɪkər ˈpænəl/ **77**–12
breakfast /ˈbrɛkfəst/
    eat... /it/ **34**–9
    have... /hæv/ **34**–9
breast /brɛst/ **133**–10
bribery /ˈbraɪbəri/ **61**–3
bricks /ˈbrɪks/
    lay... /leɪ/ **165**–5
bridge /brɪʤ/ **214**–17
briefcase /ˈbrifˌkeɪs/ **109**–16
briefs /brifs/ **107**–27
British /ˈbrɪtɪʃ/ **44**–10
British Columbia /ˈbrɪtɪʃ kəˈlʌmbiə/ **172**–2
broccoli /ˈbrakəli/ **84**–1
    steam... /stim/ **92**–10
broil /ˈbrɔɪl/ **92**–9
broken /ˈbroʊkən/ **77**–10
broom /brʊm/ **80**–28
brother /ˈbrʌðər/ **27**–17
brother-in-law /ˈbrʌðər-ɪn-ˌlɔ/ **27**–14
brown /braʊn/ **10**–16
brown hair /braʊn hɛr/ **33**–2
bruise /bruz/ **135**–30
brush /brʌʃ/ **34**–3
brush /brʌʃ/
    hair... /hɛr/ **144**–10
bucket /ˈbʌkɪt/ **80**–16
buckle /ˈbʌkəl/ **114**–11
bud /ˈbʌd/ **179**–17
buffalo /ˈbʌfəloʊ/ **185**–17
bugle /ˈbyugəl/ **207**–10
bug spray /bʌg spreɪ/ **80**–15
build /bɪld/ **198**–3, **224**–28
building material /ˈbɪldɪŋ məˈtɪriəl/ **162**
bulb /bʌlb/ **179**–18
bull /bʊl/ **152**–7
bulletin board /ˈbʊlətn bɔrd/ **19**–7
bumper /ˈbʌmpər/ **121**–9
bun /bʌn/ **33**–22
bunch /ˈbʌnʧ/
    ...of carrots /ʌv ˈkærəts/ **97**–29
Bunsen burner /ˈbʌnsʌn ˈbɜrnər/ **194**–14
burglary /ˈbɜrgləri/ **61**–4
burn /bɜrn/ **136**–6
burn /bɜrn/ **135**–24
burned out /ˈbɜrnd aʊt/ **77**–6
burrito /bɛˈritoʊ/ **91**–25
bus /bʌs/ **102**–25
bus /bʌs/ **128**–9
busboy /ˈbʌsˌbɔɪ/ **101**–5
bus driver /bʌs ˈdraɪvər/ **128**–8
bush /bʊʃ/ **185**–16
    lilac... /ˈlaɪˌlæk/ **179**–7
business card /ˈbɪznɪs kard/ **43**–20
business card file /ˈbɪznɪs kard faɪl/ **155**–14
business center /ˈbɪznɪs ˈsɛntər/ **159**–7
businessman /ˈbɪznɪsˌmæn/ **146**–23
business suit /ˈbɪznɪs sut/ **104**–29
businesswoman /ˈbɪznɪsˌwʊmən/ **146**–23
busser /ˈbʌsər/ **101**–5
bus stop /bʌs stap/ **128**–7
butcher /ˈbʊʧər/ **146**–20
butter /ˈbʌtər/ **102**–8
butter /ˈbʌtər/ **88**–23

butterfly /ˈbʌtərˌflaɪ/ **182**–21
buttocks /ˈbʌtəks/ **133**–47
button /ˈbʌtn/ **114**–10
button /ˈbʌtn/ **117**–15
button-down /ˈbʌtn-ˌdaʊn/
    ...shirt /ʃɜrt/ **111**–6
buttonhole /ˈbʌtnˌhoʊl/ **117**–14
buy /baɪ/ **114**–5
    ...a house /ə haʊs/ **31**–13
buying a house /ˈbaɪɪŋ ə haʊs/ **65**
buying clothes /ˈbaɪɪŋ klouz/ **114**–**115**
cab /kæb/ **128**–4
cabbage /ˈkæbɪʤ/ **84**–8
cab driver /ˈkæb ˈdraɪvər/ **128**–5
cabin /ˈkæbɪn/
    log... /lɔg/ **63**–4
cabinet /ˈkæbənɪt/ **70**–2
    file... /faɪl/ **155**–17
    supply... /səˈplaɪ/ **155**–21
cable /ˈkeɪbəl/ **25**–11
cactus /ˈkæktəs/ **181**–16
café /kæˈfeɪ/ **58**–8, **216**–1
cafeteria /ˌkæfəˈtɪriə/ **23**–7
cake /keɪk/ **88**–16, **229**–25
    piece of... /pis ʌv/ **97**–15
cake pan /keɪk pæn/ **95**–30
calculator /ˈkælkyəˌleɪtər/ **155**–10
calendar /ˈkæləndər/ **6**–7
call /kɔl/ **40**–16
    ...a realtor /ə ˈriəltər/ **65**–16
    ...the doctor /ðə ˈdaktər/ **137**–20
call button /kɔl ˈbʌtn/ **139**–21
caller /ˈkɔlər/ **16**–13
call in /kɔl ɪn/
    ...sick /sɪk/ **151**–22
calling card /ˈkɔlɪŋ kard/ **16**–6
calm /kam/ **38**–5
camcorder /ˈkæmˌkɔrdər/ **226**–3
camel /ˈkæməl/ **181**–8
camera /ˈkæmrə/ **226**–1
camisole /ˈkæməsoʊl/ **107**–22
camp /ˈkæmp/ **213**–29
camper /ˈkæmpər/ **213**–27
campfire /ˈkæmpfaɪr/ **213**–28
camping /ˈkæmpɪŋ/ **212**–**213**
camping stove /ˈkæmpɪŋ stoʊv/ **213**–15
can /kæn/
    ...of soda /ʌv ˈsoʊdə/ **97**–27
Canada /ˈkænədə/ **172**–**173**
Canadian /kænˈeɪdiən/ **44**–1
candidate /ˈkændəˌdeɪt/
    political... /pəˈlɪtɪkəl/ **200**–1
candle /ˈkændl/ **70**–28
    light a... /laɪt ə/ **102**–3
candles /ˈkændls/
    blow out... /ˈbloʊ aʊt/ **229**–31
    light... /laɪt/ **229**–30
candy bar /ˈkændi bar/ **99**–25
cane /keɪn/ **142**–17
canned goods /kænd gʊds/ **99**–12
canoe /kəˈnu/ **213**–8
can opener /kæn ˈoʊpənər/ **94**–16
cantaloupe /ˈkæntlˌoʊp/ **83**–12
canteen /kænˈtin/ **213**–19
canvas /ˈkænvəs/ **203**–12
canyon /ˈkænyən/ **169**–13
Capitol (Building) /ˈkæpətl (ˈbɪldɪŋ)/ **200**–6
capsule /ˈkæpsəl/ **142**–2
car /kar/
    compact... /kəmˈpækt/ **118**–30
    park the... /park ðə/ **123**–25

wash the... /wɑʃ ðə/ **79**–16
card /kɑrd/ **228**–6
   remove your... /rəˈmuv yər/ **51**–28
car dealership /kɑr ˈdilərʃɪp/ **47**–23
cardigan /ˈkɑrdɪgən/
   ...sweater /ˈswɛtər/ **111**–15
cardinal /ˈkɑrdnəl/ **190**–2
cardiologist /ˌkɑrdɪˈɑləʤɪst/ **141**–8
cardiopulmonary resuscitation
   /ˌkɑrdiouˈpəlmənæri riˌsəsəˈteɪʃən/ **139**–24
cards /kɑrʤ/ **224**–1
caring for clothes /ˈkɛrɪŋ fər klouz/ **114**–**115**
carnival /ˈkɑrnəvəl/ **216**–18
carousel /ˌkærəˈsɛl/ **214**–14
carpenter /ˈkɑrpəntər/ **147**–26
carpet /ˈkɑrpɪt/ **74**–3
   vacuum the... /ˈvækˌyum ðə/ **79**–7
carrot /ˈkærət/ **84**–19
carrots /ˈkærəts/
   bunch of... /ˈbʌnʧ ʌv/ **97**–29
   chop... /ʧɑp/ **93**–23
   peel... /pil/ **93**–22
carry /ˈkæri/ **29**–6
   ...a bag /ə bæg/ **165**–18
   ...a tray /ə treɪ/ **102**–4
carry-on bag /ˈkæri-ɑn bæg/ **125**–16
   stow your... /stou yər/ **126**–10
carton /ˈkɑrtn/
   ...of eggs /ʌv ɛgz/ **97**–23
   ...of orange juice /ʌv ˈɔrɪnʤ/ **97**–10
cartoon /kɑrˈtun/ **209**–14
cash /kæʃ/ **9**–25, **51**–6
   withdraw... /wɪðˈdrɔ/ **51**–26
cashier /kæˈʃɪr/ **9**–15, **99**–21, **147**–24
cashmere /ˈkæʒˌmɪr/ **113**–9
cash register /kæʃ ˈrɛʤɪstər/ **9**–17, **99**–16
casserole (dish) /ˈkæsəˌroul (dɪʃ)/ **95**–25
cast /kæst/ **141**–15
castle /ˈkæsəl/ **63**–19
casual /ˈkæʒuəl/
   ...clothes /klouz/ **111**–24
cat /kæt/ **152**–17
catalog /ˈkætlˌɔg/ **52**–14
catcher /ˈkæʧər/ **220**–8
caterpillar /ˈkætəˌpɪlər/ **182**–20
cauliflower /ˈkɔlɪˌflauər/ **84**–16
caulking gun /ˈkɔkɪŋ gʌn/ **160**–8
cave /keɪv/ **169**–14
cavity /ˈkævəti/ **141**–32
C-clamp /si-klæmp/ **160**–2
CD /ˌsiˈdi/ **226**–11
CD player /ˌsiˈdi ˈpleɪər/ **226**–10
CD-ROM /ˌsiˌdi-ˈrɑm/ **25**–1
CD-ROM drive /ˌsiˌdi-ˈrɑm draɪv/ **25**–28
ceiling /ˈsilɪŋ/ **72**–17
ceiling fan /ˈsilɪŋ fæn/ **72**–16
celebrate /ˈsɛləˌbreɪt/ **31**–20
celebrations /ˌsɛləˈbreɪʃənz/ **228**–**229**
celery /ˈsɛləri/ **84**–14
cello /ˈʧɛlou/ **207**–20
cell phone /sɛl foun/ **16**–19
   turn off your... /tɜrn ɔf yər/ **126**–11
Celsius /ˈsɛlsiəs/ **166**–1
centimeter /ˈsɛntəˌmitər/ **163**–2
century /ˈsɛnʧəri/ **4**
Certificate of Naturalization /sərˈtɪfɪkɪt ʌv ˌnæʧərələzeɪʃən/ **43**–26
chain /ʧeɪn/ **163**–32
chair /ʧɛr/ **19**–27, **70**–22
chairlift /ˈʧɛrlɪft/ **222**–8
chalet /ʃæˈleɪ/ **63**–5
chalk /ˈʧɔk/ **19**–15

change /ˈʧeɪnʤ/
   ...diapers /ˈdaɪəpərz/ **29**–8
   ...the sheets /ðə ʃits/ **79**–2
   ...the tire /ˈðə taɪr/ **123**–22
changing table /ˈʧeɪnʤɪŋ ˈteɪbəl/ **57**–26
charger /ˈʧɑrʤər/ **16**–7
cheap /ʧip/ **14**–16
cheat /ʧit/
   ...on a test /ɑn ə tɛst/ **18**–30
check /ʧɛk/ **21**–24
   ...his blood pressure /hɪz blʌd ˈprɛʃər/ **137**–23
   ...the monitors /ðə ˈmɑnətər/ **126**–6
   ...the oil /ðə ɔɪl/ **123**–16
   ...your baggage /yər ˈbægɪʤ/ **126**–3
check /ʧɛk/ **51**–13, **101**–31
   ask for the... /æsk fər ðə/ **102**–17
   pay the... /peɪ ðə/ **102**–24
   personal... /ˈpɜrsənəl/ **9**–24
checkbook /ˈʧɛkˌbʊk/ **51**–12
checked /ˈʧɛkt/ **113**–18
checker /ˈʧɛkər/ **99**–21
checkers /ˈʧɛkərz/ **224**–15
check in /ʧɛk ɪn/ **126**–1, **159**–25
check-in counter /ʧɛk-ɪn ˈkaʊntər/ **124**–4
checking account number /ˈʧɛktɪŋ əˈkaʊnt ˈnʌmbər/ **51**–11
check out /ʧɛk aʊt/ **159**–27
   ...books /bʊks/ **54**–26
checkout counter /ˈʧɛkˌaʊt ˈkaʊntər/ **99**–15
checkout desk /ˈʧɛkaʊt dɛsk/ **55**–15
checkup /ˈʧɛkˌʌp/ **141**–18
cheddar cheese /ˈʧɛdər ʧiz/ **88**–22
cheek /ʧik/ **133**–36
cheerleader /ˈʧɪrˌlidər/ **220**–26
cheese /ʧiz/
   cheddar... /ˈʧɛdər/ **88**–22
   grate... /greɪt/ **92**–11
   Swiss... /swɪs/ **88**–24
cheetah /ˈʧitə/ **185**–13
chef /ʃɛf/ **101**–1
chemist /ˈkɛməst/ **194**–4
chemistry /ˈkɛməstri/ **194**–3
cherries /ˈʧɛriz/ **83**–21
   pound of... /paʊnd ʌv/ **97**–19
chess /ʧɛs/ **224**–12
chest /ʧɛst/ **133**–46
chicken /ˈʧɪkən/ **87**–31, **152**–28
   baste... /beɪst/ **92**–16
   roast... /roust/ **92**–15
   season... /ˈsizən/ **92**–14
chicken breasts /ˈʧɪkən brɛsts/ **87**–29
chicken pox /ˈʧɪkən pɑks/ **135**–6
chicken teriyaki /ˈʧɪkən tɛriˈaki/ **91**–21
chickpeas /ˈʧɪkpiz/ **84**–10
child /ʧaɪld/ **30**
childcare worker /ˈʧaɪldkɛr ˈwɜrkər/ **57**–17
child car seat /ʧaɪld kɑr sit/ **121**–1
children's program /ˈʧɪldrənz ˈproʊˌgræm/ **209**–19
Chilean /ʧɪlˈeɪən/ **44**–8
chimney /ˈʧɪmni/ **69**–1
chimpanzee /ˌʧɪmpænˈzi/ **182**–3
chin /ʧɪn/ **133**–38
Chinese /ʧaɪˈniz/ **44**–23
chin-up /ʧɪn-ʌp/ **218**–11
chipmunk /ˈʧɪpˌmʌŋk/ **190**–21
chips /ʧɪps/
   potato... /pəˈteɪtou/ **99**–27
chisel /ˈʧɪzəl/ **160**–14
chocolates /ˈʧɔklɪts/ **228**–5
choke /ʧoʊk/ **136**–7
choose /ʧuz/ **126**–20
chop /ʧɑp/ **93**–23

chopsticks /ˈʧɑpˌstɪks/ **90**–18
Christmas /ˈkrɪsməs/ **229**–19
Christmas tree /ˈkrɪsməs tri/ **229**–22
chrysanthemums /krɪˈsænθəməmz/ **179**–21
church /ˈʧɜrʧ/ **47**–13
cider /ˈsaɪdər/
     gallon of... /ˈgælən ʌv/ **97**–21
cinnamon /ˈsɪnəmən/
     sift... /sɪft/ **93**–28
circle /ˈsɜrkəl/ **21**–28
circle /ˈsɜrkəl/ **193**–16
circuit breaker /ˈsɜrkɪt/ **77**–13
circular saw /ˈsɜrkyələr sɔ/ **161**–31
circulation desk /ˌsɜrkyəˈleɪʃən dɛsk/ **55**–15
circumference /sərˈkʌmfrəns/ **193**–13
circus /ˈsɜrkəs/ **216**–15
citizen /ˈsɪtəzən/ **200**–4
citizenship /ˈsɪtəzənˌʃɪp/ **200–201**
city /ˈsɪti/ **43**–12, **63**–20
city hall /ˈsɪti hɔl/ **47**–17
city park /ˈsɪti park/ **214–215**
city square /ˈsɪti skwɛr/ **58–59**
claim /kleɪm/
     ...your bags /yər bægz/ **126**–24
clams /klæmz/ **87**–16
clap /klæp/ **204**–26
clarinet /ˌklærəˈnɛt/ **207**–14
classical /ˈklæsɪkəl/ **209**–28
classroom /ˈklæsˌrum/ **18–19**, **23**–18
claw /klɔ/ **187**–22
clay /kleɪ/ **203**–21
clean /klin/ **14**–6
clean /klin/ **79**–10
cleaner /ˈklinər/ **48**–17
     vacuum... /ˈvækˌyum/ **80**–5
cleaning supplies /ˈklinɪŋ/ **80–81**
cleanser /ˈklɛnzər/ **80**–19
clear /klɪr/ **102**–25
clerk /clɜrk/
     postal... /ˈpoustəl/ **52**–20
click /klɪk/ **24**–33
cliff /klɪf/ **169**–27
climb /klaɪm/ **165**–14
clock /klak/ **19**–8
clock times /klak taɪmz/ **5**
clog /klag/ **109**–23
clogged /klagd/ **77**–2
close /klouz/ **20**–9
closed /klouzd/ **15**–38
closet /ˈklazɪt/ **74**–1
close to /klous tə/ **13**–15
cloth diaper /klaθ ˈdaɪəpər/ **57**–29
clothes /klouðz/ **104–105**
     casual... /ˈkæʒuəl/ **111**–24
     dress... /drɛs/ **111**–25
     fold the... /fould ðə/ **79**–5
     formal... /ˈfɔrməl/ **111**–25
     informal... /ɪnˈfɔrməl/ **111**–24
clothesline /ˈklouzˌlaɪn/ **107**–1
clothespin /ˈklouzˌpɪn/ **107**–2
CLOTHING /ˈklouðɪŋ/ **104–117**
clothing store /ˈklouðɪŋ stɔr/ **48**–2
cloud /klaud/ **166**–12
cloudy /ˈklaudi/ **167**–26
club /klʌb/ **224**–9
     golf... /galf/ **220**–13
clutch /klʌʧ/ **121**–25
coach /kouʧ/ **23**–1
coach (class) /kouʧ (klæs)/ **125**–23
coal /koul/ **171**–26
coat /kout/ **104**–30

cockroaches /ˈkakˌrouʧɛz/ **76**–27
coconut /ˈkoukəˌnʌt/ **83**–13
cod /kad/ **87**–22, **189**–16
coffee /ˈkɔfi/ **90**–12
     cup of... /kʌp ʌv/ **97**–13
     pot of... /pat ʌv/ **97**–12
coffee break /ˈkɔfi breɪk/
     take a... /teɪk ə/ **34**–12
coffeemaker /ˈkɔfimeɪkər/ **70**–10
coffee shop /ˈkɔfi ʃap/ **48**–19
coffee table /ˈkɔfi ˈteɪbəl/ **72**–12
coins /kɔɪnz/ **8**
colander /ˈkaləndər/ **95**–27
cold (illness) /kould/ **135**–5
cold (temperature) /kould/ **15**–30, **166**–6
cold cuts /kould kʌts/ **88**–21
collar /ˈkalər/ **117**–12
collect /kəˈlɛkt/ **20**–3
college /ˈkalɪʤ/ **47**–9
     go to... /gou tu/ **31**–6
college degree /ˈkalɪʤ dəˈgri/ **43**–27
Colombian /kəˈlʌmbiən/ **44**–5
colon /ˈkoulən/ **196**–17
colors /ˈkʌlərz/ **10–11**
comb /koum/ **34**–5
comb /koum/ **144**–8
comedy /ˈkamədi/ **208**–2
comet /ˈkamɪt/ **176**–19
comfort /ˈkʌmfərt/ **29**–12, **40**–13
comfortable /ˈkʌmftəbəl/ **39**–24
comforter /ˈkʌmfərtər/ **74**–16
comma /ˈkamə/ **196**–11
COMMUNITY /kəˈmyunəti/ **46–61**
compact car /ˈkamˌpækt kar/ **118**–30
compact disc /ˈkamˌpækt dɪsk/ **226**–13
compass /ˈkʌmpəs/ **213**–1
compliment /ˈkampləmənt/ **40**–10, **102**–13
composes /kəmˈpouzəz/ **198**–10
computer /kəmˈpyutər/ **155**–7
     desktop... /ˈdɛskˌtap/ **25**–17
     handheld... /ˈhændˌhɛld/ **25**–16
     laptop... /ˈlæpˌtap/ **25**–23
     notebook... /ˈnoutbuk/ **25**–23
     use a... /yuz ə/ **151**–21
computerized catalog /kəmˈpyutəˌraɪzd ˈkætlˌɔg/
55–5
computer program /kəmˈpyutər ˈprouˌgræm/ **25**–25
computers /kəmˈpyutərz/ **24–25**
computer technician /kəmˈpyutər tɛkˈnɪʃən/ **146**–10
concert /ˈkansərt/
     rock... /rak/ **205**–10
concierge /kɔˈsyɛrʒ/ **159**–13
concrete /kanˈkrit/
     pour... /pɔr/ **165**–7
conditioner /kənˈdɪʃənər/ **144**–3
condo /ˈkandou/ **63**–10
condominium /ˌkandəˈmɪniəm/ **63**–10
conductor /kənˈdʌktər/ **128**–13, **204**–7
cone /koun/ **193**–24
confused /kənˈfyuzd/ **39**–18
congratulate /kənˈgræʧəˌleɪt/ **40**–24
Congress /ˈkaŋgrɪs/ **201**
congressman /ˈkaŋgrɪsmən/ **200**–9
congresswoman /ˈkaŋgrɪswumən/ **200**–9
constellation /ˌkanstəˈleɪʃən/ **176**–2
construction worker /kənˈstrʌkʃən ˈwɜrkər/ **146**–6
contact (lens) /ˈkanˌtækt (lɛnz)/ **141**–22
container /kənˈteɪnər/ **97**–25
containers /kənˈteɪnərz/ **96–97**
continents /ˈkantənənts/ **174**
controller /kənˈtroulər/ **226**–18

conversation /ˌkɑnvərˈseɪʃən/
    have a... /hæv ə/ **17**–26, **40**–6
convertible /kənˈvɜrtəbəl/ **118**–31
conveyor belt /kənˈveɪər bɛlt/ **156**–6
cook /kʊk/ **79**–22, **93**–24, **150**–1
cook /kʊk/ **146**–4
cookbook /ˈkʊkˌbʊk/ **55**–21
cookie sheet /ˈkʊki ʃit/ **95**–21
    grease a... /gris ə/ **93**–26
cooking /ˈkʊkɪŋ/ **92**–93
    do the... /du ððə/ **79**–22
cooking equipment /ˈkʊkɪŋ ɪˈkwɪpmənt/ **94**–95
cool /kul/ **166**–5
cooler /ˈkulər/ **211**–18
cop /kɑp/
    traffic... /ˈtræfɪk/ **58**–6
copier /ˈkɑpiər/ **155**–3
copies /ˈkɑpiz/
    make... /meɪk/ **151**–20
copy /ˈkɑpi/ **20**–4
copy /ˈkɑpi/ **155**–4
copy machine /ˈkɑpi məˈʃin/ **155**–3
copy shop /ˈkɑpi ʃɑp/ **48**–15
coral /ˈkɔrəl/ **10**–3
coral reef /ˈkɔrəl rif/ **189**–26
cord /kɔrd/ **16**–15
    extension... /ɪkˈstɛnʃən/ **160**–20
cordless phone /ˈkɔrdlɪs foʊn/ **16**–18
corduroy /ˈkɔrdəˌrɔɪ/ **113**–2
corn /kɔrn/ **84**–24
corner /ˈkɔrnər/ **47**–25
cornrows /ˈkɔrnˌroʊz/ **33**–25
correct /kəˈrɛkt/ **21**–25
correction fluid /kəˈrɛkʃən ˈfluɪd/ **155**–27
costume /ˈkɑsˌtum/ **204**–5, **228**–14
cottage /ˈkɑtɪdʒ/ **63**–3
cotton /ˈkɑtn/ **113**–1
couch /kaʊtʃ/ **72**–8
cough /kɔf/ **137**–16
cough /kɔf/ **135**–3
cough drops /kɔf drɑps/ **142**–10
cough syrup /kɔf ˈsɪrəp/ **142**–7
counselor /ˈkaʊnslər/
    guidance... /ˈgaɪdns/ **23**–17
counter(top) /ˈkaʊntər(tɑp)/ **70**–5
country /ˈkʌntri/ **63**–23
country and western /ˈkʌntri ənd ˈwɛstərn/ **209**–29
courthouse /ˈkɔrtˌhaʊs/ **47**–19
courtroom /ˈkɔrtˌrum/ **61**–26
courtyard /ˈkɔrtˌyard/ **67**–17
cousin /ˈkʌzən/ **27**–11
cow /kaʊ/ **152**–26
coyote /kaɪˈoʊti/ **181**–4
CPR /si pi ar/ **139**–24
crab /kræb/ **87**–18, **189**–24
cracked /krækt/ **77**–4
crate /kreɪt/ **97**–30
crater /ˈkreɪtər/ **169**–10
crawl /krɔl/ **29**–22, **37**–23
crayons /ˈkreɪˌɑnz/ **224**–18
cream /krim/ **10**–21, **88**–14
creamer /ˈkrimər/ **101**–8
credit card /ˈkrɛdɪt kard/ **9**–27
crescent moon /ˈkrɛsənt mun/ **177**–30
crew neck /kru nɛk/
    ...sweater /ˈswɛtər/ **111**–14
crib /krɪb/ **57**–3
cricket /ˈkrɪkɪt/ **181**–22
crime /kraɪm/ **60**–61
criminal /ˈkrɪmənəl/ **61**–19
crochet /kroʊˈʃeɪ/ **224**–26

crochet hook /kroʊˈʃeɪ hʊk/ **224**–22
crocodile /ˈkrɑkəˌdaɪl/ **182**–19
crop /krɑp/ **152**–11
cross /krɔs/ **37**–12
cross-country skiing /krɔs-ˈkʌntri ˈskiɪŋ/ **222**–11
cross out /krɔs aʊt/ **21**–23
crosswalk /ˈkrɔsˌwɔk/ **58**–18
crutch /ˈkrʌtʃ/ **141**–14
cry /kraɪ/ **29**–23
cub /kʌb/
    bear... /bɛr/ **187**–9
cubby /ˈkʌbi/ **57**–12
cube /kyub/ **193**–22
cucumber /ˈkyuˌkʌmbər/ **84**–25
cuff /kʌf/ **117**–17
cup /kʌp/ **96**, **97**–2, **101**–18
    ...of coffee /ʌv ˈkɔfi/ **97**–13
curb /kɜrb/ **58**–15
curlers /ˈkɜrlər/ **144**–9
curling iron /ˈkɜrlɪŋ ˈaɪərn/ **144**–5
curly hair /ˈkɜrli hɛr/ **33**–18
cursor /ˈkɜrsər/ **25**–6
curtain rod /ˈkɜrtn rɑd/ **72**–15
curtain /ˈkɜrtn/ **72**–20
curved line /kɜrvd laɪn/ **193**–8
cushion /ˈkʊʃən/ **72**–2
custodian /kʌˈstoʊdiən/ **146**–11
customer /ˈkʌstəmər/ **51**–7, **101**–7
customs /ˈkʌstəmz/ **125**–17
customs (declaration) form /ˈkʌstəmz (ˌdɛkləˈreɪʃən) fɔrm/
    125–18
cut /kʌt/
    ...a pipe /ə paɪp/ **165**–21
    ...yourself /yɛrˈsɛlf/ **136**–8
cut /kʌt/ **135**–23
cut off /kʌt ɔf/ **114**–7
cutting board /ˈkʌtɪŋ bɔrd/ **94**–1
cyclist /ˈsaɪklɪst/ **214**–25
cylinder /ˈsɪləndər/ **193**–25
    graduated... /ˈgrædʒuˌeɪtɪd/ **194**–20
cymbals /ˈsɪmbəlz/ **207**–2
daffodils /ˈdæfəˌdɪls/ **179**–22
daily activities /ˈdeɪli ækˈtɪvətiz/ **34**–35
dairy products /ˈdɛri ˈprɑdəkts/ **99**–3
daisies /ˈdeɪziz/ **179**–31
dance /dæns/ **40**–22
dancer /dænsər/ **204**–3
darken /ˈdarkən/ **21**–29
dartboard /ˈdartˌbɔrd/ **218**–29
darts /ˈdarts/ **218**–30
dashboard /ˈdæʃˌbɔrd/ **121**–16
date /deɪt/ **31**–9
date /deɪt/ **6**–1
date book /deɪt bʊk/ **155**–13
date of birth /deɪt ʌv bɜrθ/ **43**–6
dates /deɪts/ **83**–24
daughter /ˈdɔtər/ **27**–22
dawn /dɔn/ **5**
day /deɪ/ **4**
daycare center /ˈdeɪˌkɛr ˈsɛntər/ **56**–57
days of the week /deɪz ʌv ðə wik/ **6**
dead /dɛd/ **14**–12
dead-bolt (lock) /ˈdɛd-ˌboʊlt (lɑk)/ **67**–28
deaf /dɛf/ **135**–21
debit card /ˈdɛbɪt kard/ **9**–26
decade /ˈdɛkeɪd/ **4**
December /dɪˈsɛmbər/ **7**–27
decision /dɪˈsɪʒən/
    make a... /meɪk ə/ **65**–18, **151**–26
deck /dɛk/ **69**–5
decorate /ˈdɛkəˌreɪt/ **64**–13

deer /dɪr/ **190**–9
defends /dɪˈfɛndz/ **198**–6
deli counter /ˈdɛli ˈkaʊntər/ **99**–6
deliver /dəˈlɪvər/ **150**–7
delivery person /dəˈlɪvəri ˈpɜrsən/ **146**–9
demonstrate /ˈdɛmənˌstreɪt/ **201**–18
denim /ˈdɛnəm/ **113**–6
dental floss /ˈdɛntl flɔs/ **144**–13
dental hygienist /ˈdɛntl haɪˈʤinɪst/ **141**–25
dentist /ˈdɛntɪst/ **141**–26, **146**–2
deodorant /diˈoʊdərənt/ **144**–20
department store /diˈpɑrtmənt stɔr/ **48**–24
deposit /diˈpɑsɪt/ **51**–16
    make a... /meɪk ə/ **51**–27
depth /dɛpθ/ **193**
describing clothes /dɪˈskraɪbɪŋ kloʊz/ **110**–111
desert /ˈdɛzərt/ **169**–11, **180**–181
design /dɪˈzaɪn/ **151**–19
designer /dɪˈzaɪnər/ **156**–1
desk /dɛsk/ **19**–22, **155**–6
desk clerk /dɛsk klɜrk/ **159**–11
desktop (computer) /ˈdɛskˌtɑp (kəmˈpyutər)/ **25**–17
dessert /dɪˈzɜrt/ **101**–28
    share a... /ʃɛr ə/ **102**–19
destination /ˌdɛstəˈneɪʃən/
    arrive at the... /əˈraɪv ət ðə/ **123**–24
detergent /dɪˈtɜrʤənt/
    laundry... /ˈlɔndri/ **116**–4
dial /ˈdaɪəl/ **17**–25
diameter /daɪˈæmətər/ **193**–15
diamond /ˈdaɪəmənd/ **224**–8
diaper /ˈdaɪəpər/ **57**–29
    cloth... /klɔθ/ **57**–29
    disposable... /dɪˈspoʊzəbəl/ **57**–27
diaper pail /ˈdaɪəpərˌpeɪl/ **57**–21
diaper pin /ˈdaɪəpərˌpɪn/ **57**–30
diapers /ˈdaɪəpərz/
    change... /ʧeɪnʤ/ **29**–8
dice /daɪs/ **92**–2
dice /daɪs/ **224**–17
dictionary /ˈdɪkʃəˌnɛri/ **55**–8
    look up a word in the... /lʊk ʌp ə wɜrd ɪn ðə/ **20**–8
die /daɪ/ **31**–24
difficult /ˈdɪfɪˌkʌlt/ **14**–8
dig /dɪg/ **165**–22
dime /daɪm/ **8**–3
dimple /ˈdɪmpəl/ **33**–9
diner /ˈdaɪnər/ **101**–7
dining area /ˈdaɪnɪŋ ˈɛriə/ **70**–71
dinner /ˈdɪnər/
    eat... /it/ **34**–19
    have... /hæv/ **34**–19
    make... /meɪk/ **34**–18
directions /dəˈrɛkʃənz/
    ask for... /æsk fər/ **123**–4
directory assistance /dɛˈrɛktəri əˈsɪstəns/ **16**–4
dirty /ˈdɜrti/ **14**–5
disabilities /ˌdɪsəˈbɪlətiz/ **134**–135
disagree /ˌdɪsəˈgri/ **40**–12
discipline /ˈdɪsəˌplɪn/ **29**–13
discovers /dɪˈskʌvərz/ **198**–9
discuss /dɪˈskʌs/
    ...your ideas /yər aɪˈdiəz/ **20**–11
dishes /ˈdɪʃəz/ **70**–3
    do the... /du ðə/ **79**–21
    dry the... /draɪ ðə/ **79**–23
    put away the... /pʊt əˈweɪ ðə/ **79**–24
    wash the... /wɑʃ ðə/ **79**–21
dish rack /dɪʃ ræk/ **70**–16
dish soap /dɪʃ soʊp/ **80**–13
dish towel /dɪʃ taʊəl/ **70**–18

dishwasher /ˈdɪʃˌwɑʃər/ **70**–14, **101**–2
dishwasher detergent /ˈdɪʃˌwɑʃər dɪˈtɜrʤənt/ **80**–12
dishwashing liquid /ˈdɪʃˌwɑʃɪŋ ˈlɪkwɪd/ **80**–13
disposable diaper /dɪˈspoʊzəbəl ˈdaɪəpər/ **57**–27
dive /daɪv/ **198**–21, **210**–31
diver /ˈdaɪvər/ **189**–13, **218**–33
divided by /dɪˈvaɪdɪd baɪ/ **193**–6
diving board /ˈdaɪvɪŋ bɔrd/ **218**–32
diving mask /ˈdaɪvɪŋ mæsk/ **211**–26
division /dɪˈvɪʒən/ **193**–29
divorced /dɪˈvɔrst/ **26**–28
dizzy /ˈdɪzi/ **135**–20
do /du/
    ...homework /ˈhoʊmˌwɜrk/ **34**–17
    ...housework /ˈhaʊsˌwɜrk/ **34**–21
    ...the cooking /ðə ˈkʊkɪŋ/ **79**–22
    ...the dishes /ðə dɪʃəz/ **79**–21
    ...the laundry /ðə ˈlɔndri/ **79**–3
dock /dɑk/ **226**–8
doctor /ˈdɑktər/ **139**–16, **146**–12
    call the... /kɔl ðə/ **137**–20
documentary /ˌdɑkyəˈmɛntəri/ **208**–10
documents /ˈdɑkyəmənts/ **42**–43
dog /dɔg/ **152**–16
doggie bag /ˈdɔgi bæg/
    offer a... /ˈɔfər ə/ **102**–20
doll /dɑl/ **224**–19
dolly /ˈdɑli/ **157**–19
dolphin /ˈdɑlfɪn/ **189**–2
dominoes /ˈdɑməˌnoʊz/ **224**–14
donkey /ˈdɑŋki/ **152**–24
do not enter /du nɑt ˈɛntər/ **118**–5
do not pass /du nɑt pæs/ **118**–4
door /dɔr/ **69**–12
doorbell /ˈdɔrˌbɛl/ **69**–13
door chain /dɔr ʧeɪn/ **67**–27
doorknob /ˈdɔrˌnɑb/ **67**–29
doorman /ˈdɔrˌmæn/ **67**–25
dorm /dɔrm/ **63**–18
dormitory /ˈdɔrmɪˌtɔri/ **63**–18
double room /ˈdʌbəl rum/ **159**–17
doughnut /ˈdoʊˌnʌt/ **90**–14
down /daʊn/ **130**–11
downhill skiing /ˈdaʊnˌhɪl ˈskiɪŋ/ **222**–12
down payment /ˈdaʊn ˈpeɪmənt/
    make a... /meɪk ə/ **65**–23
draft /dræft/
    type your... /taɪp yər/ **196**–25
    write a... /raɪt ə/ **196**–22
dragonfly /ˈdrægənˌflaɪ/ **190**–23
drain /dreɪn/ **75**–20
drama /ˈdrɑmə/ **208**–4
drama club /ˈdrɑmə klʌb/ **23**–23
draw /drɔ/ **203**–24
    ...blood /blʌd/ **137**–24
drawer /drɔr/ **74**–5
dress /drɛs/ **29**–11
dress /drɛs/ **104**–1
    ...clothes /kloʊz/ **111**–25
dresser /ˈdrɛsər/ **74**–6
dressing /ˈdrɛsɪŋ/
    salad... /ˈsæləd/ **88**–19
dressing room /ˈdrɛsɪŋ rum/
    go into a... /goʊ ˈɪntu ə/ **114**–3
drill /drɪl/ **165**–4
drill /drɪl/ **141**–31, **161**–28
drill bit /drɪl bɪt/ **161**–29
drink /drɪŋk/ **102**–12, **137**–28
drink /drɪŋk/
    spill a... /spɪl ə/ **102**–9

drips /drɪps/ **77**–5
drive /draɪv/ **123**–3, **151**–25
driver's license /ˈdraɪvərz ˈlaɪsəns/ **43**–18
drive-up window /ˈdraɪv-ˌʌp ˈwɪndoʊ/ **51**–21
driveway /ˈdraɪvˌweɪ/ **69**–18
drop-down menu /drɑp daʊn ˈmɛnyu/ **25**–8
drop off /drɑp ɔf/ **29**–18
dropper /ˈdrɑpər/ **194**–21
drought /draʊt/ **171**–3
drown /draʊn/ **136**–9
drug dealing /drʌg ˈdilɪŋ/ **61**–6
drugstore /ˈdrʌgˌstɔr/ **48**–25
drummer /ˈdrʌmər/ **205**–12
drums /drʌmz/ **207**–1
drumsticks /ˈdrʌmˌstɪks/ **87**–33
drunk driving /drʌnk ˈdraɪvɪŋ/ **61**–7
dry /draɪ/ **114**–19
    ...the dishes /ðə dɪʃəz/ **79**–23
dry clean /draɪ klin/ **115**–20
dry cleaner /draɪ ˈklinər/ **48**–17
dry clothes /draɪ kloʊz/ **116**–9
dryer /ˈdraɪər/ **116**–6
drying rack /ˈdraɪɪŋ ræk/ **70**–16
drywall /ˈdraɪwɔl/ **163**–4
    put up... /pʊt ʌp/ **165**–1
duck /dʌk/ **87**–32, **190**–14
duct tape /dʌkt teɪp/ **163**–31
dumpster /ˈdʌmpstər/ **67**–2
dump truck /dʌmp trʌk/ **118**–21
duplex /ˈduplɛks/ **63**–6
dusk /dʌsk/ **5**
dust /dʌst/ **79**–8
dust cloth /dʌst klɔθ/ **80**–10
dust mop /dʌst mɑp/ **80**–27
dustpan /ˈdʌstˌpæn/ **80**–2
DVD /ˌdiˌviˈdi/ **226**–1
DVD player /ˌdiˌviˈdi ˈpleɪər/ **226**–20
eagle /ˈigəl/ **190**–5
ear /ɪr/ **133**–35
earache /ˈɪrˌeɪk/ **135**–1
earmuffs /ˈɪrˌmʌfs/ **109**–28
    safety... /ˈseɪfti/ **157**–29
earplugs /ˈɪrˌplʌgz/ **157**–24
earrings /ˈɪrɪŋz/ **109**–9
Earth /ɜrθ/ **176**–25
EARTH AND SPACE /ɜrθ ənd speɪs/ **166**–**177**
earthquake /ˈɜrθˌkweɪk/ **171**–5
Earth's atmosphere /ɜrθs ˈætməsˌfɪr/ **176**–15
Earth's surface /ɜrθs ˈsɜrfəs/ **168**–**169**
easel /ˈizəl/ **203**–11
east /ist/ **130**–20
easy /ˈizi/ **14**–7
easy chair /ˈizi ʧɛr/ **72**–3
eat /it/ **102**–15
    ...breakfast /ˈbrɛkfəst/ **34**–9
    ...dinner /ˈdɪnər/ **34**–19
    ...lunch /lʌnʧ/ **34**–13
eclipse /ɪˈklɪps/ **176**–5
economy (class) /ɪˈkɑnəmi (klæs)/ **125**–23
edit /ˈɛdɪt/ **196**–24
editor /ˈɛdɪtər/ **146**–16
eel /il/ **189**–18
eggplant /ˈɛgˌplænt/ **84**–12
egg roll /ɛg roʊl/ **91**–22
eggs /ɛgz/ **88**–25
    carton of... /ˈkɑrtn ʌv/ **97**–23
    fry... /fraɪ/ **92**–8
    scramble... /ˈskræmbəl/ **92**–7
Egyptian /əˈʤɪpʃən/ **44**–18
eight /eɪt/ **2**
eighteen /eɪˈtin/ **2**

eighteenth /eɪˈtinθ/ **3**
eighth /eɪtθ/ **3**
eighty /ˈeɪti/ **2**
EKG /ˈiˌkeɪˈʤi/ **141**–9
elastic bandage /ɪˈlæstɪk ˈbændɪʤ/ **142**–19
elbow /ˈɛlboʊ/ **133**–9
electrical /ɪˈlɛktrəkəl/ **161**
electrical hazard /ɪˈlɛktrəkəl ˈhæzərd/ **156**–31
electrical tape /ɪˈlɛktrəkəl teɪp/ **160**–19
electrician /ɪˌlɛkˈtrɪʃən/ **77**–14, **147**–27
electric keyboard /ɪˈlɛktrɪk ˈkibɔrd/ **207**–25
electric pencil sharpener /ɪˈlɛktrɪk ˈpɛnsəl
    ʃɑrpənər/ **155**–20
electric razor /ɪˈlɛktrɪk ˈreɪzər/ **144**–19
electric shaver /ɪˈlɛktrɪk ˈʃeɪvər/ **144**–19
electric shock /ɪˈlɛktrɪk ʃɑk/
    get an... /gɛt ən/ **136**–14
electrocardiogram /ɪˌlɛktrəˈkɑrdiəˌgræm/ **141**–9
electronics store /ɪlɛkˈtrɑnɪks stɔr/ **48**–1
elects /ɪˈlɛkt/ **198**–20
element /ˈɛləmənt/ **194**–16
elephant /ˈɛləfənt/ **185**–10
elevator /ˈɛləˌveɪtər/ **67**–23
eleven /ɪˈlɛvən/ **2**
eleventh /ɪˈlɛvənθ/ **3**
elm (tree) /ɛlm (tri)/ **179**–6
e-mail (message) /ˈiˌmeɪl (ˈmɛsɪʤ)/ **25**–22
e-mail address /ˈiˌmeɪl əˈdrɛs/ **43**–10
embarrassed /ɛmˈbærəsd/ **38**–7
embroider /ɛmˈbrɔɪdər/ **224**–27
embroidered /ɛmˈbrɔɪdərd/ **113**–21
embroidery thread /ɛmˈbrɔɪdəri θrɛd/ **224**–23
emergency assistance /ɪˈmɜrʤənsi əˈsɪstəns/ **16**–3
emergency brake /ɪˈmɜrʤənsi breɪk/ **121**–28
emergency exit /ɪˈmɜrʤənsi ˈɛgzɪt/ **125**–25
emergency room /ɪˈmɜrʤənsi rum/ **139**–25
empty /ˈɛmpti/ **79**–13
empty /ˈɛmpti/ **14**–20
EMT /ˌiˌɛmˈti/ **139**–26
encourage /ɛnˈkɜrəʤ/ **29**–15
encyclopedia /ɛnˌsaɪkləˈpidiə/ **55**–9
ends /ɛndz/ **198**–14
end table /ɛnd ˈteɪbəl/ **72**–4
energy /ˈɛnərʤi/ **170**–**171**
    geothermal... /ˌʤioʊˈθɜrməl/ **171**–25
    nuclear... /ˈnukliər/ **171**–28
    solar... /ˈsoʊlər/ **171**–27
engine /ˈɛnʤɪn/ **121**–32
engineer /ˌɛnʤəˈnɪr/ **146**–22
enter /ˈɛntər/ **37**–3
    ...your password /yər ˈpæsˌwɜrd/ **24**–31
    ...your PIN /yər pɪn/ **51**–25
envelope /ˈɛnvəˌloʊp/ **52**–8
equals /ˈikwəlz/ **193**–3
Equator /ɪˈkweɪtər/ **174**–3
erase /ɪˈreɪs/ **20**–17
eraser /ɪˈreɪsər/ **19**–23
    blackboard... /ˈblækˌbɔrd/ **19**–4
escalator /ˈɛskəˌleɪtər/ **159**–10
essay /ˈɛseɪ/ **196**–5
    edit your... /ˈɛdɪt yər/ **196**–24
Europe /ˈyʊrəp/ **174**–10
evening /ˈivnɪŋ/ **5**
exam /ɪgˈzæm/ **19**–28
examine /ɪgˈzæmən/ **150**–2
    ...the patient /ðə ˈpeɪʃənt/ **137**–22
exchange /ɪksˈʧeɪnʤ/ **20**–5
excited /ɪkˈsaɪtɪd/ **39**–20
exclamation mark /ˌɛkskləˈmeɪʃən mɑrk/ **196**–13
exclamation point /ˌɛkskləˈmeɪʃən pɔɪnt/ **196**–13
Executive branch /ɪkˈzɛkyətɪv brænʧ/ **201**

exercise /ˈɛksərˌsaɪz/ **34**–16
expensive /ɪkˈspɛnsɪv/ **14**–15
explores /ɪkˈsplɔr/ **198**–8
explosive materials /ɪkˈsploʊsɪv məˈtɪriəlz/ **156**–32
extension cord /ɪkˈstɛnʃən kɔrd/ **160**–20
exterminator /ɪkˈstɜrməˌneɪtər/ **77**–18
eye /aɪ/ **133**–39
eyebrow /ˈaɪˌbraʊ/ **133**–34
eye chart /aɪ tʃɑrt/ **141**–21
eyedrops /ˈaɪˌdrɑps/ **142**–13
eyeglasses /ˈaɪglæsɪz/ **141**–24
eye hook /aɪ hʊk/ **163**–19
eyelashes /ˈaɪˌlæʃəs/ **133**–40
eyeliner /ˈaɪˌlaɪnər/ **144**–31
eye shadow /aɪ ˈʃædoʊ/ **144**–29
fabrics /ˈfæbrɪks/ **112**–113
fabric softener /ˈfæbrɪk ˈsɔfənər/ **116**–3
face /feɪs/ **32**–33, **133**–31
face powder /ˈfeɪs ˈpaʊdər/ **144**–26
factory /ˈfæktəri/ **47**–1, **156**–157
Fahrenheit /ˈfærənˌhaɪt/ **166**–2
fail /feɪl/
        ...a test /ə tɛst/ **18**–31
falcon /ˈfælkən/ **187**–19
fall /fɔl/ **7**–14
fall /fɔl/ **37**–10, **136**–15
fall in love /fɔl ɪn lʌv/ **31**–10
falls /fɔlz/ **198**–19
FAMILY /ˈfæməli/ **26**–31
family /ˈfæməli/ **26**–27
        raise a... /reɪz ə/ **31**–16
family name /ˈfæməli neɪm/ **43**–2
famine /ˈfæmɪn/ **171**–4
fan /fæn/ **220**–20
        ceiling... /ˈsilɪŋ/ **72**–16
fantasy /ˈfæntəsi/ **208**–8
fare /fɛr/ **128**–3
fare card /fɛr kɑrd/ **128**–21
far from /fɑr frəm/ **13**–2
farm /fɑrm/ **152**–153
farmer /ˈfɑrmər/ **152**–14
farmhand /ˈfɑrmhænd/ **152**–6
farmhouse /ˈfɑrmhaʊs/ **63**–8, **152**–15
farmworker /ˈfɑrmˌwɜrkər/ **152**–6
fast /fæʃ/ **15**–34
fasten /ˈfæsən/ **126**–12
fast food restaurant /fæst fud ˈrɛstərənt/ **48**–23
fat /fæt/ **15**–25
father /ˈfɑðər/ **27**–6
father-in-law /ˈfɑðər-ɪn-ˌlɔ/ **27**–10
faucet /ˈfɔsɪt/ **75**–27
        ...drips /ˈdrɪps/ **77**–5
fax machine /fæks məˈʃin/ **155**–2
feather duster /ˈfɛðər ˈdʌstər/ **80**–1
feather /ˈfɛðər/ **187**–23
February /ˈfɛbyuˌɛri/ **7**–17
feed /fid/ **29**–5, **153**–33
feedback /ˈfidˌbæk/
        get... /gɛt/ **196**–23
feel /fil/
        ...better /ˈbɛtər/ **137**–29
feelings /ˈfilɪŋz/ **38**–39
feet /fit/ **162**
female /ˈfiˌmeɪl/ **42**
fence /fɛns/ **69**–24
fender /ˈfɛndər/ **121**–31
fern /ˈfɜrn/ **182**–16
Ferris wheel /ˈfɛrɪs wil/ **214**–15
ferry /ˈfɛri/ **128**–17
fever /ˈfivər/ **135**–15

fiction section /ˈfɪkʃən ˈsɛkʃən/ **55**–6
field /fild/ **152**–9
fifteen /ˌfɪfˈtin/ **2**
fifteenth /ˌfɪfˈtinθ/ **3**
fifth /fɪfθ/ **3**
fifty /ˈfɪfti/ **2**
fifty cents /ˈfɪfti sɛnts/ **8**–5
fifty-dollar bill /ˈfɪfti-ˈdɑlər bɪl/ **8**–10
fifty dollars /ˈfɪfti ˈdɑlərz/ **8**–10
figs /fɪgz/ **83**–22
file /faɪl/ **151**–24
file /faɪl/ **25**–7, **160**–7
file cabinet /faɪl ˈkæbənɪt/ **155**–17
file folder /faɪl ˈfoʊldər/ **155**–19
filet of sole /fɪˈleɪ ʌv soʊl/ **87**–21
Filipino /fɪləˈpinoʊ/ **44**–28
fill in /ˈfɪl ɪn/ **21**–26
filling /ˈfɪlɪŋ/ **141**–27
film /fɪlm/
        roll of... /roʊl ʌv/ **226**–1
films /fɪlmz/ **208**–209
fin /fɪn/ **189**–5
find /faɪnd/ **126**–9
finding a place to live /ˈfaɪndɪŋ ə pleɪs tə lɪv/ **64**–65
fine arts /faɪn ɑrts/ **202**–203
finger /ˈfɪŋgər/ **133**–5
fingernail /ˈfɪŋgərˌneɪl/ **133**–23
fins /fɪnz/ **211**–27
fire /faɪr/ **72**–30
        forest... /ˈfɔrɪst/ **171**–1
firecracker /ˈfaɪrˌkrækər/ **228**–2
fire engine /faɪr ˈɛnʤɪn/ **118**–28
fire escape /faɪr ɪˈskeɪp/ **67**–19
fire extinguisher /faɪr ɪkˈstɪŋgwɪʃər/ **157**–17
firefighter /ˈfaɪrˌfaɪtər/ **147**–28
fire hydrant /faɪr ˈhaɪdrənt/ **58**–11
fireplace /ˈfaɪrˌpleɪs/ **72**–27
fire screen /faɪr skrin/ **72**–28
fire station /faɪr ˈsteɪʃən/ **47**–16
fireworks /ˈfaɪrˌwɜrks/ **228**–8
first /fɜrst/ **3**
first-aid kit /fɜrst-eɪd kɪt/ **143**–23
first class /fɜrst klæs/ **125**–22
first name /fɜrst neɪm/ **43**–3
fish /fɪʃ/ **213**–30
fish /fɪʃ/ **87**
fish and chips /fɪʃ ənd tʃɪps/ **90**–6
fisherman /ˈfɪʃərmən/ **213**–6
fishing pole /ˈfɪʃɪŋ poʊl/ **213**–5
fitness center /ˈfɪtnɪs ˈsɛntər/ **159**–19
fitness class /ˈfɪtnɪs klæs/ **218**–31
fittings /ˈfɪtɪŋz/ **160**–24
five /faɪv/ **2**
five after six /faɪv ˈæftər sɪks/ **5**
five cents /faɪv sɛnts/ **8**–2
five-dollar bill /faɪv-ˈdɑlər bɪl/ **8**–7
five dollars /faɪv ˈdɑlərz/ **8**–7
five of seven /faɪv ʌv ˈsɛvən/ **5**
five past six /faɪv pæst sɪks/ **5**
five to seven /faɪv tə ˈsɛvən/ **5**
fix /fɪks/ **150**–15
flag /flæg/ **19**–9
flamingo /fləˈmɪŋgoʊ/ **182**–15
flammable materials /ˈflæməbəl məˈtɪriəl/ **156**–33
flared /flɛrd/
        ...jeans /ʤinz/ **111**–10
flash drive /flæʃ draɪv/ **24**–16
flashlight /ˈflæʃˌlaɪt/ **163**–8
flask /flæsk/ **194**–24
flat tire /flæt taɪr/
        have a... /hæv ə/ **123**–21

flea market /fli 'markɪt/ 48-28
flight attendant /flaɪt ə'tɛndənt/ 125-26
flip flops /'flɪp,flaps/ 107-10
flipper /'flɪpər/ 187-18
float /floʊt/ 210-33
flood /flʌd/ 171-6
flooded /'flʌdəd/ 77-9
floor /flɔr/ 72-14
    mop the... /map ðə/ 79-12
    sweep the... /swip ðə/ 79-4
floral /'flɔrəl/ 113-16
florist /'flɔrɪst/ 146-14
flower /'flaʊər/ 179-14
flowers /'flaʊərz/ 228-12
    bouquet of... /boʊ'keɪ ʌv/ 97-6
flower stand /'flaʊər stænd/ 48-18
flu /flu/ 135-14
fluids /'fluɪdz/
    drink... /drɪŋk/ 137-28
flute /flut/ 207-12
fly /flaɪ/ 37-1, 198-13
fly /flaɪ/ 181-20
flyswatter /'flaɪ,swatər/ 80-22
fog /fɔg/ 166-16
foggy /'fɔgi/ 167-29
fold /foʊld/ 92-12
    ...the clothes /ðə kloʊz/ 79-5
folder /'foʊldər/ 25-5, 155-19
follow /'faloʊ/ 37-16
FOOD /fud/ 82-103
food processor /fud 'pra,sɛsər/ 94-8
food to go /'fud tə goʊ/ 90-91
foot (body) /fʊt/ 133-14
foot (measurement) /fʊt/ 162
football /'fʊt,bɔl/ 220-23, 220-27
football helmet /'fʊt,bɔl 'hɛlmɪt/ 220-25
forceps /'fɔr,sɛps/ 194-8
forehead /'fɔr,hɛd/ 133-33
forest /'fɔrɪst/ 169-16
forest fire /'fɔrɪst faɪr/ 171-1
fork /fɔrk/ 101-21
forklift /'fɔrk,lɪft/ 157-10
form /fɔrm/
    registration... /,rɛʤɪs'treɪʃən/ 43
formal /'fɔrməl/
    ...clothes /kloʊz/ 111-25
formula /'fɔrmyələ/ 57-19, 194-19
forty /'fɔrti/ 2
fossil /'fasəl/ 185-2
fountain /'faʊntn/ 58-7
four /fɔr/ 2
411 /fɔr wʌn wʌn/ 16-4
fourteen /,fɔr'tin/ 2
fourteenth /,fɔr'tinθ/ 3
fourth /fɔrθ/ 3
fox /faks/ 187-11
fraction /'frækʃən/ 193-30
fractions /'frækʃənz/ 3
frame /freɪm/ 203-1
freckles /'frɛkəl/ 33-6
freezer /'frizər/ 70-19
freezing /'frizɪŋ/ 166-7
French /frɛnʧ/ 44-12
french fries /frɛnʧ fraɪz/ 90-7
French horn /frɛnʧ hɔrn/ 207-7
Friday /'fraɪdeɪ/ 6-9
frog /frɔg/ 182-12
front office /frʌnt 'ɔfɪs/ 156-2
frozen /'froʊzən/ 77-8
frozen foods /'froʊzən fudz/ 99-4
frozen vegetables /'froʊzən 'vɛʤtəbəlz/ 88-1

frozen waffles /'froʊzən 'wafəlz/ 88-2
fruits /fruts/ 82-83
frustrated /'frʌ,streɪtəd/ 39-12
fry /fraɪ/ 92-8
frying pan /'fraɪɪŋ pæn/ 94-3
full /fʊl/ 14-19, 38-9
full moon /fʊl mun/ 177-32
full price /fʊl praɪs/ 9-21
funnel /'fʌnl/ 194-27
fur /fɜr/ 185-28
furnace /'fɜrnɪs/ 67-5
furnished apartment /'fɜrnɪʃd ə'partmənt/ 67-21
furniture /'fɜrnɪʧər/
    arrange the... /ə'reɪnʤ ðə/ 64-12
    polish the... /'palɪʃ ðə/ 79-9
furniture polish /'fɜrnɪʧər 'palɪʃ/ 80-9
furniture store /'fɜrnɪʧər stɔr/ 48-8
galaxy /'gæləksi/ 176-7
gallon /'gælən/ 97-21
gallon /'gælən/ 96
game system /geɪm 'sɪstəm/
    video... /'vɪdioʊ/ 226-17
games /geɪmz/ 224-225
game show /geɪm ʃoʊ/ 209-15
gang violence /gæŋ 'vaɪələns/ 61-14
garage /gə'raʒ/ 69-16
garage sale /gə'raʒ seɪl/ 216-9
garbage can /'garbɪʤ kæn/ 69-19, 214-9
garbage disposal /'garbɪʤ dɪ'spoʊzəl/ 70-17
garbage truck /'garbɪʤ trʌk/ 118-14
garbanzo beans /gar'banzoʊ binz/ 84-10
garden /'gardn/ 68-69, 69-21, 178-179
    weed the... /wid ðə/ 79-15
gardener /'gardnər/ 146-8
garden hose /'gardn hoʊz/ 69-27
garlic /'garlɪk/ 85-29
    dice... /daɪs/ 92-2
    whisk... /wɪsk/ 92-3
garment worker /'garmənt 'wɜrkər/ 147-29
gas /gæs/ 194-12
    get... /gɛt/ 123-15
    natural... /'næʧərəl/ 171-22
gas gauge /gæs geɪʤ/ 121-15
gas meter /gæs 'mitər/ 77-20
gas pedal /gæs 'pɛdl/ 121-27
gas station /gæs 'steɪʃən/ 47-20
gas tank /gæs tæŋk/ 121-7
gate /geɪt/ 69-23, 125-14
    wait at the... /weɪt ət ðə/ 126-7
gauze /gɔz/ 143-24
gazelle /gə'zɛl/ 185-15
gearshift /'gɪr,ʃɪft/ 121-23
gender /'ʤɛndər/ 43-5
general practitioner /'ʤɛnərəl præk'tɪʃənər/ 141-20
geometry /ʤi'amətri/ 193-31
geothermal energy /,ʤioʊ'θɜrməl 'ɛnərʤi/ 171-25
geraniums /ʤə'reɪniəmz/ 179-30
German /'ʤɜrmən/ 44-11
get /gɛt/
    ... a speeding ticket /ə 'spidɪŋ 'tɪkɪt/ 123-6
    ...a job /ə ʤab/ 31-8
    ...a(n electric) shock /ə(n ɪ'lɛktrɪk) ʃak/ 136-14
    ...a text /ə tɛkst/ 17-29
    ...feedback /'fid,bæk/ 196-23
    ...gas /gæs/ 123-15
    ...the key /ðə ki/ 64-8
    ...your boarding pass /yər 'bɔrdɪŋ pæs/ 126-4
get dressed /gɛt drɛsd/ 34-8
get engaged /gɛt ɛn'geɪʤd/ 31-11
get in /gɛt ɪn/ 37-7
get married /gɛt 'mærid/ 31-12

get off /gɛt ɔf/ **37**-14
   ...the highway /ðə ˈhaɪˌweɪ/ **123**-9
   ...the plane /ðə pleɪn/ **126**-23
get on /gɛt ɑn/ **37**-13
   ...the highway /ðə ˈhaɪˌweɪ/ **123**-12
get out (of) /gɛt aʊt (ʌv)/ **37**-6
get sick /gɛt sɪk/ **31**-18
get up /gɛt ʌp/ **34**-2
gift /gɪft/ **228**-11
   give a... /gɪv ə/ **40**-7
gift shop /gɪft ʃɑp/ **48**-4, **159**-22
gills /gɪlz/ **189**-4
giraffe /ʤəˈræf/ **185**-6
girdle /ˈgɜrdl/ **107**-21
girl /gɜrl/ **57**-13
give /gɪv/
   ...a gift /ə gɪft/ **40**-7
   ...a shot /ə ʃɑt/ **137**-25
glacier /ˈgleɪʃər/ **169**-4
glass /glæs/ **70**-25
   refill the... /ˈriˌfɪl ðə/ **102**-14
   water... /ˈwɔtər/ **101**-16
glass cleaner /glæs ˈklinər/ **80**-11
glasses /ˈglæsɪz/ **33**-28, **141**-24
   safety... /ˈseɪfti/ **157**-25
globe /ˈgloʊb/ **19**-10
glove compartment /glʌv kəmˈpartmənt/ **121**-18
gloves /glʌvz/ **109**-1
glue /glu/ **155**-24
glue /glu/ **165**-24
go /goʊ/
   ...home /hoʊm/ **34**-14
   ...to bed /tə bɛd/ **34**-23
   ...to college /tə ˈkalɪʤ/ **31**-6
   ...to the board /tə ðə bɔrd/ **20**-16
   ...to work /tə wɜrk/ **34**-11
goal /goʊl/ **223**-21
goalpost /ˈgoʊlˌpoʊst/ **220**-24
goat /goʊt/ **152**-21
go down /goʊ daʊn/ **37**-22
goggles /ˈgagəlz/
   safety... /ˈseɪfti/ **157**-23
go in /goʊ ɪn/ **37**-3
go into /goʊ ˈɪntu/
   ...a dressing room /ə ˈdrɛsɪŋ rum/ **114**-3
gold /goʊld/ **10**-13
golf /galf/ **220**-12
golf club /galf klʌb/ **220**-13
golf course /galf kɔrs/ **220**-15
golfer /galfər/ **220**-14
goose /gus/ **152**-19, **187**-1
gopher /ˈgoʊfər/ **185**-19
gorilla /gəˈrɪlə/ **182**-7
go shopping /goʊ ˈʃapɪŋ/ **114**-1
go through /goʊ θru/
   ...security /səˈkyʊrəti/ **126**-5
go up /goʊ ʌp/ **37**-21
gown /gaʊn/ **104**-5
GP /ʤi pi/ **141**-20
grade /greɪd/ **19**-27
graduate /ˈgræʤuˌeɪt/
   ...from high school /frəm haɪ skul/ **31**-5
graduated cylinder /ˈgræʤuˌeɪtɪd ˈsɪləndər/ **194**-20
graduation /ˌgræʤuˈeɪʃən/ **23**-12
graffiti /grəˈfiti/ **61**-9
gram /græm/ **96**
grandchildren /ˈgrænˌʧɪldrən/ **27**-23
grandfather /ˈgrænˌfaðər/ **27**-1
grandmother /ˈgrænˌmʌðər/ **27**-2
grandparent /ˈgrænˌpɛrənt/
   become a... /bɪˈkʌm ə/ **31**-21

grandparents /ˈgrænˌpɛrəntz/ **27**-24
grapefruit /ˈgreɪpˌfrut/ **83**-9
grapes /greɪps/ **83**-5
graphic artist /ˈgræfɪk ˈartɪst/ **146**-7
grass /græs/ **69**-8
   mow the... /moʊ ðə/ **79**-17
grasshopper /ˈgræsˌhapər/ **181**-19
grasslands /ˈgræsˌlændz/ **184**-185
grate /greɪt/ **92**-11
grater /ˈgreɪtər/ **94**-13
gray /greɪ/ **10**-23
gray hair /greɪ hɛr/ **33**-5
grease /gris/ **93**-26
Greek /grik/ **44**-15
green /grin/ **10**-5
green beans /grin binz/ **85**-28
green card /grin kard/ **43**-17
greenhouse /ˈgrinˌhaʊs/ **179**-8
green onions /grin ˈʌnyənz/ **85**-27
greet /grit/ **40**-2
greeting card /ˈgritɪŋ kard/ **52**-3
grill /grɪl/ **92**-6
grill /grɪl/ **69**-6, **94**-4
grizzly bear /ˈgrɪzli bɛr/ **187**-5
groceries /ˈgroʊsəri/ **99**-22
ground beef /graʊnd bif/ **87**-8
groundhog /ˈgraʊndˌhɔg/ **190**-10
group /grup/
   talk with a... /tɔk wɪð ə/ **21**-20
grow /groʊ/ **29**-26, **198**-5
grow up /groʊ ʌp/ **29**-27
guest /gɛst/
   hotel... /hoʊˈtɛl/ **159**-4
guidance counselor /ˈgaɪdns ˈkaʊnslər/ **23**-17
guitar /gɪˈtar/ **207**-22
guitarist /gɪˈtarɪst/ **205**-15
gums /gʌmz/ **141**-30
gun /gʌn/
   caulking... /kɔkɪŋ/ **160**-8
gym /ʤɪm/ **23**-4, **48**-13, **67**-15, **216**-14
gymnast /ˈʤɪmˌnəst/ **218**-24
gymnastics /ʤɪmˈnæstɪks/ **218**-23
hacksaw /ˈhækˌsɔ/ **160**-11
hail /heɪl/ **166**-18
hailstone /ˈheɪlˌstoʊn/ **166**-21
hair /hɛr/ **32**-33, **133**-32
   comb... /koʊm/ **34**-5
hairbrush /ˈhɛrˌbrʌʃ/ **144**-10
hairdresser /ˈhɛrˌdrɛsər/ **146**-5
hair dryer /hɛr ˈdraɪər/ **144**-6
hair gel /hɛr ʤɛl/ **144**-4
hairnet /ˈhɛrˌnɛt/ **157**-20
hair salon /hɛr səˈlan/ **48**-11
hairspray /ˈhɛrˌspreɪ/ **144**-1
hairstylist /ˈhɛrˌstaɪlɪst/ **146**-5
half /hæf/ **3**
half dollar /hæf ˈdalər/ **8**-5
half past six /hæf pæst sɪks/ **5**
half sister /hæf ˈsɪstər/ **27**-13
halibut /ˈhæləbət/ **189**-30
Halloween /ˌhæləˈwin/ **228**-13
hallway /ˈhɔlˌweɪ/ **67**-12
ham /hæm/ **87**-4
hamburger /ˈhæmˌbɜrgər/ **90**-4
hammer /ˈhæmər/ **165**-9
hammer /ˈhæmər/ **160**-9
hammock /ˈhæmək/ **69**-7
hand /hænd/ **133**-4
   raise your... /reɪz yər/ **20**-1
handbag /ˈhændˌbæg/ **109**-2

hand cream /hænd krim/
    tube of... /tub ʌv/ **97**–9
handcuffs /ˈhændˌkʌfs/ **61**–20
handicapped parking space /ˈhændiˌkæpt parkɪŋ speɪs/
    58–14
hand in /hænd ɪn/
    ...your paper /yər ˈpeɪpər/ **20**–2
hand mixer /hænd ˈmɪksər/ **95**–19
hand out /hænd aʊt/
    ...papers /ˈpeɪpərz/ **21**–18
handsaw /ˈhændˌsɔ/ **160**–6
hand tools /hænd tulz/ **160**
hand truck /hænd trʌk/ **157**–19
handyman /ˈhændiˌmæn/ **77**–17
hang /hæŋ/ **183**–28
hang (up) /hæŋ (ʌp)/ **115**–24
hanger /ˈhæŋər/ **117**–11
hang up /hæŋ ʌp/
    ...the phone /ððə foʊn/ **17**–27
happy /ˈhæpi/ **38**–2
hard /hard/ **14**–9
hardcover (book) /ˈhardˌkʌvər (bʊk)/ **55**–12
hard hat /hard hæt/ **156**–8
hardware /ˈhardˌwɛr/ **163**
harmonica /harˈmanɪkə/ **207**–17
harp /harp/ **207**–24
hat /hæt/ **104**–17
    hard... /hard/ **156**–8
    knit... /nɪt/ **109**–26
have /hæv/
    ...a conversation /ə ˌkanvərˈseɪʃən/ **17**–26, **40**–6
    ...a flat tire /ə flæt taɪr/ **123**–21
    ...a heart attack /ə hart əˈtæk/ **136**–13
    ...an accident /ən ˈæksədənt/ **123**–19
    ...an allergic reaction /ən əˈlɜrdzɪk riˈækʃən/
        136–12
    ...breakfast /ˈbrɛkfəst/ **34**–9
    ...dinner /ˈdɪnər/ **34**–19
    ...lunch /lʌntʃ/ **34**–13
have a baby /hæv ə ˈbeɪbi/ **31**–15
hawk /hɔk/ **181**–1
hay /heɪ/ **152**–13
hazardous waste /ˈhæzərdəs weɪst/ **171**–18
head /hɛd/ **133**–19
headache /ˈhɛdˌeɪk/ **135**–13
headlight /ˈhɛdˌlaɪt/ **121**–37
headlights /ˈhɛdˌlaɪts/
    turn on the... /tɜrn an ði/ **123**–7
headline /ˈhɛdˌlaɪn/ **55**–17
headphones /ˈhɛdˌfoʊnz/ **226**–9
    put on your... /pʊt an yər/ **126**–16
headset /ˈhɛdˌsɛt/ **16**–16
healing /ˈhilɪŋ/ **136**–137
HEALTH /hɛlθ/ **132**–145
health aide /hɛlθ eɪd/ **146**–21
health club /hɛlθ klʌb/ **48**–13
hear /hɪr/ **17**–24
heart /hart/ **133**–26, **224**–10
heart attack /hart əˈtæk/
    have a... /hæv ə/ **136**–13
heater /ˈhitər/ **121**–20
    ...doesn't work /ˈdʌzənt wɜrk/ **77**–7
heating pad /ˈhitɪŋ pæd/ **142**–21
heavy /ˈhɛvi/ **14**–23, **15**–25
    ...jacket /ˈdʒækɪt/ **111**–2
hedge clippers /hɛdʒ ˈklɪpərz/ **69**–25
heel /hil/ **133**–17
    high... /haɪ/ **109**–18
heels /hilz/
    high... /haɪ/ **111**–22
    low... /loʊ/ **111**–23

height /haɪt/ **193**
helicopter /ˈhɛliˌkaptər/ **125**–12
helmet /ˈhɛlmɪt/
    football... /ˈfʊtˌbɔl/ **220**–25
help /hɛlp/ **29**–16, **40**–19
hem /hɛm/ **117**–18
high /haɪ/
    ...heels /hilz/ **111**–22
high chair /haɪ tʃɛr/ **57**–18, **101**–17
high heel /haɪ hil/ **109**–17
high rise (building) /haɪ raɪz (ˈbɪldɪŋ)/ **47**–22
high school /haɪ skul/
    graduate from... /ˈgrædʒuˌeɪt frəm/ **31**–5
high school diploma /haɪ skul dɪˈploʊmə/
    43–28
highway /ˈhaɪˌweɪ/
    get off the... /gɛt ɔf ðə/ **123**–9
    get on the... /gɛt an ðə/ **123**–12
hike /haɪk/ **213**–31
hiker /ˈhaɪkər/ **213**–4
hiking boot /ˈhaɪkɪŋ but/ **109**–21
hiking trail /ˈhaɪkɪŋ treɪl/ **213**–14, **216**–11
hill /hɪl/ **169**–22
hinge /hɪndʒ/ **163**–25
hip /hɪp/ **133**–12
hip hop /hɪp hap/ **209**–27
hippopotamus /ˌhɪpəˈpatəməs/ **185**–7
hire /haɪr/ **150**–13
hobbies /ˈhabiz/ **224**–225
hockey /ˈhaki/
    ice... /aɪs/ **223**–17
hockey player /ˈhaki ˈpleɪər/ **223**–22
hockey puck /ˈhaki pʌk/ **223**–24
hockey stick /ˈhaki stɪk/ **223**–23
hold /hoʊld/ **29**–4
hole /hoʊl/
    drill a... /drɪl ə/ **165**–4
hole punch /hoʊl pʌntʃ/ **155**–29
holidays /ˈhaləˌdeɪz/ **228**–229
home /hoʊm/
    go... /goʊ/ **34**–14
home attendant /hoʊm əˈtɛndənt/ **146**–21
home health aide /hoʊm hɛlθ eɪd/ **146**–21
homemaker /ˈhoʊmˌmeɪkər/ **146**–13
homesick /ˈhoʊmˌsɪk/ **39**–16
homework /ˈhoʊmˌwɜrk/
    do... /du/ **34**–17
homework assignment /ˈhoʊmˌwɜrk əˈsaɪnmənt/
    19–5
honey /ˈhʌni/
    jar of... /dʒar ʌv/ **97**–24
honk /haŋk/ **123**–14
hood /hʊd/ **121**–30
hoof /hʊf/ **185**–22
hook /hʊk/ **163**–27
hop /hap/ **183**–27
horn /hɔrn/ **121**–21, **185**–23
    honk the... /haŋk ððə/ **123**–14
hornet /ˈhɔrnɪt/ **190**–26
horror /ˈhɔrər/ **208**–9
horse /hɔrs/ **152**–22
horseback rider /ˈhɔrsˌbæk ˈraɪdər/ **213**–3
hose /hoʊz/
    garden... /ˈgardn/ **69**–27
hospital /ˈhaspɪtl/ **47**–8, **118**–3, **138**–139
hospital gown /ˈhaspɪtl gaʊn/ **139**–20
hot /hat/ **15**–29, **166**–3
hot dog /hat dɔg/ **90**–8
hotel /hoʊˈtɛl/ **58**–1, **158**–159
hotel guest /hoʊˈtɛl gɛst/ **159**–4
hour /ˈaʊər/ **4**

house /haʊs/ **63**–1, **68–69**
    buy a... /baɪ ə/ **31**–13
    inspect the... /ɪnˈspɛkt ðə/ **65**–21
    wire a... /waɪr ə/ **165**–8
houseboat /ˈhaʊsˌboʊt/ **63**–13
household chores /ˈhaʊsˌhoʊld ʧɔrz/ **78–79**
household cleaners /ˈhaʊsˌhoʊld ˈklinərz/ **99**–9
household problems /ˈhaʊsˌhoʊld ˈprɑbləmz/ **76–77**
housekeeper /ˈhaʊsˌkipər/ **146**–15, **159**–1
housekeeping cart /ˈhaʊsˌkipɪŋ kɑrt/ **159**–2
House of Representatives /haʊs ʌv ˌrɛprəˈzɛntətɪvz/ **201**
house painter /ˈhaʊsˌpeɪntər/ **148**–14
house payment /ˈhaʊs ˈpeɪmənt/
    make the... /meɪk ðə/ **65**–26
house plant /ˈhaʊsˌplænt/ **72**–29
houses /ˈhaʊzɪz/
    look at... /lʊk ət/ **65**–17
housework /ˈhaʊsˌwɜrk/
    do... /du/ **34**–21
HOUSING /ˈhaʊzɪŋ/ **62–81**
hug /hʌg/ **40**–17
human body /ˈhyumən ˈbɑdi/ **132–133**
humidifier /hyuˈmɪdəˌfaɪər/ **143**–32
hummingbird /ˈhʌmɪŋˌbɜrd/ **182**–10
hungry /ˈhʌŋgri/ **38**–10
hurricane /ˈhɜrəˌkeɪn/ **171**–8
hurting /ˈhɜrtɪŋ/ **136–137**
husband /ˈhʌzbənd/ **27**–18
hydrant /ˈhaɪdrənt/
    fire... /faɪr/ **58**–11
hydroelectric power /ˌhaɪdroʊɪˈlɛktrɪk ˈpaʊər/ **171**–29
hydrogen peroxide /ˈhaɪdrəʤən pəˈrɑkˌsaɪd/ **142**–22
hyena /haɪˈinə/ **185**–5
hygienist /haɪˈʤinɪst/
    dental... /ˈdɛntl/ **141**–25
hyphen /ˈhaɪfən/ **196**–19
ice /aɪs/ **166**–24
iceberg /ˈaɪsˌbɜrg/ **187**–10
ice cream /aɪs krim/ **88**–3
ice cream stand /aɪs krim stænd/ **48**–27
iced tea /aɪsd ti/ **88**–9
ice hockey /aɪs ˈhɑki/ **223**–17
ice pack /aɪs pæk/ **143**–33
ice (skating) rink /aɪs (ˈskeɪtɪŋ) rɪŋk/ **223**–20
ice skater /aɪs ˈskeɪtər/ **222**–10
ice skates /aɪs ˈskeɪts/ **223**–25
ice skating /aɪs ˈskeɪtɪŋ/ **222**–9
ice tray /aɪs treɪ/ **88**–4
icons /ˈaɪˌkɑnz/ **25**–9
ID /ˈaɪˈdi/
    photo... /ˈfoʊtoʊ/ **124**–3
    show your... /ʃoʊ yər/ **126**–2
    student... /ˈstudnt/ **43**–19
ideas /aɪˈdiəz/
    brainstorm... /ˈbreɪnˌstɔrm/ **196**–20
    discuss your... /dɪˈskʌs yər/ **20**–11
identity theft /aɪˈdɛntətiˌθɛft/ **60**–1
igloo /ˈɪglu/ **63**–15
ignition /ɪgˈnɪʃən/ **121**–22
ill /ɪl/ **39**–14
illnesses /ˈɪlnɪsɪz/ **134–135**
immigrate /ˈɪməˌgreɪt/ **31**–4
immigration /ˌɪməˈgreɪʃən/ **125**–20
in /ɪn/ **13**–5
inch /ɪnʧ/ **163**–1
indentation /ˌɪndɛnˈteɪʃən/ **196**–6
Independence Day /ˌɪndəˈpɛndəns deɪ/ **228**–7
Indian /ˈɪndiən/ **44**–22
indoor sports and fitness /ˈɪnˌdɔr spɔrts ənd ˈfɪtnɪs/ **218–219**
infant /ˈɪnfənt/ **30, 56**–32
informal /ɪnˈfɔrməl/

...clothes /kloʊz/ **111**–24
information /ˌɪnfərˈmeɪʃən/ **16**–4
in front of /ɪn frʌnt ʌv/ **13**–17
inhaler /ɪnˈheɪlər/ **142**–11
injuries /ˈɪn ʤəriz/ **134–135**
in-line skates /ˈɪn-ˌlaɪn skeɪts/ **214**–24
in love /ɪn lʌv/ **38**–8
insect repellent /ˈɪnsɛkt rəˈpɛlənt/ **213**–22
insect spray /ˈɪnsɛkt spreɪ/ **80**–15
insert /ɪnˈsɜrt/ **51**–24
inside /ˈɪnˌsaɪd/ **13**–5
inside the refrigerator /ˈɪnˌsaɪd ðə rɪˈfrɪʤəˌreɪtər/ **88–89**
inspect /ɪnˈspɛkt/
    ...the house /ði haʊs/ **65**–21
install /ɪnˈstɔl/ **165**–13
instructor /ɪnˈstrʌktər/ **148**–9
instruments /ˈɪnstrəmənts/ **206–207**
insulation /ˌɪnsəˈleɪʃən/ **163**–6
intensive care unit /ɪnˈtɛnsɪv kɛr ˈyunɪt/ **138**–3
intercom /ˈɪntərˌkɑm/ **67**–30
interest /ˈɪntrɪst/ **51**–15
interested /ˈɪntrɪstɪd/ **38**–4
international call /ˌɪntərˈnæʃənəl kɔl/ **16**–11
Internet /ˈɪntərˌnɛt/ **25**–29
intersection /ˈɪntərˌsɛkʃən/ **47**–26
into /ˈɪntu/ **130**–3
intravenous drip /ˌɪntrəˈvinəs drɪp/ **138**–4
introduce /ˌɪntrəˈdus/ **40**–15
introduces /ˌɪntrəˈdusɪz/ **198**–17
invents /ɪnˈvɛnts/ **198**–12
invite /ɪnˈvaɪt/ **40**–23
Iranian /ɪˈraniən/ **44**–17
irises /ˈaɪrɪsɪz/ **179**–19
iron /ˈaɪərn/ **115**–23
iron /ˈaɪərn/ **116**–2
ironing board /ˈaɪərnɪŋ bɔrd/ **116**–1
island /ˈaɪlənd/ **169**–8
Italian /ɪˈtælyən/ **44**–14
IV /ˈaɪˈvi/ **138**–4
ivory /ˈaɪvəri/ **10**–21
ivy /ˈaɪvi/ **179**–27
jack /ʤæk/ **121**–2, **224**–5
jacket /ˈʤækɪt/ **104**–16
    heavy... /ˈhɛvi/ **111**–2
    light... /laɪt/ **111**–1
jack-o-lantern /ˈʤæk-ə-ˌlæntərn/ **229**–15
jail /ʤeɪl/ **61**–27
jam /ʤæm/ **88**–17
jammed /ʤæmd/ **77**–11
janitor /ˈʤænətər/ **146**–11
January /ˈʤænyuˌɛri/ **7**–16
Japanese /ˌʤæpəˈniz/ **44**–25
jar /ʤɑr/ **97**–24
jazz /ʤæz/ **209**–23
jeans /ʤinz/ **104**–27
    flared... /flɛrd/ **111**–10
    straight leg... /streɪt lɛg/ **111**–11
jellyfish /ˈʤɛliˌfɪʃ/ **189**–11
jewelry /ˈʤuəlri/ **109**–13
jewelry store /ˈʤuəlri stɔr/ **48**–5
job /ʤɑb/
    get a... /gɛt ə/ **31**–8
jobs /ʤɑbz/ **146–149**
jockstrap /ˈʤɑkˌstræp/ **107**–28
jog /ʤɑg/ **37**–8
jogger /ˈʤɑgər/ **214**–20
joker /ˈʤoʊkər/ **224**–6
judge /ʤʌʤ/ **61**–24
Judicial branch /ʤuˈdɪʃəl brænʧ/ **201**
July /ʤuˈlaɪ/ **7**–22
jump /ʤʌmp/ **37**–20

jumper cables /ˈʤʌmpər ˈkeɪbəlz/ **121**–34
June /ʤun/ **7**–21
jungle gym /ˈʤʌŋɡəl ʤɪm/ **214**–6
Jupiter /ˈʤupətər/ **176**–23
jury /ˈʤʊri/ **61**–23
   serve on a... /sɜrv ɑn ə/ **201**–17
justice /ˈʤʌstɪs/ **60**–61
justices /ˈʤʌstɪsəz/ **200**–13
kangaroo /ˌkæŋɡəˈru/ **185**–4
ketchup /ˈkɛʧəp/ **90**–17
kettle /ˈkɛtl/ **70**–7
key /ki/ **25**–18, **67**–31
keyboard /ˈkibɔrd/ **25**–21, **207**
   electric... /ɪˈlɛktrɪk/ **207**–25
key chain /ki ʧeɪn/ **109**–29
kidney /ˈkɪdni/ **133**–30
kidney beans /ˈkɪdni binz/ **84**–18
killer whale /ˈkɪlər weɪl/ **189**–7
kilogram /ˈkɪləˌɡræm/ **96**
kilometer /kɪˈlɑmɪtər/ **162**
king /kɪŋ/ **224**–3
kiss /kɪs/ **40**–21
kitchen /ˈkɪʧən/ **70**–71
kitchen timer /ˈkɪʧən ˈtaɪmər/ **94**–7
kite /kaɪt/ **214**–1
kiwi /ˈkiwi/ **83**–2
knee /ni/ **133**–45
knee brace /ni breɪs/ **142**–18
kneel /nil/ **37**–24
knife /naɪf/ **101**–24
   pocket... /ˈpɑkɪt/ **213**–21
knit /nɪt/ **224**–25
knit hat /nɪt hæt/ **109**–26
knitting needles /ˈnɪtɪŋ ˈnidlz/ **224**–20
koala /koʊˈɑlə/ **185**–3
Korean /kəˈriən/ **44**–24
lab /læb/ **139**–14
label /ˈleɪbəl/ **155**–31
laboratory /ˈlæbrəˌtɔri/ **139**–14
lab technician /læb tɛkˈnɪʃən/ **139**–15
lace /leɪs/ **113**–11
ladder /ˈlædər/
   climb a... /klaɪm ə/ **165**–14
ladle /ˈleɪdl/ **94**–11
ladybug /ˈleɪdiˌbʌɡ/ **190**–27
lake /leɪk/ **169**–7
lamb /læm/ **86**
   leg of... /lɛɡ ʌv/ **87**–2
lamb chops /læm ʧɑpz/ **87**–1
lamp /læmp/ **72**–5
lampshade /ˈlæmpˌʃeɪd/ **72**–6
land /lænd/ **126**–21
landlord /ˈlændˌlɔrd/
   meet the... /mit ðə/ **64**–3
landscape /ˈlændˌskeɪp/ **203**–4
language lab /ˈlæŋɡwɪʤ læb/ **23**–3
lantern /ˈlæntərn/ **213**–16
laptop (computer) /ˈlæpˌtɑp (kəmˈpyutər)/ **25**–23
large /lɑrʤ/ **14**–2
lasagna /ləˈzanyə/ **90**–2
last name /læst neɪm/ **43**–2
latex gloves /ˈleɪˌtɛks ɡlʌvz/ **139**–12
launches /lɔnʧez/ **198**–15
laundromat /ˈlɔndrəˌmæt/ **48**–22
laundry /ˈlɔndri/ **116**–117
   do the... /du ðə/ **79**–3
laundry basket /ˈlɔndri ˈbæskɪt/ **116**–10
laundry detergent /ˈlɔndri dɪˈtɜrʤənt/ **116**–4
laundry room /ˈlɔndri rum/ **67**–18
law /lɔ/
   obey the... /oʊˈbeɪ ðə/ **201**–15

lawn /lɔn/ **69**–8
   mow the... /moʊ ðə/ **79**–17
   water the... /ˈwɔtər ðə/ **79**–18
lawn mower /lɔn moʊər/ **69**–9
lawyer /ˈlɔyər/ **61**–25, **148**–3
lay /leɪ/
   ...bricks /ˈbrɪks/ **165**–5
lead /lid/ **37**–17
leaf /lif/ **179**–13
leaks /liks/ **77**–3
learn /lɜrn/ **31**–2
lease /lis/
   sign the... /saɪn ðə/ **64**–6
leather /ˈlɛðər/ **113**–5
leave /liv/ **37**–2, **123**–2
   ...a tip /ə tɪp/ **102**–23
leaves /livz/
   rake the... /reɪk ðə/ **79**–20
lecture /ˈlɛkʧər/ **216**–12
left /lɛft/ **130**–15
leg /lɛɡ/ **133**–14
   break a... /breɪk ə/ **136**–5
Legislative branch /ˈlɛʤɪsˌleɪtɪv brænʧ/ **201**
leg of lamb /lɛɡ ʌv læm/ **87**–2
legs /lɛɡz/ **87**–33
lemon /ˈlɛmən/ **83**–14
lemonade /ˌlɛmənˈeɪd/
   pitcher of... /ˈpɪʧər ʌv/ **97**–14
lens /lɛnz/
   contact... /ˈkɑnˌtækt/ **141**–22
leopard /ˈlɛpərd/ **185**–11
leotard /ˈliəˌtard/ **107**–18
letter /ˈlɛtər/ **52**–2, **196**–1
   write a... /raɪt ə/ **40**–8
letter carrier /ˈlɛtər ˈkæriər/ **52**–10
letterhead /ˈlɛtərˌhɛd/ **155**–12
lettuce /ˈlɛtəs/ **84**–5
level /ˈlɛvəl/ **160**–16
librarian /laɪˈbrɛriən/ **55**–10
library /ˈlaɪˌbrɛri/ **47**–18, **54**–55
   school... /skul/ **23**–6
library card /ˈlaɪˌbrɛri kard/ **55**–11
lice /laɪs/ **135**–4
license plate /ˈlaɪsəns pleɪt/ **121**–8
lid /lɪd/ **94**–6
life events /laɪf ɪˈvɛnts/ **30**–31
lifeguard /ˈlaɪfˌɡard/ **211**–17
life jacket /laɪf ˈʤækɪt/ **211**–14
light /laɪt/ **102**–3
   ...candles /ˈkændls/ **229**–30
light /laɪt/ **14**–24
   ...jacket /ˈʤækɪt/ **111**–1
lightbulb /ˈlaɪtˌbʌlb/ **160**–22
   ...is burned out /ɪz ˈbɜrnd aʊt/ **77**–6
lighthouse /ˈlaɪtˌhaʊs/ **211**–7
lightning /ˈlaɪtnɪŋ/ **166**–15
lights /laɪts/ **229**–21
light switch /laɪt swɪʧ/ **72**–24
lilac bush /ˈlaɪˌlæk bʊʃ/ **179**–7
lilies /ˈlɪliz/ **179**–20
lima beans /ˈlaɪmə binz/ **84**–21
lime /laɪm/ **83**–20
lime green /laɪm grin/ **10**–7
limo /ˈlɪmoʊ/ **118**–18
limousine /ˌlɪməˈzin/ **118**–18
line /laɪn/ **125**–21
   curved... /kɜrvd/ **193**–8
   straight... /streɪt/ **193**–7
   subway... /ˈsʌbˌweɪ/ **128**–16
   wait in... /weɪt ɪn/ **51**–23
linen /ˈlɪnən/ **113**–7

lines /laɪnz/
    parallel... /ˈpærəˌlɛl/ **193**–12
    perpendicular... /ˌpɜrpənˈdɪkyələr/ **193**–11
lion /ˈlaɪən/ **185**–20
lip /lɪp/ **133**–42
lipstick /ˈlɪpˌstɪk/ **144**–27
liquid /ˈlɪkwɪd/ **194**–11
listen /ˈlɪsən/ **20**–12, **126**–17
liter /ˈlitər/ **97**–17
liter /ˈlitər/ **96**
litter /ˈlɪtər/ **171**–21
little /ˈlɪtl/ **14**–1
liver /ˈlɪvər/ **87**–12, **133**–28
living room /ˈlɪvɪŋ rum/ **72**–73
lizard /ˈlɪzərd/ **181**–10
load /loʊd/ **150**–6
    ...a van or truck /ə væn ɔr trʌk/ **64**–10
loading dock /loʊdɪŋ dak/ **157**–18
loaf /loʊf/ **97**–16
loafer /ˈloʊfər/ **109**–20
loan /loʊn/ **65**–22
loan documents /loʊn ˈdakyəmənts/
    sign the... /saɪn ðə/ **65**–24
loan officer /loʊn ˈɔfəsər/ **51**–9
lobby /ˈlabi/ **67**–22, **159**–9
lobster /ˈlabstər/ **87**–14
local call /ˈloʊkəl kɔl/ **16**–9
lock /lak/
    dead-bolt... /dɛd-boʊlt/ **67**–28
    ...is jammed /ɪz ʤæmd/ **77**–11
locker /ˈlækər/ **23**–15
locker room /ˈlækər rum/ **218**–35
locksmith /ˈlakˌsmɪθ/ **77**–22, **148**–7
log cabin /lɔg ˈkæbɪn/ **63**–4
lonely /ˈloʊnli/ **39**–17
long /lɔŋ/
    ...skirt /skɜrt/ **111**–21
long-distance call /lɔŋ-ˈdɪstəns kɔl/ **16**–10
long hair /lɔŋ hɛr/ **33**–13
long-sleeved /lɔŋ-slivd/
    ...shirt /ʃɜrt/ **111**–5
long underwear /lɔŋ ˈʌndərˌwɛr/ **107**–15
look at /lʊk ət/
    ...a map /ə mæp/ **123**–11
    ...houses /haʊsɛz/ **65**–17
    ...the menu /ðə ˈmɛnyu/ **102**–7
look for /lʊk fər/
    ...a book /ə bʊk/ **54**–25
    ...a jacket /ə ʤækɪt/ **114**–2
    ...an apartment /ən əˈpartmənt/ **64**–1
look up /lʊk ʌp/
    ...a word /ə wərd/ **20**–8
loose /lus/
    ...pants /pænts/ **111**–12
lotion /ˈloʊʃən/ **144**–23
    baby... /ˈbeɪbi/ **57**–23
loud /laʊd/ **15**–35
loudspeaker /ˈlaʊdˌspikər/ **23**–14
love /lʌv/ **29**–1
love seat /lʌv sit/ **72**–11
low /loʊ/
    ...heels /hilz/ **111**–23
lozenges /ˈlazənʤɛz/ **142**–9
luggage /ˈlʌgɪʤ/ **124**–5
luggage cart /ˈlʌgɪʤ kart/ **159**–16
lumber /ˈlʌmbər/ **163**
    board... /bɔrd/ **163**–30
lunch /lʌnʧ/
    eat... /it/ **34**–13
    have... /hæv/ **34**–13
lung /lʌŋ/ **133**–27

machine operator /məˈʃin ˈapəˌreɪtər/ **157**–14
magazine /ˌmægəˈzin/ **55**–2
magnet /ˈmægnɪt/ **194**–30
magnifying glass /ˈmægnəˌfaɪŋ glæs/ **194**–26
mah-jongg /ˈma-ʒɔŋ/ **224**–13
mail /meɪl/ **53**–24
mail /meɪl/
    open... /ˈoʊpən/ **150**–5
mailbox /ˈmeɪlˌbaks/ **52**–9
mail carrier /meɪl ˈkæriər/ **52**–10
mailing address /ˈmeɪlɪŋ ˈəˌdrɛs/ **52**–6
mail truck /meɪl trʌk/ **52**–11
main course /meɪn kɔrs/ **101**–27
make /meɪk/
    ...a decision /ə dɪˈsɪʒən/ **65**–18, **151**–26
    ...a deposit /ə dɪˈpazɪt/ **51**–27
    ...a down payment /ə daʊn ˈpeɪmənt/ **65**–23
    ...an appointment /ən əˈpɔɪntmənt/ **64**–2, **137**–21
    ...an offer /ən ˈɔfər/ **65**–19
    ...a reservation /ə ˌrɛzərˈveɪʃən/ **102**–1, **159**–24
    ...copies /ˈkapiz/ **151**–20
    ...dinner /ˈdɪnər/ **34**–18
    ...the bed /ðə bɛd/ **79**–1
    ...the (house) payment /ðə (haʊs) ˈpeɪmənt/ **65**–26
makeup /ˈmeɪkˌʌp/ **144**
Malaysian /məˈleɪʒən/ **44**–29
male /meɪl/ **42**
mall /mɔl/ **47**–3
man /mæn/ **15**–39
manage /ˈmænɪʤ/ **151**–18
mane /meɪn/ **185**–26
mango /ˈmæŋgoʊ/ **83**–8
manicurist /ˈmæniˌkyʊrɪst/ **148**–2
mantle /ˈmæntəl/ **72**–26
manufacture /ˌmænyəˈfækʧər/ **151**–23
map /mæp/ **19**–13
    look at a... /lʊk ət ə/ **123**–11
    trail... /treɪl/ **213**–18
maple (tree) /ˈmeɪpəl (tri)/ **179**–4
maracas /məˈrakəz/ **207**–5
march /marʧ/ **37**–4
March /marʧ/ **7**–18
margarine /ˈmarʤərɪn/ **88**–6
margin /ˈmarʤɪn/ **196**–7
marigolds /ˈmærəˌgoʊldz/ **179**–26
marimba /məˈrɪmbə/ **207**–4
marinate /ˈmærəˌneɪt/ **92**–5
marker /ˈmarkər/ **19**–3
maroon /məˈrun/ **10**–2
marriage certificate /ˈmærɪʤ sərˈtɪfɪkɪt/ **43**–25
married /ˈmærid/ **26**–27
Mars /marz/ **176**–24
martial arts /ˈmarʃəl arts/ **218**–1
mascara /mæˈskærə/ **144**–30
mask /mæsk/ **204**–4
    diving... /ˈdaɪvɪŋ/ **211**–26
    surgical... /ˈsɜrʤɪkəl/ **139**–13
masking tape /ˈmæskɪŋ teɪp/ **163**–13
match /mæʧ/ **21**–22
matches /mæʧəz/ **213**–23
maternity dress /məˈtɜrnəti drɛs/ **104**–24
math /mæθ/ **192**–193
mattress /ˈmætrɪs/ **74**–13
    air... /ɛr/ **213**–26
May /meɪ/ **7**–20
mayonnaise /ˈmeɪəˌneɪz/ **88**–7
meal /mil/
    choose a... /ʧuz ə/ **126**–20
measles /ˈmizəlz/ **135**–9
measure /ˈmɛʒər/ **92**–1, **165**–11
measurements /ˈmɛʒərmənts/ **96**–97

measuring cups /ˈmɛʒərɪŋ kʌps/ **95**-23
measuring spoons /ˈmɛʒərɪŋ spunz/ **95**-24
meat /mit/ **86-87**
meats /mits/ **99**-2
meat thermometer /mit θərˈmɑmətər/ **94**-17
mechanic /məˈkænɪk/ **148**-10
medical center /ˈmɛdɪkəl ˈsɛntər/ **140-141**
medical chart /ˈmɛdɪkəl tʃɑrt/ **141**-2
medicine cabinet /ˈmɛdəsən ˈkæbənɪt/ **75**-21
meet /mit/
    ...the landlord /ðə ˈlænd.lɔrd/ **64**-3
    ...the neighbors /ðə ˈneɪbərz/ **64**-15
meeting room /ˈmitɪŋ rum/ **159**-6
melons /ˈmɛlənz/
    crate of... /kreɪt ʌv/ **97**-30
mend /mɛnd/ **115**-21
menu /ˈmɛnyu/ **101**-20
    drop down... /drɑp daʊn/ **25**-8
    look at the... /lʊk ət ðə/ **102**-7
Mercury /ˈmɜrkyəri/ **176**-27
merry-go-round /ˈmɛri-goʊ-raʊnd/ **214**-14
mesa /ˈmeɪsə/ **169**-15
message /ˈmɛsɪdʒ/
    e-mail... /ˈi-.meɪl/ **25**-22
    take a... /teɪk ə/ **150**-12
metal detector /ˈmɛtl dɪˈtɛktər/ **125**-9
meteor /ˈmitiər/ **176**-16
meter /ˈmitər/ **128**-2
    parking... /ˈpɑrkɪŋ/ **58**-20
meter reader /ˈmitər ˈridər/ **77**-21
methods of payment /ˈmɛθədz ʌv ˈpeɪmənt/ **9**
Mexican /ˈmɛksɪkən/ **44**-3
mice /maɪs/ **76**-24
microphone /ˈmaɪkrəˌfoʊn/ **205**-13
microscope /ˈmaɪkrəˌskoʊp/ **194**-25
microwave /ˈmaɪkrəˌweɪv/ **92**-13
microwave (oven) /ˈmaɪkrəˌweɪv (ˈʌvən)/ **70**-1
Mid-Atlantic States /mɪd-ətˈlæntɪk steɪts/ **172**-10
midday /ˈmɪdˌdeɪ/ **5**
middle initial /ˈmɪdl ɪˈnɪʃəl/ **43**-4
midnight /ˈmɪdˌnaɪt/ **5**
Midwest /ˌmɪdˈwɛst/ **172**-9
migrate /ˈmaɪˌgreɪt/ **198**-1
mile /maɪl/ **162**
military /ˈmɪləˌtɛri/
    serve in the... /sɜrv ɪn ðə/ **201**-19
milk /mɪlk/ **153**-32
milk /mɪlk/ **88**-26
    quart of... /kwɔrt ʌv/ **97**-18
millennium /məˈlɛniəm/ **4**
miniature golf /ˈmɪniətʃər gɑlf/ **216**-16
minivan /ˈmɪniˌvæn/ **118**-17
minus /ˈmaɪnəs/ **193**-2
minute /ˈmɪnɪt/ **4**
mirror /ˈmɪrər/ **74**-7
misbehave /ˌmɪsbɪˈheɪv/ **29**-25
mittens /ˈmɪtnz/ **109**-3
mix /mɪks/ **93**-29
mixer /ˈmɪksər/
    hand... /hænd/ **95**-19
mixing bowl /ˈmɪksɪŋ ˈboʊl/ **94**-12
mobile home /ˈmoʊbəl hoʊm/ **63**-7
mobile phone /ˈmoʊbəl foʊn/ **16**-19
model /ˈmɑdl/ **203**-5
    build a... /bɪld ə/ **224**-28
molding /ˈmoʊldɪŋ/ **163**-29
mole /moʊl/ **33**-27, **190**-16
molecule /ˈmɑlɪˌkyul/ **194**-18
Monday /ˈmʌnˌdeɪ/ **6**-5
money /ˈmʌni/ **8-9**, **51**-6
money order /ˈmʌni ˈɔrdər/ **51**-19

monitor /ˈmɑnətər/ **25**-19
monitors /ˈmɑnətərz/
    check the... /tʃɛk ðə/ **126**-6
monkey /ˈmʌnki/ **182**-6
monkey bars /ˈmʌnki bɑrz/ **214**-3
month /mʌnθ/ **4**
monthly statement /ˈmʌnθli ˈsteɪtmənt/ **51**-10
months of the year /mʌnθs ʌv ðə yɪr/ **7**
monument /ˈmɑnyəmənt/ **58**-10
moon /mun/ **176**-12
    crescent... /krɛsənt/ **177**-30
    full... /fʊl/ **177**-32
    new... /nu/ **177**-29
    quarter... /ˈkwɔrtər/ **177**-31
moose /mus/ **187**-2
mop /mɑp/ **79**-12
mop /mɑp/ **80**-26
morning /ˈmɔrnɪŋ/ **5**
mosque /mɑsk/ **47**-5
mosquito /məˈskitoʊ/ **190**-24
moss /mɔs/ **187**-6
motel /moʊˈtɛl/ **47**-4
moth /mɔθ/ **181**-21
mother /ˈmʌðər/ **27**-7
    single... /ˈsɪŋgəl/ **27**-29
mother-in-law /ˈmʌðər-ɪn-ˌlɔ/ **27**-9
Mother's Day /ˈmʌðərz deɪ/ **228**-10
motor /ˈmoʊtər/ **121**-32
motorboat /ˈmoʊtərˌboʊt/ **211**-4
motorcycle /ˈmoʊtərˌsaɪkəl/ **118**-32
mountain /ˈmaʊntn/ **169**-2
mountain lion /ˈmaʊntn ˈlaɪən/ **181**-5
mouse /maʊs/ **25**-27, **190**-29
mousetrap /ˈmaʊsˌtræp/ **80**-24
mouth /maʊθ/ **133**-41
    ...of the river /ʌv ðə ˈrɪvər/ **169**-19
move /muv/ **31**-17
move in /muv ɪn/ **65**-25
movie theater /ˈmuvi θiətər/ **47**-12, **216**-21
mow /moʊ/ **79**-17
MP3 player /ˌɛmˈpi θri ˈpleɪər/ **226**-7
mudslide /ˈmʌdslaɪd/ **171**-9
muffin /ˈmʌfɪn/ **90**-15
mug /mʌg/ **70**-30
mugging /ˈmʌgɪŋ/ **61**-10
multiplication /ˌmʌltəpləˈkeɪʃən/ **193**-28
multiplied by /ˈmʌltəˌplaɪd baɪ/ **193**-5
mumps /mʌmps/ **135**-7
mural /ˈmyʊrəl/ **203**-15
murder /ˈmɜrdər/ **61**-11
muscle /ˈmʌsəl/ **133**-2
museum /myuˈziəm/ **59**-24, **216**-19
mushroom /ˈmʌʃrum/ **85**-32
music /ˈmyuzɪk/ **209**
    listen to... /ˈlɪsən tə/ **126**-17
musician /myuˈzɪʃən/ **148**-24
music store /ˈmyuzɪk stɔr/ **48**-10
mussel /ˈmʌsəl/ **189**-27
mussels /ˈmʌsəlz/ **87**-17
mustache /ˈmʌˌstæʃ/ **33**-8
mustard /ˈmʌstərd/ **90**-16
mystery /ˈmɪstəri/ **208**-3
nail /neɪl/ **163**-20
    hammer a... /ˈhæmər ə/ **165**-9
nail clipper /neɪl ˈklɪpər/ **144**-12
nail polish /neɪl ˈpɑlɪʃ/ **144**-11
nail salon /neɪl səˈlɑn/ **48**-16
name /neɪm/ **43**-1
    spell your... /spɛl yər/ **20**-13
    write your... /raɪt yər/ **20**-6

nap /næp/
    take a... /teɪk ə/ **34**-15
napkin /'næpkɪn/ **70**-31, **101**-22
narrow /'næroʊ/
    ...tie /taɪ/ **111**-9
nasal (decongestant) spray /'neɪzəl (ˌdikən'dʒɛstənt) spreɪ/
    142-12
nationalities /ˌnæʃə'nælətiz/ **44-45**
natural disasters /'næʧərəl dɪ'zæstərz/ **170-171**
natural gas /'næʧərəl gæs/ **171**-22
nature program /'neɪʧər 'proʊˌgræm/ **209**-18
nauseous /'nɔʃəs/ **135**-19
navy (blue) /'neɪvi (blu)/ **10**-11
near /nɪr/ **13**-15
neck /nɛk/ **133**-20
necklace /'nɛklɪs/ **109**-8
needle /'nidl/ **117**-29, **224**-24
negotiate /nɪ'goʊʃiˌeɪt/
    ...the price /ðə praɪs/ **65**-20
neighbors /'neɪbərz/
    meet the... /mit ðə/ **64**-15
nephew /'nɛfyu/ **27**-20
Neptune /'nɛptun/ **176**-20
nervous /'nɜrvəs/ **38**-6
nest /nɛst/ **190**-3
net /nɛt/ **25**-29
    volleyball... /'valiˌbɔl/ **220**-11
new /nu/ **15**-31
newborn /'nuˌbɔrn/ **56**-31
New England /nu 'ɪŋlænd/ **172**-11
new moon /nu mun/ **177**-29
news /nuz/ **209**-12
newspaper /'nuzˌpeɪpər/ **55**-16
newsstand /'nuzˌstænd/ **59**-25
New Year /nu yɪr/ **228**-1
next-day mail /nɛkst-deɪ meɪl/ **52**-19
next to /nɛkst tə/ **13**-11
nickel /'nɪkəl/ **8**-2
niece /nis/ **27**-19
Nigerian /naɪ'dʒɪriən/ **44**-20
night /naɪt/ **5**
nightgown /'naɪtˌgaʊn/ **107**-14
nightshirt /'naɪtˌʃɜrt/ **107**-12
night table /naɪt 'teɪbəl/ **74**-10
nine /naɪn/ **2**
911 /naɪn wʌn wʌn/ **16**-3
nineteen /ˌnaɪn'tin/ **2**
nineteenth /ˌnaɪn'tinθ/ **3**
ninety /'naɪnti/ **2**
ninth /naɪnθ/ **3**
nipple /'nɪpəl/ **57**-1
noisy /'nɔɪzi/ **15**-35
no left turn /noʊ lɛft tɜrn/ **118**-6
nonfiction section /ˌnan'fɪkʃən 'sɛkʃən/ **55**-7
noon /nun/ **5**
north /nɔrθ/ **130**-19
North America /nɔrθ ə'mɛrɪkə/ **174**-8
Northern Canada /'nɔrðərn 'kænədə/ **172**-1
Northern Hemisphere /'nɔrðərn 'hɛməˌsfɪr/ **174**-6
North Pole /nɔrθ poʊl/ **174**-1
nose /noʊz/ **133**-37
    bloody... /'blʌdi/ **135**-29
note /'noʊt/
    absence... /'æbsəns/ **23**-27
notebook /'noʊtbʊk/ **19**-20
notebook (computer) /'noʊtbʊk (kəm'pyutər)/
    25-23
no U-turn /noʊ 'yu-ˌtɜrn/ **118**-11
novel /'navəl/ **55**-19
November /noʊ'vɛmbər/ **7**-26
nuclear energy /'nukliər 'ɛnərdʒi/ **171**-28

number /'nʌmbər/
    dial a... /'daɪəl ə/ **17**-23
numbers /'nʌmbərz/ **1-2**
nurse /nɜrs/ **29**-2
nurse /nɜrs/ **138**-2, **148**-19
    school... /skul/ **23**-8
nursery /'nɜrsəri/ **216**-4
nurses' station /'nɜrsɪz 'steɪʃən/ **138**-1
nut /nʌt/ **163**-23
    wing... /wɪŋ/ **163**-24
nuts /nʌts/ **82-83**
nylon /'naɪˌlan/ **113**-10
nylons /'naɪˌlanz/ **107**-5
oak (tree) /oʊk (tri)/ **179**-5
oasis /oʊ'eɪsɪs/ **181**-15
obey /oʊ'beɪ/ **201**-15
oboe /'oʊboʊ/ **207**-13
observatory /əb'zɜrvəˌtɔri/ **176**-8
obstetrician /ˌabstə'trɪʃən/ **141**-10
ocean /'oʊʃən/ **169**-24, **211**-5
October /ak'toʊbər/ **7**-25
octopus /'aktəpəs/ **189**-17
off /ɔf/ **13**-7
offer /'ɔfər/ **102**-20
offer /'ɔfər/
    make an... /meɪk ən/ **65**-19
office /'ɔfɪs/ **154-155**
office assistant /ɔfɪs ə'sɪstənt/ **155**-18
office building /'ɔfɪs 'bɪldɪŋ/ **47**-15
office manager /'ɔfɪs 'mænɪdʒər/ **155**-5
oil /ɔɪl/ **171**-23
    check the... /ʧɛk ðə/ **123**-16
oil gauge /ɔɪl geɪdʒ/ **121**-13
oil spill /ɔɪl spɪl/ **171**-15
old /oʊld/ **14**-21, **15**-32
olive green /'alɪv grin/ **10**-6
olive oil /'alɪv ɔɪl/
    bottle of... /'batl ʌv/ **97**-7
    measure... /'mɛʒər/ **92**-1
olives /'alɪvz/ **83**-23
on /an/ **13**-3
one /wʌn/ **2**
one-bedroom apartment /wʌn-'bɛdˌrum ə'partmənt/
    67-13
one cent /wʌn sɛnt/ **8**-1
one dollar /wʌn 'dalər/ **8**-6
one-dollar bill /wʌn-'dalər bɪl/ **8**-6
one-half /wʌn-hæf/ **3**
one hundred /wʌn 'hʌndrɪd/ **2**
one hundred-dollar bill /'wʌn 'hʌndrɪd-'dalər bɪl/ **8**-11
one hundred dollars /'wʌn 'hʌndrɪd 'dalərz/ **8**-11
one hundred thousand /'wʌn 'hʌndrɪd 'θaʊzənd/ **2**
one million /wʌn 'mɪlyən/ **2**
one-quarter /wʌn-'kwɔrtər/ **3**
one thousand /wʌn 'θaʊzənd/ **2**
one way /wʌn weɪ/ **118**-1
onion /'ʌnyən/ **84**-15
    slice... /slaɪs/ **93**-18
online /ˌan'laɪn/
    be... /bi/ **24**-30
online catalog /ˌan'laɪn 'kætlˌɔg/ **55**-5
Ontario /an'tɛrioʊ/ **172**-4
on the left of /an ðə lɛft ʌv/ **13**-8
on the right of /an ðə raɪt ʌv/ **13**-9
on top of /an tap ʌv/ **13**-1
open /'oʊpən/
    ...a present /ə 'prɛzənt/ **229**-32
    ...mail /meɪl/ **150**-5
    ...your book /yər bʊk/ **20**-10
open /'oʊpən/ **15**-37
opens /'oʊpənz/ **198**-11

opera /ˈɑprə/ **205**-25
operate /ˈɑpəˌreɪt/ **165**-15
operating room /ˈɑpəˌreɪtɪŋ rum/ **138**-5
operating table /ˈɑpəˌreɪtɪŋ ˈteɪbəl/ **138**-8
operation /ˌɑpəˈreɪʃən/ **139**-11
operator /ˈɑpəˌreɪtər/ **16**-17
opossum /əˈpɑsəm/ **190**-7
opposites /ˈɑpəzɪts/ **14**-15
optometrist /ɑpˈtɑmətrɪst/ **141**-23
orange /ˈɔrɪndʒ/ **10**-19, **83**-3
orange juice /ˈɔrɪndʒ dʒus/ **88**-27
    carton of... /ˈkɑrtn ʌv/ **97**-10
orangutan /əˈræŋəˌtæŋ/ **182**-13
orbit /ˈɔrbɪt/ **176**-6
orca /ˈɔrkə/ **189**-7
orchard /ˈɔrtʃərd/ **152**-1
orchestra /ˈɔrkəstrə/ **204**-8
orchid /ˈɔrkɪd/ **182**-11
order /ˈɔrdər/ **102**-10
    ...room service /rum ˈsɜrvɪs/ **159**-26
order /ˈɔrdər/
    take an... /teɪk ən/ **102**-11
orderly /ˈɔrdərli/ **139**-22
organ /ˈɔrgən/ **207**-27
orthopedist /ˌɔrθəˈpidɪst/ **141**-17
ostrich /ˈɑstrɪtʃ/ **185**-14
otter /ˈɑtər/ **187**-7
ottoman /ˈɑtəmən/ **72**-13
ounce /aʊns/ **96, 97**-3
out /aʊt/
    power is... /ˈpaʊər ɪz/ **77**-1
outdoor sports and fitness /ˈaʊtˌdɔr spɔrts ənd ˈfɪtnɪs/ **220**-**221**
outlet /ˈaʊtˌlɛt/ **72**-32
outline /ˈaʊtˌlaɪn/
    write an... /raɪt ən/ **196**-21
out of /aʊt ʌv/ **130**-5
outside (of) /ˌaʊtˈsaɪd (ʌv)/ **13**-6
oval /ˈoʊvəl/ **193**-17
oven /ˈʌvən/ **70**-8
    microwave... /ˈmaɪkrəˌweɪv/ **70**-1
over /ˈoʊvər/ **13**-10, **130**-14
overalls /ˈoʊvərˌɔlz/ **104**-12
overdose /ˈoʊvərˌdoʊs/ **136**-11
overhead compartment /ˈoʊvərˌhɛd kəmˈpɑrtmənt/ **125**-24
overhead light /ˈoʊvərˌhɛd laɪt/
    turn on the... /tɜrn ɑn ðə/ **126**-15
overhead projector /ˈoʊvərˌhɛd prədʒɛktər/ **19**-17
overnight mail /ˌoʊvərˈnaɪt meɪl/ **52**-19
over-the-counter medication /ˈoʊvər-ðə-ˈkaʊntər ˌmɛdɪˈkeɪʃən/ **142**-6
owl /aʊl/ **181**-2
oysters /ˈɔɪstərz/ **87**-15
pacifier /ˈpæsəˌfaɪər/ **57**-25
pack /pæk/ **64**-9, **123**-1
package /ˈpækɪdʒ/ **52**-17
packer /ˈpækər/ **156**-7
pad /pæd/ **155**-30
paddle /ˈpædl/ **213**-9
padlock /ˈpædˌlɑk/ **163**-34
pail /peɪl/ **80**-16, **211**-28
pain /peɪn/
    be in... /bi ɪn/ **136**-1
paint /peɪnt/ **165**-3, **203**-25
paint /peɪnt/ **163**-14, **203**-10
paintbrush /ˈpeɪntˌbrʌʃ/ **163**-10, **203**-8
painter /ˈpeɪntər/ **203**-9
    house... /haʊs/ **148**-14
painting /ˈpeɪntɪŋ/ **203**-7
paint roller /peɪnt roʊlər/ **163**-16

paint supplies /peɪnt səˈplaɪz/ **162**
paint tray /peɪnt treɪ/ **163**-15
pair of scissors /pɛr ʌv ˈsɪzərz/ **117**-23
paisley /ˈpeɪzli/ **113**-17
pajamas /pəˈdʒɑməz/ **107**-17
palace /ˈpælɪs/ **63**-14
palette /ˈpælɪt/ **203**-6
palm tree /pɑm tri/ **181**-7
pan /pæn/
    frying... /ˈfraɪɪŋ/ **94**-3
pan pipes /pæn paɪps/ **207**-16
panther /ˈpænθər/ **182**-17
panties /ˈpæntiz/ **107**-20
pants /ˈpænts/ **104**-22
    baggy... /ˈbægi/ **111**-12
    loose... /lus/ **111**-12
pantyhose /ˈpæntiˌhoʊz/ **107**-5
papaya /pəˈpaɪə/ **83**-18
paper /ˈpeɪpər/ **196**-5
    hand in your... /hænd ɪn yər/ **20**-2
paperback (book) /ˈpeɪpərˌbæk (bʊk)/ **55**-13
paper bag /ˈpeɪpər bæg/ **99**-14
paper clip /ˈpeɪpər klɪp/ **155**-28
paper products /ˈpeɪpər ˈprɑdʌkts/ **99**-8
papers /ˈpeɪpərz/
    collect the... /kəˈlɛkt ðə/ **20**-3
    exchange... /ɪksˈtʃeɪndʒ/ **20**-5
    hand out... /hænd aʊt/ **21**-18
paper shredder /ˈpeɪpər ʃrɛdər/ **155**-15
paper towels /ˈpeɪpər ˈtaʊəlz/ **80**-7
parade /pəˈreɪd/ **228**-3
paragraph /ˈpærəˌgræf/ **196**-4
parakeet /ˈpærəˌkit/ **182**-1
parallel lines /ˈpærəˌlɛl laɪnz/ **193**-12
paramedic /ˌpærəˈmɛdɪk/ **139**-26
parent /ˈpɛrənt/ **57**-8
parentheses /pəˈrɛnθəsiz/ **196**-15
parents /ˈpɛrənts/ **27**-25
park /pɑrk/ **123**-25
park /pɑrk/ **47**-28
park bench /pɑrk bɛntʃ/ **214**-18
parking /ˈpɑrkɪŋ/
    valet... /væˈleɪ/ **159**-23
parking garage /ˈpɑrkɪŋ gəˈrɑʒ/ **47**-21
parking meter /ˈpɑrkɪŋ ˈmitər/ **58**-20
parking space /ˈpɑrkɪŋ speɪs/ **67**-8
parrot /ˈpærət/ **182**-5
particle mask /ˈpɑrtɪkəl mæsk/ **157**-26
parts /ˈpɑrts/ **157**-13
parts of a car /pɑrts ʌv ə kɑr/ **120**-**121**
parts of a fish /pɑrts ʌv ə fɪʃ/ **188**
pass /pæs/
    ...a test /ə tɛst/ **19**-34
    ...a truck /ə trʌk/ **123**-13
pass away /pæs əˈweɪ/ **31**-24
passbook /ˈpæsˌbʊk/
    savings account... /ˈseɪvɪŋz əˈkaʊnt/ **51**-14
passenger /ˈpæsəndʒər/ **124**-6, **128**-6
passport /ˈpæsˌpɔrt/ **43**-22
password /ˈpæsˌwɜrd/
    enter your... /ˈɛntər yər/ **24**-31
past /pæst/ **130**-2
pastries /ˈpeɪstriz/
    tray of... /treɪ ʌv/ **97**-11
path /pæθ/ **214**-27
patient /ˈpeɪʃənt/ **139**-18
    examine the... /ɪgˈzæmən ðə/ **137**-22
patio /ˈpætiˌoʊ/ **69**-22
patterns /ˈpætərnz/ **112**-**113**
paw /pɔ/ **185**-27

pay /peɪ/
    ...a security deposit /ə səˈkyʊrəti dɪˈpɑsɪt/ **64**–7
    ...a toll /ə toʊl/ **123**–23
    ...taxes /ˈtæksɪz/ **201**–16
    ...the bills /ðə bɪlz/ **79**–6
    ...the check /ðə ʧɛk/ **102**–24
    ...the rent /ðə rɛnt/ **64**–14
payment /ˈpeɪmənt/
    make the... /meɪk ðə/ **65**–26
peach /piʧ/ **83**–19
peacock /ˈpiˌkɑk/ **182**–8
peak /pik/ **169**–1
peanuts /ˈpiˌnəts/ **83**–33
pear /pɛr/ **83**–1
peas /piz/ **85**–30
pebble /ˈpɛbəl/ **181**–17
pecans /pɪˈkɑnz/ **83**–30
pedestrian /pəˈdɛstriən/ **58**–17
pedestrian crossing /pəˈdɛstriən ˈkrɔsɪŋ/ **118**–9
pediatrician /ˌpidiəˈtrɪʃən/ **141**–7
peel /pil/ **93**–22
peephole /ˈpipˌhoʊl/ **67**–26
pen /pɛn/ **19**–21
pencil /ˈpɛnsəl/ **19**–20
pencil sharpener /ˈpɛnsəl ˈʃɑrpənər/
    electric... /ɪˈlɛktrɪk/ **155**–20
penguin /ˈpɛŋgwɪn/ **187**–13
peninsula /pəˈnɪnsələ/ **169**–17
penny /ˈpɛni/ **8**–1
PEOPLE /ˈpipəl/ **32**–45
pepper shaker /ˈpɛpər ˈʃeɪkər/ **101**–13
percent /pərˈsɛnt/ **193**–4
percussion /pərˈkʌʃən/ **207**
perform /pərˈfɔrm/ **150**–10
performing arts /pərˈfɔrmɪŋ ɑrts/ **204**–205
perfume /ˈpərˌfyum/ **144**–21
period /ˈpɪriəd/ **196**–10
periodical section /ˌpɪriˈɑdɪkəl ˈsɛkʃən/ **55**–1
periodic table /ˌpɪriˈɑdɪk ˈteɪbəl/ **194**–15
periods of time /ˈpɪriədz ʌv taɪm/ **4**
permission slip /pərˈmɪʃən slɪp/ **23**–26
perpendicular lines /ˌpərpənˈdɪkyələr laɪnz/ **193**–11
personal check /ˈpərsənəl ʧɛk/ **9**–25
Peruvian /pəˈruviən/ **44**–6
pesticide poisoning /ˈpɛstəˌsaɪd ˈpɔɪzənɪŋ/ **171**–16
petal /ˈpɛtl/ **179**–16
pet food /pɛt fud/ **99**–10
petri dish /ˈpitri dɪʃ/ **194**–29
petroleum /pəˈtroʊliəm/ **171**–23
pet store /pɛt stɔr/ **48**–20
pharmacist /ˈfɑrməsɪst/ **142**–5
pharmacy /ˈfɑrməsi/ **48**–25, **142**–143
phone /foʊn/
    answer the... /ˈænsər ðə/ **17**–25
    hang up the... /hæŋ ʌp ðə/ **17**–27
    pick up the... /pɪk ʌp ðə/ **17**–22
phone book /foʊn bʊk/ **16**–8
phone card /foʊn kard/ **16**–6
phone jack /foʊn ʤæk/ **16**–14
phone number /foʊn ˈnʌmbər/ **16**–21
photocopier /ˈfoʊtəˌkɑpiər/ **155**–3
photocopy /ˈfoʊtəˌkɑpi/ **155**–4
photograph /ˈfoʊtəˌgræf/ **203**–26
photograph /ˈfoʊtəˌgræf/ **203**–22
    take a... /teɪk ə/ **203**–26
photographer /fəˈtɑgrəfər/ **148**–12, **203**–23
photo ID /ˈfoʊtoʊ ˈaɪˈdi/ **124**–3
physical (exam) /ˈfɪzɪkəl (ɪgˈzæm)/ **141**–18
physical therapist /ˈfɪzɪkəl ˈθɛrəpɪst/ **148**–6
physicist /ˈfɪzəsɪst/ **194**–6
physics /ˈfɪzɪks/ **194**–5

piano /piˈænoʊ/ **207**–26
pick /pɪk/ **153**–31
pickles /ˈpɪkəlz/ **88**–10
pick up /pɪk ʌp/ **29**–10, **29**–19
    ...the phone /ðə foʊn/ **17**–24
pickup truck /ˈpɪkˌʌp trʌk/ **118**–15
picnic /ˈpɪknɪk/ **214**–11
picnic basket /ˈpɪknɪk ˈbæskɪt/ **214**–12
picnic table /ˈpɪknɪk ˈteɪbəl/ **214**–13
picture book /ˈpɪkʧər bʊk/ **55**–24
piece /pis/
    ...of cake /ʌv keɪk/ **97**–15
pie pan /paɪ pæn/ **95**–29
pier /pɪr/ **211**–2
pierced ears /pɪrsd ɪrz/ **33**–20
pig /pɪg/ **152**–25
pigeon /ˈpɪʤən/ **214**–29
pigtails /ˈpɪgˌteɪlz/ **33**–26
pile /paɪl/
    ...of tomatoes /ʌv təˈmeɪtoʊz/ **97**–28
pill /pɪl/ **142**–3
    take a... /teɪk ə/ **137**–27
pillow /ˈpɪloʊ/ **74**–12
    ask for a... /æsk fər ə/ **126**–14
pillowcase /ˈpɪloʊˌkeɪs/ **74**–11
pilot /ˈpaɪlət/ **125**–15, **148**–23
PIN /pɪn/
    enter... /ˈɛntər/ **51**–25
pin /pɪn/ **109**–12, **117**–21
pincushion /pɪn ˈkʊʃən/ **117**–22
pine (tree) /paɪn (tri)/ **179**–1
pineapple /ˈpaɪˌnæpəl/ **83**–7
pinecone /paɪn koʊn/ **179**–9
ping-pong /ˈpɪŋ-ˌpɑŋ/ **218**–8
ping-pong paddle /ˈpɪŋ-ˌpɑŋ pædl/
    218–9
ping-pong table /ˈpɪŋ-ˌpɑŋ ˈteɪbəl/ **218**–10
pink /pɪŋk/ **10**–4
pint /paɪnt/ **96**, **97**–1
pinto beans /pɪntoʊ binz/ **84**–9
pipe /paɪp/ **161**–26
    cut a... /kʌt ə/ **165**–21
pipe fittings /paɪp ˈfɪtɪŋz/ **160**–24
pipes /paɪps/
    ...are frozen /ər ˈfroʊzən/ **77**–8
pipe wrench /paɪp rɛnʧ/ **161**–25
pistachios /pɪˈstæʃiˌoʊz/ **83**–32
pitcher /ˈpɪʧər/ **97**–14
pizza /ˈpitsə/ **90**–1
placemat /ˈpleɪsmæt/ **70**–26
place of birth /pleɪs ʌv bərθ/ **43**–7
places around town /ˈpleɪsɪz əˈraʊnd taʊn/
    46–47
places to visit /ˈpleɪsɪz tə ˈvɪzɪt/ **216**–217
plaid /plæd/ **113**–19
plains /pleɪnz/ **169**–26
plan /plæn/ **150**–16
plane /pleɪn/
    ...wood /wʊd/ **165**–23
plane /pleɪn/ **125**
    board the... /bɔrd ðə/ **126**–8
    get off the... /gɛt ɔf ðə/ **126**–23
planetarium /ˌplænəˈtɛriəm/ **216**–3
planets /ˈplænɪts/ **176**
plant /plænt/ **153**–29
plaster /ˈplæstər/ **165**–2
plastic bag /ˈplæstɪk bæg/ **99**–20
plate /pleɪt/ **70**–23, **101**–23
plateau /plæˈtoʊ/ **169**–12
platform /ˈplætˌfɔrm/ **128**–19
play /pleɪ/ **205**–17

player /ˈpleɪər/
    basketball... /ˈbæskɪtˌbɔl/ **218**–6
    hockey... /ˈhɑki/ **223**–22
playground /ˈpleɪˌɡraʊnd/ **214**–4
playpen /ˈpleɪˌpɛn/ **57**–4
play with /pleɪ wɪð/ **29**–9
pleated /ˈplitəd/
    ...skirt /skɜrt/ **111**–19
pliers /ˈplaɪərz/ **160**–15
plow /plaʊ/ **152**–5
plug /plʌɡ/ **226**–5
plum /plʌm/ **83**–15
plumber /ˈplʌmər/ **77**–15, **148**–15
plumbing /ˈplʌmɪŋ/ **161**
plunger /ˈplʌndʒər/ **75**–23
plus /plʌs/ **193**–1
plywood /ˈplaɪˌwʊd/ **163**–28
P.O. Box /ˌpiˈoʊ bɑks/ **52**–13
pocket /ˈpɑkɪt/ **117**–13
pocket knife /ˈpɑkɪt naɪf/ **213**–21
poison /ˈpɔɪzən/
    swallow... /ˈswɑloʊ/ **136**–10
poisoning /ˈpɔɪzənɪŋ/
    pesticide... /ˈpɛstəˌsaɪd/ **171**–16
poisonous materials /ˈpɔɪzənəs məˈtɪriəlz/ **156**–34
polar bear /ˈpoʊlər bɛr/ **187**–8
polar lands /ˈpoʊlər lændz/ **186**–187
police car /pəˈlis kɑr/ **118**–26
police officer /pəˈlis ˈɔfəsər/ **61**–21, **148**–11
police station /pəˈlis ˈsteɪʃən/ **47**–10
polish /ˈpɑlɪʃ/ **79**–9
political candidate /pəˈlɪtɪkəl ˈkændəˌdeɪt/ **200**–1
polka dot /ˈpoʊlkə dɑt/ **113**–15
pollution /pəˈluʃən/ **170**–171
    air... /ɛr/ **171**–13
    water... /ˈwɔtər/ **171**–19
polo /ˈpoʊloʊ/
    ...shirt /ʃɜrt/ **111**–7
pomegranate /ˈpɑməˌɡrænɪt/ **83**–4
poncho /ˈpɑnʧoʊ/ **104**–11
pond /pɑnd/ **214**–19
ponytail /ˈpoʊniˌteɪl/ **33**–24
pool /pul/
    swimming... /ˈswɪmɪŋ/ **159**–21, **218**–34
pool hall /pul hɔl/ **216**–7
poor /pʊr/ **15**–28
pop /pɑp/ **209**–22
popcorn /ˈpɑpˌkɔrn/ **99**–28
poppies /ˈpɑpiz/ **179**–32
porch /pɔrʧ/ **69**–14
porcupine /ˈpɔrkyəˌpaɪn/ **190**–11
pork /pɔrk/ **86**
pork chops /pɔrk ʧɑps/ **87**–3
pork roast /pɔrk roʊst/ **87**–7
portrait /ˈpɔrtrɪt/ **203**–3
postal clerk /ˈpoʊstəl klɜrk/ **52**–20
postal scale /ˈpoʊstəl skeɪl/ **52**–15
postcard /ˈpoʊstˌkɑrd/ **52**–16
poster /ˈpoʊstər/ **19**–16
postmark /ˈpoʊstˌmɑrk/ **52**–18
post office /poʊst ˈɔfɪs/ **47**–14, **52**–53
post office box /poʊst ˈɔfɪs bɑks/ **52**–13
pot /pɑt/ **94**–5
    ...of coffee /ʌv ˈkɔfi/ **97**–12
potato /pəˈteɪtoʊ/ **84**–26
potato chips /pəˈteɪtoʊ ʧɪps/ **99**–27
potatoes /pəˈteɪtoʊz/
    bag of... /bæɡ ʌv/ **97**–22
    boil... /bɔɪl/ **92**–17
potholder /ˈpɑtˌhoʊldər/ **70**–9
potter /ˈpɑtər/ **203**–19

potter's wheel /ˈpɑtərz wil/ **203**–20
pottery /ˈpɑtəri/ **203**–18
potty chair /ˈpɑti ʧɛr/ **57**–20
poultry /ˈpoʊltri/ **86**–87, **99**–2
pound /paʊnd/ **96**, **97**–19
pour /pɔr/
    ...concrete /kənˈkrit/ **165**–7
    ...water /ˈwɔtər/ **102**–2
powder /ˈpaʊdər/
    baby... /ˈbeɪbi/ **57**–22
power /ˈpaʊər/
    hydroelectric... /ˌhaɪdroʊɪˈlɛktrɪk/ **171**–29
    ...is out /ɪz aʊt/ **77**–1
power sander /ˈpaʊər ˈsændər/ **161**–32
power strip /ˈpaʊər ˌstrɪp/ **25**–12
power tools /ˈpaʊər tulz/ **161**
Prairie Provinces /ˈprɛri ˈprɑvɪnsəz/ **172**–3
praise /preɪz/ **29**–17
pregnant /ˈprɛɡnənt/
    be... /bi/ **31**–14
pregnant woman /ˈprɛɡnənt ˈwʊmən/ **141**–11
preschooler /ˈpriˌskulər/ **56**–34
prescription /prɪˈskrɪpʃən/ **142**–15
prescription medicine /prɪˈskrɪpʃən ˈmɛdəsən/ **142**–4
present /ˈprɛzənt/ **228**–11
    open a... /ˈoʊpən ə/ **229**–32
    wrap a... /ræp ə/ **229**–29
president /ˈprɛzədənt/ **200**–11
press /prɛs/ **115**–23
pretzels /ˈprɛtsəlz/ **99**–26
price /praɪs/ **9**–18
    negotiate the... /nɪˈɡoʊsiˌeɪt ðə/ **65**–20
price tag /praɪs tæɡ/ **9**–16
primary colors /ˈpraɪˌmɛri ˈkʌlərz/ **10**
principal /ˈprɪnsəpəl/ **23**–16
print (out) /prɪnt (aʊt)/ **24**–35
print /prɪnt/ **113**–14
printer /ˈprɪntər/ **25**–15
prism /ˈprɪzəm/ **194**–7
prison /ˈprɪzən/ **61**–27
prisoner /ˈprɪzənər/ **61**–28
produce /prəˈdus/ **198**–2
produce /ˈproʊˌdus/ **99**–1
program /ˈproʊˌɡræm/ **205**–23
    computer... /kəmˈpyutər/ **25**–25
projector /prəˈʤɛktər/ **25**–13
    overhead... /ˌoʊvərˈhɛd/ **19**–16
protect /prəˈtɛkt/ **29**–14
protest /prəˈtɛst/ **201**–18
proud /praʊd/ **38**–1
psychologist /saɪˈkɑləʤɪst/ **141**–5
public transportation /ˈpʌblɪk ˌtrænspərˈteɪʃən/ **128**–129
puck /pʌk/
    hockey... /ˈhɑki/ **223**–24
pull /pʊl/ **37**–27, **165**–6
pull over /pʊl ˈoʊvər/ **123**–20
pullover /ˈpʊlˌoʊvər/ **104**–20
pump /pʌmp/ **109**–19
pumpkin pie /ˈpʌmpkɪn paɪ/ **229**–18
punching bag /ˈpʌnʧɪŋ bæɡ/ **218**–20
punctuation /ˌpʌŋkʧuˈeɪʃən/ **196**–9
puppet show /ˈpʌpɪt ʃoʊ/ **214**–10
puree /pyʊˈreɪ/ **93**–25
purple /ˈpɜrpəl/ **10**–14
purse /pɜrs/ **109**–2
push /pʌʃ/ **37**–25, **165**–20
push-up /ˈpʌʃˌʌp/ **218**–12
put /pʊt/
    ...air in the tires /ɛr ɪn ðə taɪrz/ **123**–18
    ...a stamp on /ə stæmp ɑn/ **53**–23
put away /pʊt əˈweɪ/ **79**–24

put down /pʊt daʊn/ **126**–18
put on /pʊt an/ **114**–8
   ...makeup /ˈmeɪkˌʌp/ **34**–7
   ...your headphones /yər ˈhɛdˌfoʊnz/ **126**–16
put out /pʊt aʊt/ **79**–19
put up /pʊt ʌp/ **165**–1
puzzle /ˈpʌzəl/ **224**–16
pyramid /ˈpɪrəmɪd/ **193**–21
pyramids /ˈpɪrəmɪdz/
   build... /bɪld/ **198**–3
quart /kwɔrt/ **96, 97**–18
quarter /ˈkwɔrtər/ **3, 8**–4
quarter after six /ˈkwɔrtər ˈæftər sɪks/ **5**
quarter moon /ˈkwɔrtər mun/ **177**–31
quarter of seven /ˈkwɔrtər ʌv ˈsɛvən/ **5**
quarter past six /ˈkwɔrtər pæst sɪks/ **5**
quarter to seven /ˈkwɔrtər tə ˈsɛvən/ **5**
Quebec /kwəˈbɛk/ **172**–5
queen /kwin/ **224**–4
question mark /ˈkwɛsʧən mark/ **196**–12
questions /ˈkwɛsʧənz/
   ask... /æsk/ **64**–5
quiet /ˈkwaɪɪt/ **15**–36
quotation marks /ˈkwoʊˈteɪʃən marks/ **196**–16
rabbit /ˈræbɪt/ **152**–18, **190**–28
raccoon /ræˈkun/ **190**–19
racket /ˈrækɪt/
   tennis... /ˈtɛnɪs/ **220**–2
radiation /ˌreɪdiˈeɪʃən/ **171**–17
radiator /ˈreɪdiˌeɪtər/ **121**–35
radio /ˈreɪdioʊ/ **121**–17
radioactive materials /ˌreɪdioʊˈæktɪv məˈtɪriəlz/ **156**–35
radish /ˈrædɪʃ/ **85**–31
radius /ˈreɪdiəs/ **193**–14
raft /ræft/ **213**–10
rag /ræg/ **80**–17
railroad crossing /ˈreɪlˌroʊd ˈkrɔsɪŋ/ **118**–7
rain /reɪn/ **166**–20
   acid... /ˈæsɪd/ **171**–14
rainbow /ˈreɪnˌboʊ/ **166**–11
raincoat /ˈreɪnˌkoʊt/ **104**–10
raindrop /ˈreɪnˌdrap/ **166**–23
rain forest /reɪn ˈfɔrɪst/ **182**–183
raining /ˈreɪnɪŋ/ **167**–30
raise /reɪz/
   ...a family /ə ˈfæməli/ **31**–16
   ...your hand /yər hænd/ **20**–1
raising a child /ˈreɪzɪŋ ə ʧaɪld/ **28**–29
raisins /ˈreɪzənz/ **83**–27
rake /reɪk/ **79**–20
rake /reɪk/ **69**–17
ranch /rænʧ/ **63**–16
rash /ræʃ/ **135**–26
raspberries /ˈræzˌbɛriz/ **83**–26
rat /ræt/ **181**–13
rats /ræts/ **76**–25
rattle /ˈrætl/ **57**–10
razor /ˈreɪzər/ **144**–18
   electric... /ɪˈlɛktrɪk/ **144**–19
R&B /ər ən bi/ **209**–26
reach /riʧ/ **198**–18
read /rid/ **20**–7, **29**–20, **55**–27
   ...blueprints /ˈbluˌprɪnts/ **165**–17
reading room /ˈridɪŋ rum/ **55**–3
real estate agent /ˈriələˈsteɪtˈeɪʤənt/ **148**–20
   call a... /kɔl ə/ **65**–16
reality show /riˈæləti ʃoʊ/ **209**–21
rearview mirror /ˈrɪrˌvyu ˈmɪrər/ **121**–11
receipt /rɪˈsit/ **9**–14
receptionist /rəˈsɛpʃənɪst/ **141**–16, **148**–5
recipe /ˈrɛsəˌpi/ **92, 93**

RECREATION /ˌrɛkriˈeɪʃən/ **210**–229
rectangle /ˈrɛkˌtæŋgəl/ **193**–18
recycling bin /riˈsaɪklɪŋ bɪn/ **80**–25
red /rɛd/ **10**–1
red hair /rɛd hɛr/ **33**–1
referee /ˌrɛfəˈri/ **218**–4
reference desk /ˈrɛfərəns dɛsk/ **55**–4
refill /ˈriˌfɪl/ **102**–14
refrigerator /rɪˈfrɪʤəˌreɪtər/ **70**–20
regions of Canada /ˈriʤənz ʌv ˈkænədə/ **172**
regions of the United States /ˈriʤənz ʌv ðə yuˈnaɪtɪd steɪts/ **172**
registration desk /ˌrɛʤɪsˈtreɪʃən dɛsk/ **159**–12
registration form /ˌrɛʤɪsˈtreɪʃən fɔrm/ **43**
regular price /ˈrɛgyələr praɪs/ **9**–21
reindeer /ˈreɪnˌdɪr/ **187**–3
remarried /riˈmærid/ **27**–30
remote control /rəˈmoʊt kənˈtroʊl/ **226**–19
remove /rəˈmuv/ **51**–28
rent /rɛnt/
   ...an apartment /ən əˈpartmənt/ **31**–7
rent /rɛnt/
   pay the... /peɪ ðə/ **64**–14
renting an apartment /ˈrɛntɪŋ ən əˈpartmənt/ **64**
repair /rəˈpɛr/ **115**–21, **150**–15
report card /rəˈpɔrt kard/ **23**–24
reporter /rəˈpɔrtər/ **148**–1
reservation /ˌrɛzərˈveɪʃən/
   make a... /meɪk ə/ **102**–1, **159**–24
Resident Alien card /ˈrɛzədənt eɪliən kard/ **43**–17
respirator /ˈrɛspəˌreɪtər/ **157**–22
rest /rɛst/ **137**–26
restaurant /ˈrɛstərənt/ **100**–101
rest mat /rɛst mæt/ **57**–5
restroom /ˈrɛstrum/ **23**–8
resume /ˈrɛzəˌmeɪ/ **155**–16
retire /rəˈtaɪr/ **31**–22
retirement /rəˈtaɪrmənt/ **229**–28
retirement home /rəˈtaɪrmənt hoʊm/ **63**–17
return /rɪˈtɜrn/ **55**–28
return address /rɪˈtɜrn əˈdrɛs/ **52**–4
revolving door /rɪˈvalvɪŋ dɔr/ **67**–24, **159**–14
rhinoceros /raɪˈnasərəs/ **185**–8
ribs /rɪbz/ **87**–9
rice /raɪs/ **91**–19
rich /rɪʧ/ **15**–27
ride /raɪd/ **37**–26
right /raɪt/ **130**–16
ring /rɪŋ/ **109**–7
river /ˈrɪvər/ **169**–21
riverbank /ˈrɪvərbæŋk/ **169**–20
road trip /roʊd trɪp/ **122**–123
roast /roʊst/ **92**–15
roast beef /roʊst bif/ **87**–11
robe /roʊb/ **107**–13
robin /ˈrabɪn/ **190**–1
robot /ˈroʊbat/ **156**–5
rock /rak/ **29**–3
rock /rak/ **181**–11, **209**–24
rock climber /rak ˈklaɪmər/ **213**–2
rock concert /rak ˈkansərt/ **205**–10
rocket /ˈrakət/ **176**–4
rocking chair /ˈrakɪŋ ʧɛr/ **72**–31
Rocky Mountain States /raki ˈmaʊntn steɪts/ **172**–8
rodeo /ˈroʊdiˌoʊ/ **216**–22
roller /ˈroʊlər/
   paint... /peɪnt/ **163**–16
roller coaster /ˈroʊlər ˈkoʊstər/ **214**–16
rollers /ˈroʊlərz/ **144**–9
rolling pin /ˈroʊlɪŋ pɪn/ **95**–22
roll up /roʊl ʌp/ **114**–12

romance /roʊˈmæns/ **208**–5
roof /ruf/ **69**–4
   ...leaks /liks/ **77**–3
roofer /ˈrufər/ **77**–16
room /rum/
   double... /ˈdʌbəl/ **159**–17
   meeting... /ˈmitɪŋ/ **159**–6
   single... /ˈsɪŋgəl/ **159**–18
roommate /ˈrumˌmeɪt/ **67**–11
room service /rum ˈsɜrvɪs/ **159**–3
   order... /ˈɔrdər/ **159**–26
rooster /ˈrustər/ **152**–20
roots /ruts/ **179**–12
rope /ˈroʊp/ **163**–9, **213**–17
   pull a... /pʊl ə/ **165**–6
roses /ˈroʊzəz/ **179**–28
rouge /ruʒ/ **144**–28
router /ˈraʊtər/ **161**–27
rowboat /ˈroʊˌboʊt/ **213**–7
rubber band /ˈrʌbər bænd/ **155**–23
rubber gloves /ˈrʌbər glʌvz/ **80**–18
rug /rʌg/ **74**–4
   shake out the... /ʃeɪk aʊt ðə/ **79**–14
ruler /ˈrulər/ **160**–17
rules /rulz/ **198**–7
run /rʌn/ **37**–11
runner /ˈrʌnər/ **220**–17
runway /ˈrʌnˌweɪ/ **125**–13
rural area /ˈrʊrəl ˈɛriə/ **63**–23
Russian /ˈrʌʃən/ **44**–21
RV /ˈarˈvi/ **118**–16
sad /sæd/ **39**–21
safe-deposit box /seɪf-dɪˈpasɪt baks/ **51**–1
safety boots /ˈseɪfti buts/ **157**–28
safety-deposit box /ˈseɪfti-dɪˈpasɪt baks/ **51**–1
safety earmuffs /ˈseɪfti ˈɪrˌmʌfs/ **157**–29
safety glasses /ˈseɪfti glæsɪz/ **157**–25
safety goggles /ˈseɪfti ˈgagəlz/ **157**–23
safety pin /ˈseɪfti pɪn/ **117**–30
safety vest /ˈseɪfti vɛst/ **157**–27
safety visor /ˈseɪfti ˈvaɪzər/ **157**–21
sail /seɪl/ **198**–4
sailboard /ˈseɪlˌbɔrd/ **211**–12
sailboarder /ˈseɪlˌbɔrdər/ **211**–13
sailboat /ˈseɪlˌboʊt/ **211**–1
salad /ˈsæləd/ **88**–18
salad bar /ˈsæləd bar/ **101**–30
salad dressing /ˈsæləd ˈdrɛsɪŋ/ **88**–19
salamander /ˈsæləˌmændər/ **190**–17
salami /səˈlami/ **87**–5
sale /seɪl/ **9**–12
sale price /seɪl praɪs/ **9**–22
salesperson /ˈseɪlzˌpərsən/ **148**–21
sales tax /ˈseɪlz tæks/ **9**–19
salmon /ˈsæmən/ **87**–24
salsa /ˈsalsə/ **91**–27
saltshaker /ˈsɔltˌʃeɪkər/ **101**–12
sand /sænd/ **165**–25
sand /sænd/ **211**–21
   shovel... /ˈʃʌvəl/ **165**–19
sandal /ˈsændl/ **109**–22
sandbox /ˈsændˌbaks/ **214**–8
sand castle /sænd ˈkæsəl/ **211**–25
sand dune /sænd dun/ **181**–6
sander /sændər/
   power... /ˈpaʊər/ **161**–32
sandpaper /ˈsændˌpeɪpər/ **163**–12
sandwich /ˈsændwɪʧ/ **90**–10
Santa Claus /ˈsæntəˌklɔz/ **229**–20
sari /ˈsari/ **104**–9
satellite /ˈsætlˌaɪt/ **176**–15

satellite dish /ˈsætlˌaɪt dɪʃ/ **226**–18
Saturday /ˈsætərˌdeɪ/ **6**–10
Saturn /ˈsætərn/ **176**–22
saucepan /ˈsɔsˌpæn/ **94**–10
saucer /ˈsɔsər/ **101**–19
Saudi Arabian /ˈsɔdi əˈreɪbiən/ **44**–19
sauna /ˈsɔnə/ **159**–20
sausages /ˈsɔsɪʤez/ **87**–6
sauté /sɔˈteɪ/ **93**–19
savings account passbook /ˈseɪvɪŋz əˈkaʊnt ˈpæsˌbʊk/ **51**–14
saw /sɔ/ **165**–10
saw /sɔ/
   circular... /ˈsɜrkyələr/ **161**–31
saxophone /ˈsæksəˌfoʊn/ **207**–11
scale /skeɪl/ **99**–7
   postal... /ˈpoʊstəl/ **52**–15
scales /skeɪlz/ **189**–6
scallions /ˈskælyənz/ **85**–27
scallops /ˈskæləps/ **87**–19
scan /skæn/ **24**–34
scanner /skænər/ **25**–14
scar /skar/ **33**–7
scarecrow /ˈskerˌkroʊ/ **152**–12
scared /skɛrd/ **39**–19
scarf /skarf/ **104**–18
schedule /ˈskɛdzul/ **128**–22
   student... /ˈstudnt/ **23**–25
SCHOOL /skul/ **18**–25
school /skul/ **47**–6
   start... /start/ **31**–3
   take your child to... /teɪk yər ʧaɪld tə/ **34**–10
school bus /skul bʌs/ **23**–13, **118**–12
school library /skul ˈlaɪˌbrɛri/ **23**–6
school nurse /skul nərs/ **23**–20
SCHOOL SUBJECTS /skul ˈsʌbʤɪkts/ **192**–201
school zone /skul zoʊn/ **118**–8
science /ˈsaɪəns/ **194**–195
science fiction /ˈsaɪəns ˈfɪkʃən/ **208**–6
scientist /ˈsaɪəntɪst/ **148**–16
scissors /ˈsɪzərz/
   pair of... /pɛr ʌv/ **117**–23
score /skɔr/ **223**–19
scoreboard /ˈskɔrˌbɔrd/ **223**–18
scorpion /ˈskɔrpiən/ **181**–23
scouring pad /skaʊrɪŋ pæd/ **80**–14
scramble /ˈskræmbəl/ **92**–7
scraper /skreɪpər/ **163**–11
screen /skrin/ **25**–20
screw /skru/ **163**–22
screwdriver /ˈskruˌdraɪvər/ **160**–18
scroll bar /skroʊl bar/ **25**–10
scrub /skrʌb/ **79**–11
scrub brush /skrʌb brʌʃ/ **80**–20
scuba diver /ˈskubə ˈdaɪvər/ **189**–13
sculptor /ˈskʌlptər/ **203**–17
sculpture /ˈskʌlpʧər/ **203**–16
sea /si/ **188**–189
sea anemone /si əˈnɛməni/ **189**–25
seafood /ˈsiˌfud/ **86**–87
seagull /ˈsiˌgʌl/ **189**–1
sea horse /si hɔrs/ **189**–14
seal /sil/ **187**–12
seam /sim/ **117**–25
seashell /ˈsiˌʃɛl/ **211**–22
season /ˈsizən/ **92**–14
seasons /ˈsizənz/ **7**
seat /sit/ **19**–27, **125**–27, **205**–20
   find your... /faɪnd yər/ **126**–9
seat belt /sit bɛlt/ **121**–12, **125**–28
   fasten... /ˈfæsən/ **126**–12
   unfasten your... /ʌnˈfæsən yər/ **126**–22

sea urchin /si ˈɜrtʃɪn/ **189**–22
seaweed /ˈsiˌwid/ **189**–9
second /ˈsɛkənd/ **3, 4**
second-hand store /ˈsɛkənd-hænd stɔr/ **48**–14
secretary /ˈsɛkrəˌteri/ **155**–18
security /səˈkyurəti/
    go through... /goʊ θru/ **126**–5
security checkpoint /səˈkyurəti ˈtʃɛkˌpɔɪnt/ **125**–10
security deposit /səˈkyurəti dɪˈpasɪt/
    pay a... /peɪ ə/ **64**–7
security guard /səˈkyurəti gard/ **51**–2, **148**–8
sedan /səˈdæn/ **118**–19
see /si/ **64**–4
seed /sid/ **179**–24
seesaw /ˈsiˌsɔ/ **214**–7
select /səˈlɛkt/ **24**–32
sell /sɛl/ **150**–14
semi /ˈsɛmi/ **118**–25
semicolon /ˈsɛmiˌkoʊlən/ **196**–18
Senate /ˈsɛnɪt/ **201**
senator /ˈsɛnətər/ **200**–10
send /sɛnd/ **53**–24
    ...a text /ə tɛkst/ **17**–28
senior (citizen) /ˈsinyər (ˈsɪtəzən)/ **31**
sentence /ˈsɛntns/ **196**–3
    copy the... /ˈkɑpi ðə/ **20**–4
September /sɛpˈtɛmbər/ **7**–24
serve /sɜrv/
    ...a meal /ə mil/ **102**–16
    ...in the military /ɪn ðə ˈmɪləˌteri/ **201**–19
    ...on a jury /ɑn ə ˈdʒʊri/ **201**–17
server /ˈsɜrvər/ **101**–4, **101**–6, **148**–18
    signal the... /ˈsɪgnəl ðə/ **102**–18
    thank the... /ˈθæŋk ðə/ **102**–21
set /sɛt/ **102**–5
set /sɛt/ **205**–19
set of knives /sɛt ʌv naɪvz/ **94**–2
seven /ˈsɛvən/ **2**
seventeen /ˌsɛvənˈtin/ **2**
seventeenth /ˌsɛvənˈtinθ/ **3**
seventh /ˈsɛvənθ/ **3**
seventy /ˈsɛvənti/ **2**
sewing /ˈsoʊɪŋ/ **117**
sewing machine /ˈsoʊɪŋ məˈʃin/ **117**–20
sew on /ˈsoʊ ɑn/ **115**–22
sex /sɛks/ **43**–5
shade /ʃeɪd/
    window... /ˈwɪndoʊ/ **74**–8
shake hands /ʃeɪk hændz/ **40**–4
shake out /ʃeɪk aʊt/ **79**–14
shampoo /ʃæmˈpu/ **144**–2
shapes /ʃeɪps/ **193**
share /ʃɛr/
    ...a book /ə bʊk/ **21**–21
    ...a dessert /ə dɪˈzɜrt/ **102**–19
shark /ʃark/ **189**–12
shave /ʃeɪv/ **34**–6
shaving cream /ʃeɪvɪŋ krim/ **144**–16
shawl /ʃɔl/ **104**–23
sheep /ʃip/ **152**–23
sheet /ʃit/ **74**–15
sheets /ʃits/
    change the... /tʃeɪndʒ ðə/ **79**–2
shelf /ʃɛlf/ **70**–4
shellfish /ˈʃɛlˌfɪʃ/ **87**
shingles /ˈʃɪŋgəlz/ **163**–5
ship /ʃɪp/ **211**–6
shipping clerk /ˈʃɪpɪŋ klɜrk/ **157**–16
shirt /ʃɜrt/ **104**–2
    button-down... /ˈbʌtn-daʊn/ **111**–6
    long-sleeved... /lɔŋ-slivd/ **111**–5

polo... /ˈpoʊloʊ/ **111**–7
short-sleeved... /ʃɔrt-slivd/ **111**–4
sleeveless... /ˈslivlɪs/ **111**–3
shish kebab recipe /ʃɪʃ kəˈbab ˈrɛsəˌpi/ **92**
shock /ʃak/
    be in... /bi ɪn/ **136**–4
    get a... /gɛt ə/ **136**–14
shoes /ʃuz/ **108**–109
shoe store /ʃu stɔr/ **48**–3
shop /ʃap/
    gift... /gɪft/ **159**–22
shoplifting /ˈʃapˌlɪftɪŋ/ **61**–12
shopper /ˈʃapər/ **9**–13, **99**–23
shopping /ˈʃapɪŋ/ **9**
shopping basket /ˈʃapɪŋ ˈbæskɪt/ **99**–24
shopping cart /ˈʃapɪŋ kart/ **99**–17
shops /ʃaps/ **48**–49
shore /ʃɔr/ **169**–18
short /ʃɔrt/ **14**–18
    ...skirt /skɜrt/ **111**–20
short hair /ʃɔrt hɛr/ **33**–11
shorts /ʃɔrts/ **104**–8
short-sleeved /ʃɔrt-slivd/
    ...shirt /ʃɜrt/ **111**–4
shot /ʃat/
    give him a... /gɪv hɪm ə/ **137**–25
shoulder /ˈʃoʊldər/ **133**–21
shoulder-length hair /ˈʃoʊldər-lɛŋθ hɛr/ **33**–12
shovel /ˈʃʌvəl/ **165**–19
shovel /ˈʃʌvəl/ **160**–4, **211**–29
show /ʃoʊ/ **126**–2
shower /ˈʃaʊər/ **75**–18
    take a... /teɪk ə/ **34**–4
shower curtain /ˈʃaʊər ˈkɜrtn/ **75**–19
shredder /ʃrɛdər/
    paper... /ˈpeɪpər/ **155**–15
shrimp /ʃrɪmp/ **87**–20, **189**–21
shrub /ʃrʌb/ **185**–16
shut /ʃʌt/ **15**–38
shutter /ˈʃʌtər/ **69**–11
sick /sɪk/ **39**–14
side /saɪd/ **193**–10
sideburns /ˈsaɪdˌbɜrnz/ **33**–15
sidewalk /ˈsaɪdˌwɔk/ **47**–24, **58**–16
sift /sɪft/ **93**–28
sign /saɪn/
    ...the lease /ðə lis/ **64**–6
    ...the loan documents /ðə loʊn ˈdakyəmənts/ **65**–24
sign /saɪn/ **58**–19
signal /ˈsɪgnəl/ **102**–18
signature /ˈsɪgnətʃər/ **43**–15
signs /saɪnz/ **118**
silk /sɪlk/ **113**–4
silo /ˈsaɪloʊ/ **152**–2
silver /ˈsɪlvər/ **10**–24
silverware /ˈsɪlvərˌwer/ **70**–27
simmer /ˈsɪmər/ **93**–21
sing /sɪŋ/ **150**–11
singer /ˈsɪŋər/ **205**–14
single mother /ˈsɪŋgəl ˈmʌðər/ **27**–29
single room /ˈsɪŋgəl rum/ **159**–18
sink /sɪŋk/ **70**–15, **75**–28
    clean the... /klin ðə/ **79**–10
sister /ˈsɪstər/ **27**–15
sister-in-law /ˈsɪstər-ɪn-lɔ/ **27**–16
sit (down) /sɪt (daʊn)/ **20**–15, **37**–19
sitar /ˈsɪtar/ **207**–18
sitcom /ˈsɪtˌkam/ **209**–13
sit-up /sɪt-ʌp/ **218**–13
six /sɪks/ **2**–6
six fifteen /sɪks ˌfɪfˈtin/ **5**

six fifty-five /sɪks ˈfɪfti-faɪv/ **5**
six forty-five /sɪks ˈfɔrti-faɪv/ **5**
six o'clock /sɪks əˈklɑk/ **5**
six-oh-five /sɪks-ou-faɪv/ **5**
six-pack /sɪks-pæk/ **97**–26
sixteen /sɪksˈtin/ **2**
sixteenth /sɪksˈtinθ/ **3**
sixth /sɪksθ/ **3**
six-thirty /sɪks-ˈθɜrti/ **5**
six thirty-five /sɪks ˈθɜrti-faɪv/ **5**
six twenty-five /sɪks ˈtwɛnti-faɪv/ **5**
sixty /ˈsɪksti/ **2**
skateboard /ˈskeɪtˌbɔrd/ **214**–21
skateboarder /ˈskeɪtˌbɔrdər/ **214**–22
skater /ˈskeɪtər/ **214**–23
skates /skeɪts/
  ice... /aɪs/ **223**–25
  in-line... /ˈɪn-ˌlaɪn/ **214**–24
skating rink /skeɪtɪŋ rɪŋk/ **223**–20
sketch /skɛtʃ/ **203**–14
sketchpad /ˈskɛtʃ pæd/ **203**–13
ski boots /ski buts/ **222**–5
skier /skiər/ **222**–13
skiing /ˈskiɪŋ/
  cross country... /krɔs ˈkʌntri/ **222**–11
  downhill... /ˈdaʊnˈhɪl/ **222**–12
skin /skɪn/ **133**–1
ski poles /ski poulz/ **222**–6
skirt /skɜrt/ **104**–15
  long... /lɔŋ/ **111**–21
  pleated... /plitɪd/ **111**–19
  short... /ʃɔrt/ **111**–20
  straight... /streɪt/ **111**–18
  tight... /taɪt/ **111**–17
skis /skiz/ **222**–4
skunk /skʌŋk/ **190**–22
sky /skaɪ/ **166**–10
skylight /ˈskaɪˌlaɪt/ **69**–3
slacks /slæks/ **104**–22
sled /slɛd/ **222**–3
sledgehammer /ˈslɛdʒˌhæmər/ **160**–3
sleep /slip/ **34**–24
sleeper /slipər/
  blanket... /ˈblæŋkɪt/ **107**–16
sleeping bag /slipɪŋ bæg/ **213**–25
sleepwear /ˈslipˌwɛr/ **106–107**
sleeve /sliv/ **117**–16
sleeveless /ˈslivlɪs/
  ...shirt /ʃɜrt/ **111**–3
slice /slaɪs/ **93**–18
slide /slaɪd/ **194**–28, **214**–5
sling /slɪŋ/ **141**–13
slip /slɪp/ **37**–9
slip /slɪp/ **107**–23
slippers /ˈslɪpərz/ **107**–11
slow /slou/ **15**–33
slow down /slou daʊn/ **123**–8
small /smɔl/ **14**–1
small town /smɔl taʊn/ **63**–22
smartphone /ˈsmɑrtˌfoʊn/ **16**–1
smile /smaɪl/ **40**–18
smog /smɔg/ **171**–13
smoke detector /smoʊk dɪˈtɛktər/ **72**–18
snacks /snæks/ **99**
snail /sneɪl/ **182**–22
snake /sneɪk/ **181**–14
sneaker /ˈsnikər/ **109**–25
sneeze /sniz/ **137**–17
snorkel /ˈsnɔrkəl/ **211**–11
snorkeler /ˈsnɔrkələr/ **211**–10
snow /snou/ **166**–19

snowboard /ˈsnouˌbɔrd/ **223**–16
snowboarder /ˈsnouˌbɔrdər/ **222**–15
snowboarding /ˈsnouˌbɔrdɪŋ/ **222**–14
snowflake /ˈsnouˌfleɪk/ **166**–22
snowing /ˈsnouɪŋ/ **167**–28
snowmobile /snou ˈmouˌbil/ **222**–1
snowshoes /ˈsnouˌʃuz/ **222**–2
soap /soup/ **144**–24
  bar of... /bɑr ʌv/ **97**–8
soap opera /soup ˈɑprə/ **209**–16
soccer /ˈsɑkər/ **220**–19
soccer field /ˈsɑkər fild/ **220**–21
Social Security card /ˈsouʃəl səˈkyʊrəti kɑrd/ **43**–8, **43**–21
socks /sɑks/ **107**–3
soda /ˈsoudə/ **88**–5
  can of... /kæn ʌv/ **97**–27
  six-pack of... /sɪks-pæk ʌv/ **97**–26
sofa /ˈsoufə/ **72**–8
soft /sɔft/ **14**–10
software /ˈsɔftˌwɛr/ **25**–25
soil /sɔɪl/ **152**–10
solar energy /ˈsoulər ˈɛnərdʒi/ **171**–27
soldier /ˈsouldʒər/ **148**–4
solid /ˈsɑlɪd/ **113**–13, **194**–10
solids /ˈsɑlɪdz/ **193**
son /sʌn/ **27**–21
sonogram /ˈsɑnəgræm/ **141**–12
sore throat /sɔr θrout/ **135**–8
soul /soul/ **209**–26
sour cream /saʊr krim/ **88**–8
South /saʊθ/ **172**–13
south /saʊθ/ **130**–21
South America /saʊθ əˈmɛrɪkə/ **174**–9
Southern Hemisphere /ˈsʌðərn ˈhɛməˌsfɪr/ **174**–7
South Pole /saʊθ poul/ **174**–5
Southwest /saʊθˈwɛst/ **172**–12
soy sauce /ˈsɔɪˌsɔs/ **91**–24
space /speɪs/ **176**–11
space shuttle /speɪs ˈʃʌtl/ **176**–17
space station /speɪs ˈsteɪʃən/ **176**–1
spade /speɪd/ **224**–7
spaghetti /spəˈgɛti/ **90**–3
Spanish /ˈspænɪʃ/ **44**–13
Spanish club /ˈspænɪʃ klʌb/ **23**–22
sparrow /ˈspærou/ **185**–18
spatula /ˈspætʃələ/ **95**–31
speak /spik/ **150**–3
speaker /spikər/ **226**–12
speeding ticket /ˈspidɪŋ tɪkɪt/
  get a... /gɛt ə/ **123**–6
speedometer /spɪˈdɑmətər/ **121**–14
speed up /ˈspidˌʌp/ **123**–5
spell /spɛl/ **20**–13
sphere /sfɪr/ **193**–23
spice rack /spaɪs ræk/ **70**–11
spider /ˈspaɪdər/ **181**–18
spill /spɪl/ **102**–9
spinach /ˈspɪnɪtʃ/ **84**–4
split peas /splɪt piz/
  stir... /stɜr/ **93**–20
sponge /spʌndʒ/ **80**–21, **189**–29
spoon /spun/ **101**–25
sporting event /ˈspɔrtɪŋ ɪˈvɛnt/ **216**–6
sporting goods store /ˈspɔrtɪŋ gʊdz stɔr/ **48**–6
sports /spɔrts/ **23**–21, **209**–20
sports car /spɔrts kɑr/ **118**–24
sports coat /spɔrts kout/ **104**–21
sports jacket /spɔrts ˈdʒækɪt/ **104**–21
spotlight /ˈspɑtˌlaɪt/ **205**–11
sprained wrist /spreɪnd rɪst/ **135**–10
spread /sprɛd/ **93**–30

spring /sprɪŋ/ **7**-12
sprinkler /ˈsprɪŋkələr/ **69**-29
square /skwɛr/ **193**-20
squash /skwɑʃ/ **84**-6
squat /skwɑt/ **37**-15
squeegee /ˈskwidʒi/ **80**-6
squid /skwɪd/ **189**-19
squirrel /ˈskwɜrəl/ **190**-8
stadium /ˈsteɪdiəm/ **47**-2
stage /steɪdʒ/ **204**-6
stairs /stɛrz/ **67**-4
stamp /stæmp/ **52**-5
        put a...on /pʊt ə...ɑn/ **53**-23
stamp machine /stæmp məˈʃin/ **52**-12
stand up /stænd ʌp/ **21**-19, **37**-18
staple /ˈsteɪpəl/ **151**-17
stapler /ˈsteɪplər/ **155**-9
staples /ˈsteɪpəlz/ **155**-26
star /stɑr/ **176**-3
starfish /ˈstɑrˌfɪʃ/ **189**-28
start /stɑrt/
        ...school /skul/ **31**-3
state /steɪt/ **43**-13
statement /ˈsteɪtmənt/
        monthly... /ˈmʌnθli/ **51**-10
stationary bike /ˈsteɪʃəˌnɛri baɪk/ **218**-14
station wagon /ˈsteɪʃən wægən/ **118**-29
statue /ˈstætʃu/ **59**-23
steak /steɪk/ **87**-10
steam /stim/ **92**-10
steamer /ˈstimər/
        vegetable... /ˈvɛdʒtəbəl/ **95**-26
steel wool /stil wʊl/ **163**-17
steering wheel /ˈstɪrɪŋ wil/ **121**-24
stem /stɛm/ **179**-15
stepfather /ˈstɛpˌfɑðər/ **27**-8
stepladder /ˈstɛpˌlædər/ **80**-23
stepmother /ˈstɛpˌmʌðər/ **27**-5
steps /stɛps/ **69**-15
stepsister /ˈstɛpˌsɪstər/ **27**-12
stereo (system) /ˈstɛriˌoʊ (ˈsɪstəm)/ **226**-13
sterile pad /ˈstɛrəl pæd/ **143**-25
sterile tape /ˈstɛrəl teɪp/ **143**-26
stethoscope /ˈstɛθəˌskoʊp/ **141**-1
sticky notes /ˈstɪki noʊtz/ **155**-25
still life /stɪl laɪf/ **203**-2
sting /stɪŋ/
        bee... /bi/ **135**-28
stingray /ˈstɪŋreɪ/ **189**-20
stir /stɜr/ **93**-20
stir-fried vegetables /stɜr-fraɪd
        ˈvɛdʒtəbəlz/ **91**-20
stitches /ˈstɪtʃez/ **139**-28
stockbroker /ˈstɑkˌbroʊkər/ **148**-13
stockings /ˈstɑkɪŋz/ **107**-6
stomach /ˈstʌmək/ **133**-29
stomachache /ˈstʌməkˌeɪk/ **135**-12
stool /stul/ **70**-21
stop /stɑp/ **118**-2
stopper /ˈstɑpər/ **194**-22
storage space /ˈstɔrɪdʒ speɪs/ **67**-1
stores /stɔrz/ **48**-49
storm /stɔrm/ **166**-14
stove /stoʊv/ **70**-6
        camping... /ˈkæmpɪŋ/ **213**-15
stow /stoʊ/ **126**-10
straight /streɪt/ **130**-1
        ...skirt /skɜrt/ **111**-18
straight hair /streɪt hɛr/ **33**-17
straight leg /streɪt lɛg/
        ...jeans /dʒinz/ **111**-11

straight line /streɪt laɪn/ **193**-7
strainer /ˈstreɪnər/ **94**-18
strap /stræp/ **128**-15
straw /strɔ/ **90**-11
strawberries /ˈstrɔˌbɛriz/ **83**-25
        box of... /bɑks ʌv/ **97**-20
stream /strim/ **169**-6
street /strit/ **47**-27
street address /strit əˈdrɛs/ **43**-11
streetlight /ˈstritˌlaɪt/ **58**-4
street musician /strit myuˈzɪʃən/ **59**-22
street vendor /strit ˈvɛndər/ **58**-12, **214**-28
stretch /strɛtʃ/ **126**-18
stretcher /ˈstrɛtʃər/ **139**-27
string /strɪŋ/ **207**
string beans /strɪŋ binz/ **85**-28
striped /straɪpt/ **113**-20
stroller /ˈstroʊlər/ **57**-11
strong /strɔŋ/ **14**-3
student /ˈstudnt/ **19**-26
student ID /ˈstudnt aɪ di/ **43**-19
student schedule /ˈstudnt ˈskɛdʒul/ **23**-25
studio (apartment) /ˈstudioʊ (əˈpɑrtmənt)/ **67**-9
study /ˈstʌdi/ **19**-33
subtraction /səbˈtrækʃən/ **193**-27
suburbs /ˈsʌbˌɜrbz/ **63**-21
subway (train) /ˈsʌbˈweɪ (treɪn)/ **128**-18
subway line /ˈsʌbˈweɪ laɪn/ **128**-16
suede /sweɪd/ **113**-8
sugar /ˈʃʊgər/
        sift... /sɪft/ **93**-28
sugar bowl /ˈʃʊgər ˈboʊl/ **101**-10
suit /sut/
        business... /ˈbɪznɪs/ **104**-29
suite /swit/ **159**-5
summer /ˈsʌmər/ **7**-13
sun /sʌn/ **166**-9, **176**-18
sunbather /ˈsʌnˌbeɪðər/ **211**-19
sunburn /ˈsʌnˌbɜrn/ **135**-27
Sunday /ˈsʌnˌdeɪ/ **6**-11
sunflowers /ˈsʌnˌflaʊərz/ **179**-29
sunglasses /ˈsʌnˌglæsɪz/ **109**-14
sunny /ˈsʌni/ **167**-25
sunrise /ˈsʌnˌraɪz/ **5**
sunscreen /ˈsʌnˌskrin/ **144**-22, **211**-24
sunset /ˈsʌnˌsɛt/ **5**
sunshine /ˈsʌnˌʃaɪn/ **166**-13
super /ˈsupər/ **67**-3
superintendent /ˌsupərɪnˈtɛndənt/ **67**-3
supermarket /ˈsupərˌmɑrkət/ **48**-26, **98**-99
supervisor /ˈsupərˌvaɪzər/ **156**-9
supplies /səˈplaɪz/ **162**-163
supply cabinet /səˈplaɪ ˈkæbənɪt/ **155**-21
Supreme Court /suˈprim kɔrt/ **200**-8
surf /sɜrf/ **210**-30
surfboard /ˈsɜrfˌbɔrd/ **211**-16
surfer /ˈsɜrfər/ **211**-15
surgeon /ˈsɜrdʒən/ **139**-10
surgical mask /ˈsɜrdʒɪkəl mæsk/ **139**-13
surname /ˈsɜrneɪm/ **43**-2
surprised /sərˈpraɪzəd/ **39**-22
sushi /ˈsuʃi/ **91**-23
suspenders /səˈspɛndərz/ **109**-5
suspense /səˈspɛns/ **208**-3
SUV /ɛs yu vi/ **118**-22
swallow /ˈswɑloʊ/ **136**-10
sweater /ˈswɛtər/ **104**-20
        cardigan... /ˈkɑrdɪˌgən/ **111**-15
        crew neck... /kru nɛk/ **111**-14
        turtleneck... /ˈtɜrtlˌnɛk/ **111**-16
        V-neck... /vi-nɛk/ **111**-13

sweatpants /swɛtpænts/ **104**–4
sweatshirt /swɛʧ3rt/ **104**–3
sweep /swip/ **79**–4
sweet potato /swit pəˈteɪtoʊ/ **84**–22
swim /swɪm/ **210**–32
swimmer /swɪmər/ **211**–8
swimming pool /ˈswɪmɪŋ pul/ **159**–21, **218**–34
swimming trunks /ˈswɪmɪŋ trʌŋks/ **107**–9
swimsuit /ˈswɪmˌsut/ **107**–7
swimwear /ˈswɪmˌwɛr/ **106**–**107**
swing /swɪŋ/ **183**–26
swings /swɪŋz/ **214**–2
Swiss cheese /swɪs ʧiz/ **88**–24
switch /swɪʧ/
   light... /laɪt/ **72**–24
swollen ankle /ˈswoʊlən ˈæŋkəl/ **135**–11
swordfish /ˈsɔrdˌfɪʃ/ **87**–23, **189**–3
symptoms /ˈsɪmptəmz/ **134**–**135**
synagogue /ˈsɪnəˌgɑg/ **47**–7
syrup /ˈsɪrəp/ **88**–13
table /ˈteɪbəl/ **19**–18, **70**–32
   bus the... /bʌs ðə/ **102**–25
   clear the ... /klɪr ðə/ **102**–25
   set the... /sɛt ðə/ **102**–5
   wipe the... /waɪp ðə/ **102**–22
tablecloth /ˈteɪbəlˌklɔθ/ **101**–11
tablespoon /ˈteɪbəlˌspun/ **97**–5
tablespoon /ˈteɪbəlˌspun/ **96**
tablet /ˈtæblɪt/ **24**–2, **142**–1
taco /ˈtakoʊ/ **91**–26
tail /teɪl/ **185**–29
taillight /ˈteɪlˌlaɪt/ **121**–5
tailor /ˈteɪlər/ **117**–19
take /teɪk/
   ...a bath /ə bæθ/ **34**–22
   ...a break /ə breɪk/ **20**–14
   ...a coffee break /ə ˈkɔfi breɪk/ **34**–12
   ...a message /ə ˈmɛsɪʤ/ **150**–12
   ...a nap /ə næp/ **34**–15
   ...an order /ən ˈɔrdər/ **102**–11
   ...a photograph /ə ˈfoʊtəˌgræf/ **203**–26
   ...a pill /ə pɪl/ **137**–27
   ...a shower /ə ˈʃaʊer/ **34**–4
   ...a test /ə tɛst/ **19**–33
   ...a vacation /ə veɪˈkeɪʃən/ **31**–19
   ...a walk /ə wɔk/ **34**–20
   ...care of /kɛr ʌv/ **150**–9
   ...home /hoʊm/ **114**–6
   ...your child to school /yər ʧaɪld tə skul/ **34**–10
   ...your temperature /yər ˈtɛmpərəʧər/ **137**–19
take off /teɪk ɔf/ **114**–17, **126**–13
take out /teɪk aʊt/ **79**–19
taking a flight /teɪkɪŋ ə flaɪt/ **126**–**127**
talk /tɔk/ **21**–20
talk show /tɔk ʃoʊ/ **209**–17
tall /tɔl/ **14**–17
tambourine /ˌtæmbəˈrin/ **207**–3
tan /tæn/ **10**–17
tangerine /ˌtænʤəˈrin/ **83**–28
tank top /tæŋk tɑp/ **107**–25
tape /teɪp/ **155**–8
   duct... /dʌkt/ **163**–31
   masking... /ˈmæskɪŋ/ **163**–13
tape measure /teɪp ˈmɛʒər/ **117**–28, **163**–3
tarantula /təˈrænʧələ/ **182**–25
taupe /toʊp/ **10**–18
taxes /ˈtæksəz/
   pay... /peɪ/ **201**–16
taxi /ˈtæksi/ **128**–4
taxi driver /ˈtæksi ˈdraɪvər/ **128**–5, **148**–17
taxi stand /ˈtæksi stænd/ **128**–1

tea /ti/ **90**–13
teacher /ˈtiʧər/ **19**–2, **148**–9
teachers' lounge /ˈtiʧərz laʊnʤ/ **23**–1
tea kettle /ti ˈkɛtl/ **70**–7
teal /til/ **10**–8
team /tim/ **23**–2
teapot /ˈtiˌpɑt/ **70**–29
tear down /tɛr daʊn/ **165**–16
teaspoon /ˈtiˌspun/ **96**, **97**–4
teenager /ˈtinˌeɪʤər/ **30**
teeth /tiθ/
   brush... /brʌʃ/ **34**–3
teething ring /tiðɪŋ rɪŋ/ **57**–7
telephone /ˈtɛləˌfoʊn/ **16**–**17**, **155**–11
telephone book /ˈtɛlə foʊn bʊk/ **16**–8
telephone number /ˈtɛlə foʊn ˈnʌmbər/ **16**–21, **43**–9
telescope /ˈtɛləˌskoʊp/ **176**–9
television /ˈtɛləˌvɪʒən/ **226**–16
   watch... /wɑʧ/ **34**–25
teller /ˈtɛlər/ **51**–4
teller window /ˈtɛlər ˈwɪndoʊ/ **51**–5
temperature /ˈtɛmpərəʧər/ **135**–15
   take your... /teɪk yər/ **137**–19
ten /tɛn/ **2**
tenant /ˈtɛnənt/ **67**–10
ten cents /tɛn sɛnts/ **8**–3
ten-dollar bill /tɛn-ˈdɑlər bɪl/ **8**–8
ten dollars /tɛn ˈdɑlərz/ **8**–8
tennis /ˈtɛnɪs/ **220**–1
tennis ball /ˈtɛnɪs bɔl/ **220**–3
tennis racket /ˈtɛnɪs ˈrækɪt/ **220**–2
tent /tɛnt/ **63**–2, **213**–24
tenth /tɛnθ/ **3**
ten thousand /tɛn ˈθaʊzənd/ **2**
terminal /ˈtɜrmənəl/ **124**–1
termites /ˈtɜrˌmaɪts/ **76**–26
test /tɛst/ **19**–28
   cheat on a... /ʧit ɑn ə/ **18**–30
   fail a... /feɪl ə/ **18**–31
   pass a... /pæs ə/ **19**–34
   study for a... /ˈstʌdi fər ə/ **19**–32
   take a... /teɪk ə/ **19**–33
test tube /tɛst tub/ **194**–13
text /tɛkst/
   select... /səˈlɛkt/ **24**–32
   ...message /ˈmɛsɪʤ/ **17**–8
textbook /ˈtɛkstˌbʊk/ **19**–25
Thai /taɪ/ **44**–26
thank /θæŋk/ **102**–21
Thanksgiving /ˈθæŋksˌgɪvɪŋ/ **229**–16
theater /ˈθiətər/ **47**–11
theft /θɛft/ **61**–5
thermometer /θərˈmɑmətər/ **143**–30, **166**–8
   meat... /mit/ **94**–17
thermostat /ˈθɜrməˌstæt/ **72**–25
thigh /θaɪ/ **133**–13
thighs /θaɪz/ **87**–27
thimble /ˈθɪmbəl/ **117**–26
thin /θɪn/ **15**–26
third /θɜrd/ **3**
thirsty /ˈθɜrsti/ **39**–11
thirteen /θərˈtin/ **2**
thirteenth /θərˈtinθ/ **3**
thirty /ˈθɜrti/ **2**
thread /θrɛd/ **117**–27
   embroidery... /ɛmˈbrɔɪdəry/ **224**–23
three /θri/ **2**
three-fourths /θri-fɔrθs/ **3**
three quarters /θri ˈkwɔrtərs/ **3**
thrift shop /θrɪft ʃɑp/ **48**–14
throat /θroʊt/ **133**–25

throat lozenges /θrout ˈlazənʤz/ **142**–9
through /θru/ **130**–4
throw pillow /θrou ˈpɪlou/ **72**–9
throw up /θrou ʌp/ **137**–18
thumb /θʌm/ **133**–6
thumbtack /ˈθʌmˌtæk/ **155**–22
Thursday /ˈθɜrzˌdeɪ/ **6**–8
tick /tɪk/ **190**–25
ticket /ˈtɪkɪt/ **124**–2, **128**–11, **205**–22
ticket counter /ˈtɪkɪt ˈkaʊntər/ **124**–4
ticket window /ˈtɪkɪt ˈwɪndou/ **128**–10
tidal wave /ˈtaɪdl weɪv/ **171**–10
tie /taɪ/ **104**–28
    narrow... /ˈnærou/ **111**–9
    wide... /waɪd/ **111**–8
tiger /ˈtaɪgər/ **182**–9
tight /taɪt/
    ...skirt /skɜrt/ **111**–17
tights /taɪts/ **107**–4
tile /taɪl/ **163**–7
time /taɪm/ **4**–5
time card /taɪm kard/ **157**–11
time clock /taɪm klak/ **157**–12
timer /ˈtaɪmər/
    kitchen... /ˈkɪʧən/ **94**–7
times /taɪmz/ **193**–5
times of day /taɪmz ʌv deɪ/ **5**
time zones /taɪm zounz/ **16**–12
tip /tɪp/
    leave a... /liv ə/ **102**–23
tire /taɪr/ **121**–4
    change the... /ʧeɪnʤ ðə/ **123**–22
tired /taɪrd/ **39**–23
tires /taɪrz/
    put air in the... /pʊt ɛr ɪn ðə/ **123**–18
tissues /ˈtɪʃuz/ **144**–25
title /ˈtaɪtl/ **55**–18, **196**–8
toad /toud/ **190**–20
toaster /ˈtoustər/ **70**–13
toboggan /təˈbagən/ **222**–7
today /təˈdeɪ/ **6**–3
toddler /ˈtadlər/ **56**–33
toe /tou/ **133**–18
tofu /ˈtoufu/ **88**–11
toilet /ˈtɔɪlɪt/ **75**–25
    ...is clogged /ɪz klagɛd/ **77**–2
    scrub the... /skrʌb ðə/ **79**–11
toilet brush /ˈtɔɪlɪt brʌʃ/ **75**–30
toilet paper /ˈtɔɪlɪt ˈpeɪpər/ **75**–24
toilet tissue /ˈtɔɪlɪt ˈtɪʃu/ **75**–24
token /ˈtoukən/ **128**–20
toll /toul/
    pay a... /peɪ ə/ **123**–23
tomato /təˈmeɪtou/ **84**–7
tomatoes /təˈmeɪtouz/
    pile of... /paɪl ʌv/ **97**–28
tomorrow /təˈmɔrou/ **6**–4
tongue /tʌŋ/ **133**–43
toolbar /tulbar/ **25**–4
tool belt /tul bɛlt/ **160**–12
tools /tulz/ **160**–161
tooth /tuθ/ **133**–44, **141**–28
toothbrush /ˈtuθˌbrʌʃ/ **144**–15
toothpaste /ˈtuθˌpeɪst/ **144**–14
tornado /tɔrˈneɪdou/ **171**–11
tortilla /tɔrˈtiə/ **91**–29
tortoise /ˈtɔrtəs/ **181**–12
total /ˈtoutl/ **9**–20
to the left of /tə ðə lɛft ʌv/ **13**–8
to the right of /tə ðə raɪt ʌv/ **13**–9
touch /tʌʧ/ **40**–5

touchpad /tʌʧpæd/ **25**–24
touch screen /tʌʧskrin/ **16**–5
tour guide /tʊr gaɪd/ **148**–22
tourist information booth /ˈtʊrɪst ˌɪnfərˈmeɪʃən buθ/
    59–21
toward /tɔrd/ **130**–7
towel /ˈtaʊəl/ **75**–26
town hall /taʊn hɔl/ **47**–17
townhouse /ˈtaʊnˌhaʊs/ **63**–12
tow truck /tou trʌk/ **118**–13
toys /tɔɪz/ **57**–15, **224**–**225**
toy store /tɔɪ stɔr/ **48**–7
track /træk/ **128**–14, **220**–16, **220**–18
trackpad /trækpæd/ **25**–24
tractor /ˈtræktər/ **152**–4
tractor trailer /ˈtræktər ˈtreɪlər/ **118**–25
traffic accident /ˈtræfɪk ˈæksədənt/ **58**–5
traffic cop /ˈtræfɪk kɑp/ **58**–6
traffic signs /ˈtræfɪk saɪnz/ **118**
trail /treɪl/
    hiking... /ˈhaɪkɪŋ/ **213**–14, **216**–11
trailer /ˈtreɪlər/ **118**–23
trail map /treɪl mæp/ **213**–18
train /treɪn/ **128**–12
    subway... /ˈsʌbˌweɪ/ **128**–18
training pants /ˈtreɪnɪŋ/ **57**–28
TRANSPORTATION /ˌtrænspərˈteɪʃən/ **118**–**131**
trash /træʃ/
    put out the... /pʊt aʊt ðə/ **79**–19
    take out the... /teɪk aʊt ðə/ **79**–19
trash bags /træʃ bægz/ **80**–8
trash can /træʃ kæn/ **69**–19, **214**–9
travel /ˈtrævəl/ **31**–23
travel agency /ˈtrævəl ˈeɪʤəbsi/ **58**–13
travel agent /ˈtrævəl ˈeɪʤənt/ **148**–27
tray /treɪ/ **101**–29
    carry a... /ˈkæri ə/ **102**–4
    ...of pastries /ʌv ˈpeɪstriz/ **97**–11
    paint... /peɪnt/ **163**–15
tray table /treɪ ˈteɪbəl/
    put down your... /pʊt daʊn yər/ **126**–19
treadmill /ˈtrɛdˌmɪl/ **218**–15
tree /tri/
    birch... /bɜrʧ/ **179**–3
    Christmas... /ˈkrɪsməs/ **229**–22
    elm... /ɛlm/ **179**–6
    maple... /ˈmeɪpəl/ **179**–4
    oak... /ouk/ **179**–5
    pine... /paɪn/ **179**–1
    willow... /ˈwɪlou/ **179**–2
trench /trɛnʧ/
    dig a... /dɪg ə/ **165**–22
trench coat /trɛnʧ kout/ **104**–19
trial /ˈtraɪəl/ **61**–22
triangle /ˈtraɪˌæŋgəl/ **193**–19
tripod /ˈtraɪˌpad/ **226**–4
trombone /tramˈboun/ **207**–8
trousers /ˈtraʊzərz/ **104**–22
trout /traʊt/ **87**–25
truck /trʌk/
    load a... /loud ə/ **64**–10
    pickup... /ˈpɪkˌʌp/ **118**–15
truck driver /trʌk ˈdraɪvər/ **148**–26
trumpet /ˈtrʌmpət/ **207**–9
trunk /trʌŋk/ **121**–3, **179**–11, **185**–25
trunks /trʌŋks/
    swimming... /swɪmɪŋ/ **107**–9
try on /traɪ an/ **114**–4
T-shirt /ˈti-ˌʃɜrt/ **104**–25
tsunami /suˈnami/ **171**–10
tuba /ˈtubə/ **207**–6

tube /tub/
   ...of hand cream /ʌv hænd krim/ **97**-9
Tuesday /ˈtuzˌdeɪ/ **6**-6
tulips /ˈtulɪps/ **179**-25
tuna /ˈtunə/ **87**-26, **189**-10
tunnel /ˈtʌnəl/
   out of the... /aʊt ʌv ðə/ **130**-5
   into the... /ˈɪntʊ ðə/ **130**-3
   through the... /θru ðə/ **130**-4
turkey /ˈtɜrki/ **87**-30, **152**-27, **190**-12, **229**-17
Turkish /ˈtɜrkɪʃ/ **44**-16
turnip /ˈtɜrnɪp/ **84**-17
turn off /tɜrn ɔf/ **126**-11
turn on /tɜrn ɑn/
   ...the headlights /ðə ˈhɛdˌlaɪts/ **123**-7
   ...the overhead light /ði ˌoʊvərˈhɛd laɪt/ **126**-15
turn signal /tɜrn ˈsɪgnəl/ **121**-36
turnstile /ˈtɜrnˌstaɪl/ **128**-23
turquoise /ˈtɜrˌkwɔɪz/ **10**-10
turtle /ˈtɜrtl/ **189**-8
turtleneck /ˈtɜrtlnɛk/
   ...sweater /ˈswɛtər/ **111**-16
tusk /tʌsk/ **185**-24, **187**-17
tuxedo /tʌkˈsidoʊ/ **104**-6
TV /tiˈvi/ **226**-16
TV programs /tiˈvi ˈproʊˌgræmz/ **209**
tweezers /ˈtwizərz/ **143**-31
twelfth /twɛlfθ/ **3**
twelve /twɛlv/ **2**
twentieth /ˈtwɛntiəθ/ **3**
twenty /ˈtwɛnti/ **2**
twenty-dollar bill /ˈtwɛnti-dɑlər bɪl/ **8**-9
twenty dollars /ˈtwɛnti dɑlərz/ **8**-9
twenty-first /ˈtwɛnti-fɜrst/ **3**
twenty-five after six /ˈtwɛnti-faɪv ˈæftər sɪks/ **5**
twenty-five cents /ˈtwɛnti-faɪv sɛnts/ **8**-4
twenty-five of seven /ˈtwɛnti-faɪv ʌv ˈsɛvən/ **5**
twenty-five past six /ˈtwɛnti-faɪv pæst sɪks/ **5**
twenty-five to seven /ˈtwɛnti-faɪv tə ˈsɛvən/ **5**
twenty-one /ˈtwɛnti-wʌn/ **2**-21
two /tu/ **2**
two-family house /tu-ˈfæməli haʊs/ **63**-6
two-thirds /tu-θɜrdz/ **3**
type /taɪp/ **150**-8, **196**-25
types of homes /taɪps ʌv hoʊmz/ **62**-63
ugly /ˈʌgli/ **14**-13
ultrasound /ˈʌltrəˌsaʊnd/ **141**-12
umbrella /ʌmˈbrɛlə/ **109**-4
unbuckle /ʌnˈbʌkəl/ **114**-16
unbutton /ʌnˈbʌtn/ **114**-14
uncle /ˈʌŋkəl/ **27**-4
uncomfortable /ʌnˈkʌmftəbəl/ **39**-25
unconscious /ʌnˈkɑnʃəs/
   be... /bi/ **136**-2
under /ˈʌndər/ **13**-13, **130**-13
underline /ˈʌndərˌlaɪn/ **21**-27
underneath /ˈʌndərˌniθ/ **13**-16
underpants /ˈʌndərˌpænts/ **107**-20
undershirt /ˈʌndərˌʃɜrt/ **107**-24
underwear /ˈʌndərˌwɛr/ **106**-107
unfasten /ʌnˈfæsən/ **126**-22
unfurnished apartment /ʌnˈfɜrnɪʃt əˈpartmənt/ **67**-20
uniform /ˈyunəˌfɔrm/ **104**-13, **220**-22
United States /yuˈnaɪtəd steɪts/ **172**-173
Universe /ˈyunəˌvɜrs/ **176**-177
unpack /ʌnˈpæk/ **64**-11
unzip /ʌnˈzɪp/ **114**-15
up /ʌp/ **130**-10
upside down /ˈʌnˌsaɪd ˈdaʊn/ **130**-12
Uranus /ˈyʊˈreɪnəs/ **176**-21

urban area /ˈɜrbən ˈɛriə/ **63**-20
USB port /ˈyuˈɛsˈpi pɔrt/ **25**-26
U.S. Constitution /ˌyuˈɛs ˌkɑnstəˈtuʃən/ **200**-5
U.S. government /ˌyuˈɛs ˈgʌvərmənt/ **200**-201
use /yuz/
   ...a computer /ə kəmˈpyutər/ **151**-21
usher /ˈʌʃər/ **205**-21
utility knife /yuˈtɪləti naɪf/ **160**-1
vacuum /ˈvækˌyum/ **79**-7
vacuum (cleaner) /ˈvækˌyum (ˌklinər)/ **80**-5
vacuum cleaner attachments /ˈvækˌyum ˌklinər əˈtæʧmənts/ **80**-4
vacuum cleaner bag /ˈvækˌyum ˌklinər ˌbæg/ **80**-3
Valentine's Day /ˈvælənˌtaɪnz ˌdeɪ/ **228**-4
valet parking /væˈleɪ ˌparkɪŋ/ **159**-23
valley /ˈvæli/ **169**-5
van /væn/ **118**-20
   load a... /loʊd ə/ **64**-10
vandalism /ˈvændlɪzəm/ **61**-13
vase /veɪs/ **101**-9
vault /vɔlt/ **51**-3
veal cutlets /vil ˌkʌtlɪts/ **87**-13
vegetable peeler /ˈvɛʤtəbəl ˌpilər/ **94**-14
vegetables /ˈvɛʤtəbəlz/ **84**-85
vegetable steamer /ˈvɛʤtəbəl ˌstimər/ **95**-26
vehicle registration card /ˈviɪkəl ˌrɛʤɪsˈtreɪʃən kard/ **43**-16
vehicles /ˈviɪkəlz/ **118**-119
velvet /ˈvɛlvɪt/ **113**-3
Venezuelan /ˌvɛnəˈzweɪlən/ **44**-4
vent /vɛnt/ **72**-23
Venus /ˈvinəs/ **176**-26
vest /vɛst/ **104**-26
   safety... /ˈseɪfti/ **157**-27
vet /vɛt/ **148**-28
veterinarian /ˌvɛtərəˈnɛriən/ **148**-28
vice president /vaɪs ˈprɛzədənt/ **200**-12
victim /ˈvɪktəm/ **61**-17
video game system /ˈvɪdioʊ geɪm ˌsɪstəm/ **226**-17
Vietnamese /ˈviyɛtnəˌmiz/ **44**-27
Vikings /ˈvaɪkɪŋz/
   ...sail /seɪl/ **198**-4
villa /ˈvɪlə/ **63**-11
vine /ˈvaɪn/ **182**-2
vineyard /ˈvɪnyərd/ **152**-8
violet /ˈvaɪələt/ **10**-15
violets /ˈvaɪələts/ **179**-23
violin /ˌvaɪəˈlɪn/ **207**-21
visa /ˈvizə/ **43**-23
vise /vaɪs/ **160**-13
visit /ˈvɪzɪt/ **40**-3
visitor /ˈvɪzətər/ **139**-17
vitamins /ˌvaɪtəmɪnz/ **142**-20
V-neck /ˈviˌnɛk/
   ...sweater /ˈswɛtər/ **111**-13
volcanic eruption /vɑlˈkænɪk ɪˈrʌpʃən/ **171**-12
volcano /vɑlˈkeɪnoʊ/ **169**-3
volleyball /ˈvaliˌbɔl/ **220**-9
volleyball /ˈvaliˌbɔl/ **220**-10
volleyball net /ˈvaliˌbɔl nɛt/ **220**-11
vomit /ˈvɑmɪt/ **137**-18
vote /voʊt/ **201**-14
voting booth /voʊtɪŋ buθ/ **200**-3
vulture /ˈvʌlʧər/ **181**-9
waist /weɪst/ **133**-11
wait /weɪt/ **126**-7
waiter /ˈweɪtər/ **101**-6
waiting room /ˈweɪtɪŋ rum/ **141**-6
wait on /weɪt ɑn/ **102**-6
waitress /ˈweɪtrɪs/ **101**-4
wake up /weɪk ʌp/ **34**-1
walk /wɔk/ **37**-5

walk /wɔk/
    learn to... /lɜrn tə/ **31**–2
    take a... /teɪk ə/ **34**–20
walk(way) /wɔk(weɪ)/ **69**–28
wall /wɔl/ **72**–21
    ...is cracked /ɪz krækt/ **77**–4
    paint a... /peɪnt ə/ **165**–3
    plaster a... /ˈplæstər ə/ **165**–2
    tear down a... /ter daʊn ə/ **165**–16
wallet /ˈwalɪt/ **109**–15
wall unit /wɔl ˈyunɪt/ **72**–7
walnuts /ˈwɔlˌnʌts/ **83**–34
walrus /ˈwɔlrəs/ **187**–15
warehouse /ˈwerˌhaʊs/ **157**–15
warm /wɔrm/ **166**–4
warning label /ˈwɔrnɪŋ ˈleɪbəl/ **142**–16
wash /waʃ/ **114**–18
    ...the car /ðə kar/ **79**–16
    ...the dishes /ðə dɪʃəz/ **79**–21
    ...the windshield /ðə ˈwɪndˌʃild/ **123**–17
washcloth /ˈwaʃˌklɔθ/ **75**–29
washer /ˈwaʃər/ **116**–7, **163**–26
washing machine /ˈwaʃɪŋ məˈʃin/ **116**–7
wasp /wasp/ **182**–23
waste /weɪst/
    hazardous... /ˈhæzərdəs/ **171**–18
wastebasket /ˈweɪstˌbæskɪt/ **75**–31
    empty the... /ˈɛmpti ðə/ **79**–13
watch /waʧ/ **34**–25
watch /waʧ/ **109**–11
water /ˈwɔtər/ **79**–18, **153**–30
water /ˈwɔtər/ **211**–5
    liter of... /ˈlitər ʌv/ **97**–17
    pour... /pɔr/ **102**–2
water bottle /ˈwɔtər ˈbatl/ **213**–13
waterfall /ˈwɔtərˌfɔl/ **169**–9
water fountain /ˈwɔtər ˈfaʊntn/ **23**–9
water glass /ˈwɔtər glæs/ **101**–16
water heater /ˈwɔtər ˈhitər/ **67**–6
watermelon /ˈwɔtər ˈmɛlən/ **83**–6
water meter /ˈwɔtər ˈmitər/ **77**–19
water park /ˈwɔtər park/ **216**–20
water pollution /ˈwɔtər pəˈluʃən/ **171**–19
water-skier /ˈwɔtərˌskiər/ **211**–3
water wing /ˈwɔtər wɪŋ/ **211**–23
wave /weɪv/ **40**–20
wave /weɪv/ **211**–9
    tidal... /ˈtaɪdl/ **171**–10
wavy hair /ˈweɪvi her/ **33**–19
weak /wik/ **14**–4
wear /wer/ **114**–13
wearing clothes /ˈwerɪŋ kloʊz/ **114–115**
weather /ˈweðər/ **166–167**
Web /wɛb/ **25**–29
Wednesday /ˈwɛnzdeɪ/ **6**–7
weed /wid/ **79**–15
week /wik/ **4**
weekdays /ˈwikˌdeɪz/ **6**
weekend /ˈwikˌɛnd/ **6**
weigh /weɪ/ **53**–22
weightlifter /ˈweɪtˌlɪftər/ **218**–26
weightlifting /ˈweɪtˌlɪftɪŋ/ **218**–25
weld /wɛld/ **165**–12
west /wɛst/ **130**–22
West Coast /wɛst koʊst/ **172**–7
western /ˈwɛstərn/ **208**–7
wet clothes /wɛt kloʊz/ **116**–8
whale /weɪl/ **187**–14
    killer... /ˈkɪlər/ **189**–7
wheel /wil/
    produce the... /ˈproʊˌdus ði/ **198**–2

wheelbarrow /ˈwilˌbæroʊ/ **69**–26
    push a... /pʊʃ ə/ **165**–20
wheelchair /ˈwilˌʧer/ **139**–23
whisk /wɪsk/ **92**–3
whisk /wɪsk/ **95**–20
whiskers /ˈwɪskərz/ **187**–16
white /waɪt/ **10**–20
whiteboard /waɪtˌbɔrd/ **19**–6
whiteboard eraser /ˈwaɪtˌbɔrd ɪˈreɪzə/ **19**–4
White House /waɪt haʊs/ **200**–7
wide /waɪd/
    ...tie /taɪ/ **111**–8
width /wɪdθ/ **193**
wife /waɪf/ **27**–26
willow (tree) /ˈwɪloʊ (tri)/ **179**–2
wind /wɪnd/ **166**–17, **171**–24
windbreaker /ˈwɪndˌbreɪkər/ **104**–7
window /ˈwɪndoʊ/ **25**–3, **69**–10
    install a... /ɪnˈstɔl ə/ **165**–13
    ...is broken /ɪz ˈbroʊkən/ **77**–10
window seat /ˈwɪndoʊ sit/ **72**–10
window shade /ˈwɪndoʊ ʃeɪd/ **74**–8
windshield /ˈwɪndˌʃild/
    wash the... /waʃ ðə/ **123**–17
windshield wiper /ˈwɪndˌʃild ˈwaɪpər/ **121**–29
windy /ˈwɪndi/ **167**–27
wine glass /waɪn glæs/ **101**–15
wing /wɪŋ/ **187**–21
wing nut /wɪŋ nʌt/ **163**–24
wings /wɪŋz/ **87**–28
wins /wɪnz/ **198**–16
winter /ˈwɪntər/ **7**–15
winter sports /ˈwɪntər spɔrts/ **222–223**
wipe /waɪp/ **102**–22
wipes /waɪps/
    baby... /ˈbeɪbi/ **57**–24
wire /waɪr/ **165**–8
wire /waɪr/ **160**–21
wire stripper /waɪr ˈstrɪpər/ **160**–23
withdraw /wɪðˈdrɔ/ **51**–26
withdrawal /wɪðˈdrɔəl/ **51**–17
witness /ˈwɪtnɪs/ **61**–18
wok /wak/ **95**–28
wolf /wʊlf/ **187**–4
woman /ˈwʊmən/ **15**–40
wood /wʊd/ **163**
    glue... /glu/ **165**–24
    plane... /pleɪn/ **165**–23
    sand... /sænd/ **165**–25
    saw... /sɔ/ **165**–10
wooden spoon /ˈwʊdn spun/ **94**–9
woodlands /ˈwʊdlənds/ **190–191**
woodpecker /ˈwʊdˌpɛkər/ **190**–13
woodwind /ˈwʊdˌwɪnd/ **207**
wool /wʊl/ **113**–12
word /wɜrd/ **196**–2
    look up a... /lʊk ʌp ə/ **20**–8
WORK /wɜrk/ **146–165**
work /wɜrk/ **77**–7
    go to... /goʊ tə/ **34**–11
workbook /ˈwɜrkˌbʊk/ **19**–19
worker /ˈwɜrkər/ **156**–4
working /ˈwɜrkɪŋ/ **150–151**
work out /wɜrk aʊt/ **34**–16
workout room /ˈwɜrkˌaʊt rum/ **67**–15
World /wɜrld/ **174–175**
World Wide Web /wɜrld waɪd wɛb/ **25**–29
worm /wɜrm/ **190**–18
worried /ˈwɜrid/ **39**–15
wrap /ræp/
    ...a present /ə ˈprɛzənt/ **229**–29

wrench /rɛnʧ/ **160**–10
    pipe... /paɪp/ **161**–25
wrestler /ˈrɛslər/ **218**–22
wrestling /ˈrɛslɪŋ/ **218**–21
wrinkle /ˈrɪŋkəl/ **33**–10
wrist /rɪst/ **133**–7
    sprained... /spreɪnd/ **135**–10
wristwatch /ˈrɪstˌwɑʧ/ **109**–11
write /raɪt/ **20**–6
    ...a draft /ə dræft/ **196**–22
    ...a letter /ə ˈlɛtər/ **40**–8
    ...an outline /ən ˈaʊtlaɪn/ **196**–21
writer /ˈraɪtər/ **55**–20, **148**–25
writes /raɪtz/ **198**–21
writing /ˈraɪtɪŋ/ **196**–**197**
X-ray /ˈɛks-reɪ/ **138**–6
yard /yɑrd/ **69**–20, **162**

yarn /ˈyɑrn/ **224**–21
year /yɪr/ **4**
yellow /ˈyɛloʊ/ **10**–12
yesterday /ˈyɛstərˌdeɪ/ **6**–2
yield /yild/ **118**–10
yoga /ˈyoʊgə/ **218**–2
yogurt /ˈyoʊgərt/ **88**–12
    container of ... /kənˈteɪnər ʌv/ **97**–25
young /yʌŋ/ **14**–22
zebra /ˈzibrə/ **185**–12
zero /ˈzɪroʊ/ **2**
zip /zɪp/ **114**–9
zip code /zɪp koʊd/ **43**–14, **52**–7
zipper /ˈzɪpər/ **117**–24
zoo /zu/ **216**–2
zoom lens /zum lɛnz/ **226**–2
zucchini /zuˈkini/ **84**–11

Credits

Illustrators

Ron Berg: pp. 220–223
Denny Bond: pp. 48–49, 106–107, 190–191, 202–203, 214–215 (©Denny Bond)
Higgins Bond: pp. 184–185
James Edwards: pp. 18–19, 34–35, 64–65, 116–117, 122–123 (©James Edwards/The Beranbaum Group)
Mike Gardner: pp. 32–33, 110–111, 145 (32–37), 146–151, 200–201, 228–229 (©Mike Gardner)
Patrick Gnan: pp. 68–69, 168–169, 178–179 (©Patrick Gnan/IllustrationOnLine.com)
Julia Green: pp. 20–21, 28–29, 56–57, 100–101, 126–127, 198–199
Gershom Griffith: pp. 26–27, 196 (20–25)
Ted Hammond: pp. 9, 38–39, 60–61, 102–103, 156–157
Sharon and Joel Harris: pp. 18–19, 36–37, 114–115, 132–133, 134–135, 138–139, 182–183, 204–205 (©Sharon and Joel Harris/IllustrationOnLine.com)
Phil Howe: pp. 3, 58–59, 70–71, 92–95 (©Phil Howe/IllustrationOnLine.com)
Ken Joudrey: pp. 52–53 (©Ken Joudrey/Munro Campagna)
Bob Kayganich: pp. 5, 12–13, 14 (21, 22, 31, 32), 15 (17, 18, 27, 28, 29, 30), 16–17, 24–25, 50–55, 76–77, 96–97, 104–105, 176–177, 180–181, 194 (1, 10, 11, 12), 195 (3, 5, 17, 19) (©Bob Kayganich/IllustrationOnLine.com)
Alan King: pp. 10–11, 46–47, 120–121, 142–143, 154–155, 210–211 (©Alan King/IllustrationOnLine.com)
Greg LaFever: pp. 152–153
Jeff Mangiat: pp. 22–23, 48–49, 90–91, 108–109, 130–131, 212–213
Mapping Specialists: pp. 44–45, 172–175 (©Mapping Specialists)
Precision Graphics: pp. 22 (24, 25), 23 (26, 27), 30–31, 42–43, 50 (10–13), 51 (14, 19), 52 (1, 2, 3, 8), 78–79, 118–119, 124–125, 136–137, 140–141, 158–159, 162 (1, 2), 164–167, 186–189, 201 (5–13), 218–219, 227 (26–31) (©Precision Graphics)
John Schreiner: pp. 80–81, 86–87 (©John Schreiner/IllustrationOnLine.com)
Dave Schweitzer: pp. 208–209 (©Dave Schweitzer/Munro Campagna)
Beryl Simon: pp. 170–171 (©Beryl Simon)
Carol Stutz: pp. 216–217 (©Carol Stutz)
Gerad Taylor: pp. 6–7, 66–67, 72–75, 88–89, 98–99, 128–129, 192–193 (©Gerad Taylor/IllustrationOnLine)
Meryl Treatner: pp. 112–113 (©Meryl Treatner/Chris Tugeau)

Photos

All photographs not otherwise credited are ©National Geographic Learning, Cengage Learning.

Unit One UNIT ICON CREDIT: ©Tom Grill/CORBIS; 2 all: ©Hemera Photo-Objects; 3 center: ©Hemera Photo-Objects; 4 center: ©Hemera Photo-Objects; 4 bottom: ©Royalty-Free/CORBIS; 5 all: ©Hemera Photo-Objects; 6 bottom: ©F.SCHLUSSER.PHOTOLINK/Getty; 8 bottom: ©C Squared Studios/Getty; 14 most: ©Hemera Photo-Objects; 14 (12): ©Thinkstock LLC/Index Stock Imagery, Inc.; 14 (14): ©Louis K. Meisel Gallery/CORBIS; 14 (33): ©Paul Sonders/CORBIS; 14 (34): ©Tom Brakefield/CORBIS; 15 (3): ©Tumar/Shutterstock.com; 15 (4): ©Randy Faris/CORBIS; 15 (5, 6, 27): ©John Coletti; 15 (15, 16): ©C Squared Studios/Getty; 15 (25): ©Melissa Goodrum; 15 (26): ©Catherine Ledner/Stone/Getty; 15 (35): ©privilege/Shutterstock.com; 15 (36): ©MillaF/Shutterstock.com; 15 (37, 38, 39, 40): ©Hemera Photo-Objects; 16 left: ©Scott Baxter/Getty; 16 center: ©David Buffington/Photodisc Green/Getty; 17 bottom left: ©COMSTOCK Images

Unit Two UNIT ICON CREDIT: ©Royalty-Free/CORBIS; 24 top right: ©Hemera Photo-Objects; 24 bottom left: ©David Shopper/Index Stock Imagery, Inc.

Unit Three UNIT ICON CREDIT: ©Thinkstock/Getty; 27: ©Royalty-Free/CORBIS; 29 top left: ©SW Productions/Photodisc Green/Getty; 29 top right: ©Royalty-Free/CORBIS; 29 center left: ©Jerry Koontz/Index Stock Imagery, Inc.; 29 center right: ©Zefa Visual Media-Germany/Index Stock Imagery, Inc.; 29 bottom left (small): ©Chris Carroll/CORBIS; 29 bottom left (big): ©Hemera Photo-Objects; 29 bottom right (small): ©Ariel Skelley/CORBIS; 29 bottom right (big): ©Royalty-Free/CORBIS

Unit Four UNIT ICON CREDIT: ©Jose Luis Pelaez, Inc./CORBIS; 40 (1): ©Ghislain & Marie David de Lossy/The Image Bank/Getty; 40 (7): ©Monkey Business Images/Shutterstock.com; 40 (8, 16, 18, 20): ©Hemera Photo-Objects; 40 (9): ©Michael Newman/PhotoEdit; 40 (10): ©Jerry Tobias/CORBIS; 40 (15): ©David Young-Wolff/PhotoEdit; 40 (17): ©Patrik Giardino/CORBIS; 40 (19): ©Don Romero/Index Stock Imagery, Inc.; 41 (3): ©Francisco Cruz/SuperStock; 41 (4, 11, 22): ©Hemera Photo-Objects; 41 (5): ©GeoStock/Photodisc Green/Getty; 41 (12): ©Royalty-Free/CORBIS; 41 (13): ©wavebreakmedia/Shutterstock.com; 41 (14): ©SuperStock; 41 (21): ©Morocco Flowers/Index Stock Imagery, Inc.; 41 (23): ©Steve Prezant/CORBIS; ©Myrleen Ferguson Cate/PhotoEdit; 42 top: ©Shuji Kobayashi/Stone/Getty; 42 center: ©Image Source/SuperStock; 42 (19): ©Thorsten Rust /Shutterstock.com; 42 bottom: ©Michael Newman/PhotoEdit; 44 top left: ©Hemera Photo-Objects; 44 top right: ©Springfield Photography/Alamy; 44 bottom left: ©Peter Guttman/CORBIS; 44 bottom right: ©Hemera Photo-Objects; 45 all: ©Hemera Photo-Objects

Unit Five UNIT ICON CREDIT: ©Photodisc Collection/Getty; 54: ©Mitchell Gerber/CORBIS; 56 top right: ©Hemera Photo-Objects; 56 center left: ©Willie Holdman/Index Stock Imagery Inc.; 56 center right: ©Stewart Cohen/Taxi/Getty; 56 bottom left: ©Chris Carroll/CORBIS; 56 bottom right: ©Hemera Photo-Objects

Unit Six UNIT ICON CREDIT: ©Cydney Conger/CORBIS; 62 (1): ©Cydney Conger/CORBIS; 62 (2): ©Dean Conger/CORBIS; 62 (3): ©Bob Krist/CORBIS; 62 (4): ©Vince Streano/CORBIS; 62 (5): ©Elfi Kluck/Index Stock Imagery Inc.; 62 (6): ©Craig Lovell/CORBIS; 62 (7): ©Michael Newman/PhotoEdit; 62 (8): ©RO-MA Stock/Index Stock Imagery Inc.; 62 (9, 10): ©Hemera Photo-Objects; 62 (11): ©Massimo Listri/CORBIS; 62 (12): ©Joseph Sohm; Visions of America/CORBIS; 62 (13): ©Reinhard Eisele/CORBIS; 62 (15): ©Yvette Cardozo/Index Stock Imagery Inc.; 62 (16): ©Philip Coblentz/Brand X Pictures; 62 (17): ©Phil Cantor/SuperStock; 63 (14): ©Pawel Libera/CORBIS; 63 (18): ©iStockphoto.com/Technotr; 63 (19): ©Mitch Diamond/Index Stock Imagery Inc.; 63 (20): ©Anselm Spring/Image Bank/Getty; 63 (21): ©Royalty-Free/CORBIS; 63 (22): ©Joseph Sohm; ChromoSohm Inc./CORBIS; 63 (23): ©Michael S. Yamashita/CORBIS; 67: ©Hemera Photo-Objects

Unit Seven UNIT ICON CREDIT: ©Burke-Triolo Pruductions/Getty; 82–85 most: ©Hemera Photo-Objects; 82 (5): ©Photodisc Collection/Getty; 82 (11): ©Seide Preis/Getty; 82 (17): ©Royalty-Free/CORBIS; 82 (24): ©Picture Arts/CORBIS; 82 (27): ©Keith Seaman/FoodPix; 82 (33): ©Maximilian Stock, LTD/FoodPix; 83 (7): ©Photodisc Inc./Getty; 83 (28): ©Paul Poplis/FoodPix; 84 (2): Africa Studio/Shutterstock.com; 84 (9, 18): ©Royalty-Free/CORBIS; 84 (10): ©John Coletti; 84 (21): ©Picture Arts/CORBIS; 84 (21): ©Evan Sklar/Food Pix; 84 (22): ©Jiang Hongyan/Shutterstock.com; 84 (30): ©istockphoto.com/ajt; 85 (25): ©Picture Arts/CORBIS

Unit Eight UNIT ICON CREDIT: ©C Squared Studios/Getty; 97 bottom right: ©Hemera Photo-Objects; 112 (1, 10): ©Veer Incorporated; 112 (2): © Royalty-Free Division/Masterfile; 112 (3): ©Nick Koudis/Getty; 112 (4): ©Barry David Marcus/SuperStock; 112 (6): ©Jules Frazier/Getty; 112 (7): ©D. Boone/CORBIS; 112 (11): ©Stacy Gold/National Geographic/Getty; 113 (5): ©Royalty-Free/CORBIS; 113 (8): ©Veer Incorporated; 113 (9): ©Reuters/CORBIS; 113 (12): ©Francisco Rojo Alvarez/Getty

Unit Nine UNIT ICON CREDIT: ©Wes Thompson/CORBIS

Unit Ten UNIT ICON CREDIT: ©Herrmann/Starke/CORBIS; 140 top center: ©Hemera Photo-Objects; 142 all: ©Hemera Photo-Objects; 144 (1): ©Amy Etra/PhotoEdit; 144 (2, 3, 12, 14, 15): ©Photodisc Collection/Getty; 144 (4, 7, 13): ©John Coletti; 144 (5, 8, 10, 11): ©Hemera Photo-Objects; 144 (6): ©Siede Preis/Photodisc Green/Getty; 144 (9): ©sweetie rice/Shutterstock.com; 145 top left: ©Stockbyte/Ablestock; 145 (16): ©Michael Newman/PhotoEdit; 145 (17, 20, 23, 26, 28): ©John Coletti; 145 (18): ©COMSTOCK Images; 145 (19, 21, 24, 25, 27): ©Hemera Photo-Objects; 145 (22): ©C Squared Studios/Photodisc Green/Getty; 145 (30, 31): ©Joe Atlas/Brand X Pictures; 145 (29): ©gresei /Shutterstock.com

Unit Eleven UNIT ICON CREDIT: ©PictureNet/CORBIS; 160–163 most: ©Hemera Photo-Objects; 160 (1, 4, 7, 8): ©COMSTOCK Images; 160 (3): ©C Squared Studios/Photodisc Green/Getty; 160 (9): ©Seide Preis/Photodisc Green/Getty; 160 (12): ©Photodisc Green/Getty; 161 (24, 30): ©C Squared Studios/Photodisc Green/Getty; 161 (26): ©Royalty-Free/CORBIS; 161 (32): ©Stockbyte; 162 (3): ©Seide Preis/Photodisc Green/Getty; 162 (4, 5, 28): ©John Coletti; 162 (6): ©Patrick Olear/Photo Edit; 162 (7, 14, 17): ©C Squared Studios/Photodisc Green/Getty; 162 (8): ©Jules Frazier/Getty; 162 (12): ©COMSTOCK Images; 163 (18): ©Royalty-Free/CORBIS; 163 (19, 29): ©John Coletti; 163 (20, 22, 24): ©Seide Preis/Photodisc Green/Getty; 163 (30): ©Widstock/Alamy

Unit Twelve UNIT ICON CREDIT: ©L. Clarke/CORBIS; 174: ©Digital Vision

Unit Thirteen UNIT ICON CREDIT: ©Digital Vision/Getty; 183 (25): ©Hemera Photo-Objects; 184 (1): ©Hemera Photo-Objects; 186 (7): ©Photodisc Collection/Getty; 191 (29): ©Jules Frazier/Getty

Unit Fourteen UNIT ICON CREDIT: ©Don Farrall/Getty; 194 (8, 14): ©Hemera Photo-Objects; 194 (9): ©Dennis MacDonald/PhotoEdit; 194 (7): ©Thinkstock LLC/Index Stock Imagery, Inc.; 194 (12): ©Seide Preis/Photodisc Green/Getty; 195 (18, 20, 21, 22, 27): ©Hemera Photo-Objects; 195 (15): ©Widstock/Alamy; 195 (17): Skinny boy/Shutterstock.com; 195 (23, 24, 25, 26): ©Seide Preis/Photodisc Green/Getty; 195 (28, 30): ©COMSTOCK Images; 195 (29): ©Myotis/Shutterstock.com

Unit Fifteen UNIT ICON CREDIT: ©Don Farrall/Getty; 203: ©Hemera Photo-Objects; 206–207 most: ©Hemera Photo-Objects; 206 (1, 6, 22): ©Photodisc Collection/Getty; 206 (8, 18, 19): ©C Squared Studios/Photodisc Green/Getty; 207 (3, 13, 15, 16, 17, 26, 28): ©Photodisc Collection/Getty; 207 (2): ©Spencer Grant/PhotoEdit; 207 (27): ©Photodisc Green/Getty

Unit Sixteen UNIT ICON CREDIT: ©Digital Vision/Getty; 212 (1): ©Hemera Photo-Objects; 216–217 (1): ©Catherine Karnow; (2): ©Justin Guariglia; (3, 12): Pavel L Photo and Video; (3): ©Albert Barr; (4): ©Velychko; (5): ©Fukuoka Irina; (6): ©Maxisport; (7): ©Kristian Sekulic/Getty; (8): ©Ekaterina Novikova; (9): ©PaulMcKinnon; (10): ©Rachal Grazias; (11): ©Robbie George; (13): ©Taylor S. Kennedy; (15): ©Mark Bowden; (15): ©Craft Vision/Getty; (16, 19, 20): ©Dreamstime; (17): ©Skip Brown; (18): ©Marcio Jose Bastos Silva; (21): ©René Mansi/Getty; (22): ©William Albert Allard; 223 (25): ©Hemera Photo-Objects; 224–226 most: ©Hemera Photo-Objects; 224 (1): ©Royalty-Free/CORBIS; 224 (21): ©John Coletti; 225 (16): ©C Squared Studios/Getty; 225 (16): ©ACE STOCK LTD/Alamy; 225 (19): ©Erin Garvey/Index Stock Imagery, Inc.; 226 (1): COMSTOCK Images; 226 (3, 8, 11, 14, 18): ©Shutterstock.com; 226 (9, 10, 19): ©iStockphoto.com; 226 (7): ©F.Schlusser/PhotoLink/Getty; 227 most: ©COMSTOCK Images; 227 (9): ©Mediacolor's/Alamy; 227 (14, 15, 19, 21, 23): ©Hemera Photo-Objects; 227 (20): ©Judith Collins/Alamy; 227 (24, 25): ©John Coletti